TROJAN TENNIS

A HISTORY OF THE STORIED MEN'S TENNIS PROGRAM AT THE
UNIVERSITY OF SOUTHERN CALIFORNIA

TROJAN TENNIS

A HISTORY OF THE STORIED MEN'S TENNIS PROGRAM AT THE
UNIVERSITY OF SOUTHERN CALIFORNIA

S. MARK YOUNG
FOREWORDS BY STAN SMITH AND STEVIE JOHNSON

New Chapter Press

Dedication

This book is dedicated to:

My father—the late Dr. Sydney S. Y. Young, a brilliant scientist—my mentor and first tennis coach

My mother—the late Doreen Young—whose affability and zest for life shaped me in more ways than she ever knew

And to every tennis player, coach, trainer, administrator, parent, relative, and fan who has contributed to, and marveled at, the men's tennis program at the University of Southern California

Table of Contents

Acknowledgements

What started out as a modest proposal, transformed into one of the most ambitious projects I have ever undertaken. Certainly, without the participation and help of many, this book would never have become a reality. First, Peter Smith, the USC men's tennis coach, allowed me into his inner sanctum so that I could understand his leadership and coaching style and gain insight into how he has created one of the very best teams in the nation. Peter also gave me unprecedented access to his players—past and present—as well as his staff, so that I could learn first-hand about their perspectives on the team. Former USC Coach Dick Leach answered my unending questions with great patience and insight about his time as a player and coach across 40 years of USC's tennis history. Both Peter and Dick also read the manuscript carefully and gave me excellent comments on it.

I was also very fortunate to interview many great USC players, including Sonny "SC" Voges (SC recently passed away and will be greatly missed), Alex Olmedo, Jim Buck, Don Eisenberg, Ed Atkinson, Dennis Ralston, Bob Lutz, Stan Smith, Steve Avoyer, Doug Adler, Tim Pawsat, John Shea, Gil Shea, Barbara Hallquist DeGroot, Beth Herr Bellamy, Eduardo Martinez Lanz, George Taylor, Sashi Menon, Dick Bornstedt, Dave Borelli, Robert Van't Hof, Bruce Manson, Chris Lewis, Bryon Black, Matt Anger, Eric Amend, Fernando Samayoa, Luke Jensen, Murphy Jensen, Prakash Amritraj, Wayne Black, Drew Hoskins, Andrew Park, Ruben Torres, Robert Farah, Kaes Van't Hof, Jamil Al-Agba, Jon Leach, Hans Gildemeister, Rick Leach, Cecil Mamiit, Stevie Johnson, Daniel Nguyen, Peter

Lucassen, Ray Sarmiento, Yannick Hanfmann, Roberto Quiroz, Lupita Novelo Osuna, Kaitlyn Christian, Sabrina Santamaria, Nick Crystal, Brandon Holt, Michael Grant, Jake Devine, Logan Smith, Tanner Smith, Riley Smith, Johnny Wang, Jack Jaede, Zoe Scandalis, Eric Johnson, Danielle Lao, Jens Sweaney, Michael Tang, Kristen Venter and Max de Vroome. Many team members on both the men's and women's teams, including, Emilio Gomez, Henry Ji, Laurens Verboven, Thibault Forget, Rob Bellamy, Greg Labanowski and David Laser also strongly supported this project.

Some of the best insights into the history of USC tennis came from interviewing relatives of some of USC's tennis greats: Katie Dempster, George Toley's daughter; Paula DiChiara and Ann Perez-Beals, daughters of Bobby Perez; Rafael Belmar Osuna, nephew of Rafael Osuna; Ellsworth Vines III, son of Ellsworth Vines, Jr.; Joseph Rafael Hunt, Joe Hunt's grand-nephew; James Eddy, Arnold Eddy's son; Laura Mako, Gene Mako's widow, and Tracy Austin Holt and Scott Holt, Brandon and Dylan Holt's parents. Margie Smith, Stan Smith's wife, engaged in another extraordinary act of kindness by sending me Stan's voluminous tennis scrapbooks compiled by Rhoda, Stan's mother. These archives were critical in helping me understand both Stan and Bob Lutz's significant contribution to the tennis program in the late 1960s. I would also like to express how much we in the Los Angeles tennis community mourn the loss of Steve Johnson, Sr. I was very fortunate to get to know Steve and interviewed him regarding Stevie Johnson's formative years. He was a very gracious and kind man.

I am also indebted to Kris Kwinta, the USC associate head coach, who schooled me in the fine points of the modern game. I have yet to find anyone more passionate about tennis than Kris. Further support was provided by Darcy Couch of

USC Sports Information, who went out of her way to help track down archived photos and whose careful reporting of recent matches on the USC tennis website helped tremendously, and Jose Eskanazi, who gave me access to USC's photo library. Claude Zachary of the USC Libraries was very helpful and found some very rare photos in the catacombs of Doheny Library, and Robert Faure and Colleen Connors of the Los Angeles Tennis Club gave me unprecedented access to the club's library and photo gallery. I also learned a great deal about college tennis by visiting the International Collegiate Tennis Hall of Fame at the University of Georgia. Other coaches and players, including the great Rod Laver, Tracy Austin, Chico Hagey, Dana Bozeman, Justin Gimelstob, Gary Young, Richard Gallien, George Husack, Brett Masi, Billy Martin and Deiton Baughman also shared their insights into the game and USC's tennis program. Stanford legendary coach Dick Gould was extremely helpful in sharing his vast knowledge of the history of college tennis.

Special thanks also goes to Professor Jack Barcal for his financial support and friendship and to Alexandra Bitterlin, Associate Athletic Director, who helped spark the idea for this book. Steve Holwell, Jamie Herndon, Phil Siordia, Wayne Bryan, Annette Buck, Bob Shafer, Jon Yamada, Jake Birnberg, Cassandra Porter, Craig Kridel, Jon Gurian, John Gordon Huber, Mike Borders, Anne Loveland, Taylor Coon, Dylan Holt, Oliver Peyron, the late Joe Jares, Sue Jares, Trent Wong, Iris Ichim Harris, Horacio Tambourini, my friends at the Flint Canyon Tennis Club, Mitch Voges, Judy Aydelott, Diane Clardy Crystal and Scott Crystal, Tracie Elle Majors and Ed Majors, Jim and Candy Yee, Mike Blue, Nancy Carnahan, Rudy Lara, Pat Haden, Steve Loeb, and Tim Tessalone, Ken Solomon and David Edges of the Tennis Channel and Erica Perkins Jasper of the Intercollegiate Tennis Association all provided strong encouragement. I also want to thank Jim Ellis, Dean of the Marshall School of Business, William Holder, Dean of the Leventhal School of Accounting, and Danielle Galvan and Audrena Goodie of the Leventhal School for their support with this project.

This book would never have been completed without data gathered by Roy Lee and Fiona Wang. Kristen Venter, a member of the USC women's tennis team, and McKenna Marshall, provided invaluable research assistance in producing the appendices and wrangling many of the photographs for this project. I am also indebted to my good friend and long-time collaborator Jill Stern for her insightful suggestions and detailed editing of the manuscript.

I am forever grateful to Stan Smith and Stevie Johnson for writing the forewords to the book. Not only are they one-in-a-million competitors, but most importantly, truly exemplary people. I am very thankful to Randy Walker, the publisher of New Chapter Press and a former walk-on tennis player at the University of Georgia, for his enthusiasm and guidance on this project. Finally I thank my wife, Dr. Sarah E. Bonner for her guidance, and my children Nathaniel and Kaylee Young. They all encouraged me to undertake this passion project even though it took much time away from them.

—S. Mark Young
2018

Foreword - Stan Smith

It's been over 50 years since I committed to play tennis under Coach George Toley at the University of Southern California. Those four years included some of my favorite times playing tennis. I had the privilege to play with a number of great athletes, including Tom Edlefsen, Tom Leonard, Jim Hobson, Jerry Cromwell, Steve Avoyer, Joaquin Loyo-Mayo, among others, and of course, my most successful doubles partner, Bob Lutz.

We didn't know it at the time, but under George Toley's tutelage, we would make tennis history by winning four straight NCAA team titles from 1966-1969. I will always be proud to have been part of the first four-peat.

Being a Trojan not only honed my skills and confidence in tennis, but this discipline enabled me to have a very successful career in the professional tennis ranks and in business. For me, while George Toley was one of the greatest tennis coaches of all time, he was also a dear friend and life coach who turned so many young boys to men. I can't thank him enough.

The history of USC tennis is truly significant and includes many legendary players. Top athletes like Tom Bundy, Gene Mako, Rafael Osuna, Joe Hunt, Dennis Ralston, Alex Olmedo, Rick Leach, and most recently Steve Johnson, are all part of the legacy of modern tennis. This book traces USC tennis history from its very beginnings as a fledgling club sport to one of the most dominant teams in American collegiate tennis history. The USC Trojans have won 21 national team titles, the most of any university in history, and boast the largest number of players (eight) in the most prestigious honorary society in the sport, The International Tennis Hall of Fame, of which I am currently the President.

This is more than a book on win-loss records and other statistics. You will certainly find your fill of that kind of material, but what makes the book come alive are the stories based on many original interviews that Mark Young has conducted. These interviews were conducted with the players, the relatives and the rivals of these young men, and the people who coached them. Young interweaves USC tennis history with the history of venerable institutions like the Los Angeles Tennis Club and the evolution of college tennis in general. Much of this information was in danger of being lost and it is wonderful to see that this important part of tennis history has now been preserved. If you love tennis, you will enjoy reading this book.

Foreword - Stevie Johnson

I came to USC in 2009 to fulfill a dream of becoming a Trojan and playing for Coach Peter Smith. I really had no idea what was in store for me, but I knew that I wanted to be part of something great.

When we won our first NCAA team title in 2009, we were all elated, but thought we were capable of more. Then we won the title again in 2010 and 2011. People ask me all the time how this was possible. I tell them that several factors were responsible. The first was the immense skill of our coaching staff – they are in a class of their own. The second was that we put the team ahead of each player's individual needs, and the third was we couldn't have been more motivated. After winning three national titles in row, it occurred to me to turn pro, but my heart told me that I had to go back to try for the four-peat. Few college teams ever win one national championship let alone four, so it was a gamble – but we did it.

At USC I learned a lot more than how to be a better tennis player. I learned that talent doesn't always win out; that it's hard work, character and respect for the people on your team that makes the difference. These aren't just lessons that apply only on the court, but to life in general. I made lifelong friendships with Kaes Van't Hof, Robert Farah, Daniel Nguyen, Ray Sarmiento, Peter Lucassen and so many of my other teammates. These guys are my brothers and I learned so much from them. My father, Steve Johnson Sr., will always be my first mentor and coach, but I also owe so much of my growth to Peter Smith. My close friendship with Peter was forged through all of the great times and struggles we had on and off the court. Peter is a truly great mentor, and in my opinion, the best tennis coach in the country.

Some question whether top junior players should skip college and go directly to the pros. My experience tells me that this might be the pathway for some, but for me, I received a first-class education *and* I was able to more than achieve my tennis goals. The tour is exciting, but grueling. While the average age of top professional players has crept up a bit lately, most players are thinking of retiring in their early 30s -- so having a college degree provides you with more options when the time comes to leave the circuit.

I first met Mark Young in 2012 while we were on our way to the four-peat. Mark told me that he wanted to write a book about the entire history of the men's tennis team, a history that began well over 100 years ago. Every time I saw Mark he would give me an update.

Now the book is a reality and I am really excited about it. It's a fascinating read that I think will be of great interest, not just to Trojan tennis fans, but also to everyone who loves tennis. I was aware of bits and pieces of USC men's tennis and knew many of the biggest names like Alex Olmedo, Stan Smith, Bob Lutz, Dennis Ralston and Rick Leach. But, as I discovered, USC's history consists of hundreds of players and thousands of contests. What I like most about this book are the stories of the greatest matches, the rivalries and the funniest moments. I am very proud that my story is now part of this illustrious history.

Author's Note

The history of the USC men's tennis team is rich and extensive. Hundreds of great athletes have participated on these teams for almost 120 years. In writing this history, I tried to include as many players as possible, but at the same time had to make some judgment calls due to space limitations. I apologize in advance if I have left specific players out of the narrative, but Appendix I contains all photos of the NCAA Championship teams, Appendix II lists every player who has played on every team, based on the extant archival record, and Appendix III lists the outstanding achievements of specific team members. Readers can also find even more statistical and descriptive information at http://usctrojans.com/roster.aspx?path=mten.

The data sources I used to compile the history were comprehensive, but sometimes incomplete or inaccurate. Where possible, I have cross-referenced information contained in media guides and annuals, *El Rodeo* yearbooks, the *Daily Trojan*, newspapers, magazine articles, Internet sites, and books. For the history from 1943 to present, I also relied on extensive, original interviews—conducted over the past five years—with players, coaches and relatives. These interviews represent the rich oral history of the team, not contained in any of the above source material. Players, relatives and institutions were also very generous in donating many never-before-seen photos that help bring the narrative to life. It goes without saying that, in the end, I am responsible for any omissions or errors in this volume.

I have also benefitted greatly from discussions about the sport with former women's tennis coach Dave Borelli and members of the USC women's team, including Barbara Hallquist, Beth Herr, Danielle Lao, Zoe Scandalis, Kaitlyn Christian and Sabrina Santamaria. The USC women's team has won seven team national titles under Coach Borelli, five national singles titles, two national doubles titles, and has produced not only the top players mentioned above, but also Stacy Margolin, Anne White, Sheila McInerney, Anna-Marie Fernandez, Anna-Lucia Fernandez, Cecilia Fernandez, Nina Voydat, Trey Lewis, Diane Desfor, Mary Norwood, Heliane Steden, Lupita Novelo Osuna, Lea Antonopolis, Leslie Allen, Kelly Henry, Caroline Kuhlman, Trisha Laux, Jewel Peterson, Lindsey Nelson, Amanda Fink, Maria Sanchez, and Guliana Olmos among many others. This team deserves a separate volume of its own.

Introduction:

The Legacy

On January 17, 2011, USC's Steve *aka* "Stevie" Johnson squared off against Bradley Klahn, one of Stanford's brightest stars and the 2010 NCAA singles champion, in the final of the prestigious Sherwood Collegiate Cup. For fifteen years, the Sherwood Country Club in Thousand Oaks, California sponsored this major contest by inviting a handful of the nation's top-ranked players to participate. Nestled against the base of the Santa Monica mountains, this bucolic setting that once hosted film sets for Hollywood stars like Errol Flynn was transformed into a stage to host some of the fiercest and most dramatic showdowns in college tennis. Klahn, known for his big left-handed serve, played well, upsetting Johnson, his friend—and rival since the juniors—6-2, 6-4, taking the title for the second straight year.

Sixteen months later, on May 27, 2012, in the NCAA singles semifinals at the Dan Magill Tennis Complex at the University of Georgia, No. 1 seed Johnson once again faced Klahn. Although Klahn had experienced a tough year and entered the tournament unseeded, he was back in good health

1

and playing well, dispatching several top players, including the fourth and eighth seeds. But Johnson was riding a tidal wave of success. Using his huge serve, one of the heaviest topspin forehands in college tennis, and an extremely aggressive style of play, Johnson had won every match since his loss to Klahn in 2011. The suspense was palpable. Would Klahn, the only competitor to beat Johnson in recent memory, be the spoiler who ended his winning streak? Those who watched the match were not disappointed. The two battled it out as they had many times before, but Johnson was not to be denied, and emerged with a 6-4, 7-5 victory that landed him in the final.

Two-time NCAA singles champion Stevie Johnson

In the last match of his college career, Johnson faced another top competitor, senior Eric Quigley. Quigley was a four-time Kentucky High School State Champion, winning 66 consecutive high school matches, and an All-American at the University of Kentucky. In the first set, both players held serve, but at 4-4, Johnson broke Quigley, held his serve, and won the set 6-4. Johnson broke again in the second set to go up 5-3. Quigley regained his composure and held, but Johnson, one of the fiercest competitors in the history of college tennis, knew it was time to end it. Serving for the match at 5-4, Johnson unleashed a series of blistering serves that took him to championship point. After a long baseline rally, Johnson hit his biting slice backhand down the line and Quigley inexplicably shanked a forehand off the top of his racket, careening the ball into the stands. Johnson dropped to his knees, arching back and releasing two long, loud screams.

No one but his inner circle knew what Johnson had endured on his way to winning his second NCAA singles title. In Johnson's quarterfinal match against Virginia's unseeded Alex Domijan, Johnson had started to cramp and felt like he might have torn a stomach muscle. Coach Peter Smith, who was sitting on the sidelines, grabbed a large jar of pickles from a table next to the court. Emptying out the pickles, he urged Johnson to drink the juice. Researchers believe the vinegar in the juice hits receptors on the tongue and instructs the brain to relax the muscles and to stop cramping. The remedy provided temporary relief for Johnson, who continued on to win the match in three sets. The first scream may have been a primal reaction releasing the intense stress he had endured, but the second was a reaction to the pain of leaning backwards and aggravating his abdominal muscle.

After the match Quigley said, "I think his lack of nerves and his ability to come up with some great shots at big moments makes him pretty special. His serve—I think he can put it on a dime. I think he did it several times today." Smith summed up Johnson's drive to the title saying, "Steve is a very special player. He has gears that I have never seen before."

Johnson's winning streak of 72 consecutive matches shattered the record held by Mikael Pernfors, the University of Georgia standout, who ran up 42 matches in a row in 1985. But the individual win was just icing on the cake for Johnson. The previous week, he and co-captain Daniel (Dwin) Nguyen led the USC team to its fourth consecutive national team title, a feat only accomplished twice before in American collegiate tennis history—once by USC from 1966-1969 and more recently by Stanford from 1995-1998.

After winning his second straight NCAA singles title, an exhausted Johnson said, "I am so happy to have won it again in singles. It's been a long two weeks, but the most special thing was winning the team event last week. Winning the fourth in a row—that's special with the guys. It's something I will never forget."

Johnson's herculean efforts did not go unrecognized. In April 2016, the seven-time All-American and the most dominant college tennis player of all time was honored as the Pac-12 Men's Tennis Player of the Century.

Stories like Johnson's perfectly encapsulate the excitement of college tennis. Fans appreciate the intense individual effort that must be directed toward the success of the team. A victory or a loss on one court can completely shift the momentum of the team match. While professional tennis can be thrilling, it's hard to rival the nerve-racking excitement of watching the country's most gifted and tenacious college players battling it out in front of their excited fans. If you're not convinced, come down to a USC home match. You will never see competitive tennis in the same light again!

The making of a successful college tennis team is not as easy as simply recruiting the top high school players. Although having exceptional players is a necessary component, when it comes to team sports, temperament, camaraderie and maturity are just as important as talent. On college teams, junior tennis players, accustomed to training for personal advancement, are thrust into an environment in which individual victory becomes secondary to the success of the team. This setting aside of personal ambition is more challenging than one might think. In today's culture, many top juniors are now home-schooled to maximize their training and tournament play. And they may choose not to play on their high school teams, unless there is a tangible benefit to their personal development. Arriving at college and becoming part of a team can either lead to the best bonding and maturing experience of a young tennis player's life—or leave a young player feeling confused and alienated. For Stevie Johnson, the satisfaction of contributing to the legacy of arguably the greatest team in American college tennis history fueled his pursuit of personal excellence.

Steve Johnson's phenomenal success at USC is not an anomaly. While Johnson is an outstanding athlete and superior competitor in his own right, he is also one in a very long line of tennis greats who have played for the University of Southern California. What has made the Trojans tennis team so hard to beat over the past century? Certainly, the historical development of tennis in Southern California has played a role, as has the commitment of the university to their athletes. But at the core of USC's success is its coaching staff.

In January of 2014, former USC Athletic Director Pat Haden unveiled a newly renovated Heritage Hall, housing the USC Hall of Fame and the Athletic Department. The southwest wall on the second floor showcases the *Coaching Legends of USC*. The eighteen exceptional coaches were chosen from a pool of hundreds across all sports beginning in 1880. To occupy a place on the wall is to be recognized as great. Three of the eighteen legends—George Toley, Dick Leach, and Peter Smith—are tennis coaches. Together, these three coaches, and the winning cultures each created, span over 60 years of USC tennis history and represent the most enviable record in American collegiate tennis history. Furthermore, eight of USC's players have been inducted into the International Tennis Hall of Fame -- including Gene Mako, Ellsworth Vines, Bob Falkenburg, Alex Olmedo, Rafael Osuna, Dennis Ralston, Joe Hunt, and Stan Smith -- the most by far of any team in the country. The spectacular Buntmann Family Tennis Center, which also houses the David X. Marks Tennis Stadium, contains a treasure trove of photos of USC greats and countless trophies and awards testifying to the numerous achievements of the men's and women's teams.

Plaques honoring USC Coaching Legends George Toley, Dick Leach and Peter Smith in Heritage Hall, USC

California has spawned the top three Division I tennis teams in the country—Stanford, UCLA and USC—each defined by exceptional tennis programs. Individually impressive, these rivals have inspired and goaded one another to achieve the highest standards of performance in the sport. At USC, men's tennis has won 21 NCAA team Championships, an impressive 20 percent of the 104 NCAA national titles earned across all USC teams, as of the start of the 2017/18 school season. Stanford is second with 17, all won under the leadership of legendary head coach Dick Gould, and UCLA is third with 16 wins. Together, this west coast trio accounts for over 76 percent (54/71) of the total NCAA team titles since the inception of the team championship in 1946.

All three of these Pac-12 schools can claim to have produced some of the greatest players in tennis history, including: Ted Schroeder, John McEnroe, Sandy Mayer, Roscoe Tanner, Tim Mayotte and the Bryan Brothers at Stanford; Jimmy Connors, Arthur Ashe, Charlie Pasarell, Jim Pugh and Peter Fleming at UCLA; and Gene Mako, Stan Smith, Bob Lutz, Alex Olmedo, Rafael Osuna, Dennis Ralston, Raul Ramirez, Rick Leach, and Stevie Johnson at USC. Each school has also been coached by some of the best coaches of all time: William Ackerman, J.D. Morgan, Glenn Bassett and Billy Martin at UCLA, Dick Gould and John Whitlinger at Stanford and George Toley, Dick Leach and Peter Smith at USC. Outside of California, universities such as Trinity University, the University of Georgia, and most recently the University of Virginia among others, have fielded extremely talented teams. The on-court battles waged by these programs are of mythic proportions and provide a level of excitement and drama that only top college competition can provide.

It is inconceivable to talk about the ascendancy of USC tennis without considering the history of the game in the region and examining why Southern California has spawned so many of the world's greatest champions. Certainly a hospitable climate, the early adoption of the game before the turn of the 20th Century, the large number of students at high schools and colleges who took to the sport, and the proliferation of tennis courts at private clubs and public parks where top juniors and seasoned players were groomed, created an environment in which tennis flourished. In particular, the legendary Los Angeles Tennis Club (LATC) in Hancock Park, and the Ojai Valley Tennis Tournament played significant roles in the development of tennis in Southern California. The LATC is an institution that has linked USC tennis with many of the greatest professional players of all time, including Pancho Segura, Bill Tilden, Budge Patty, Jack Kramer, Pancho Gonzales, Bobby Riggs, Don Budge and countless others. The Ojai tournament, one of the most venerable and respected tournaments in the nation, boasts many of the nation's top players as its former champions.

For well over 100 years, USC has produced champions who played truly significant and dominant roles in the sport. The story began in 1899 and continued to 1925 when tennis at USC went from a club team to a minor sport, before emerging as a major sport in 1931. At the turn of the 20th Century, the first star player for USC was Tom Bundy, who went on to become a finalist at the U.S. Championships (the modern-day U.S. Open) in 1919. Former player-turned-coach Harold Godshall took over the team in 1927 and coached many of USC's great players including Gene Mako and Joe Hunt. In the decade following Godshall's untimely death in 1942, four successive coaches, George Toley (for one season), Arnold Eddy, Bill Moyle and

Lou Wheeler, took over the Trojan squad. With the exception of Toley, none of these coaches were notable tennis players, yet all served to stabilize the team while garnering two national championships in the process.

When Toley, a former player and professional coach, returned to helm the team from 1954 to 1980, USC's tennis program coalesced and rose to national prominence. During this period, many of USC's greatest champions emerged, including Dennis Ralston, Rafael Osuna, Alex Olmedo, Stan Smith and Bob Lutz. In addition, Toley forged an unprecedented connection between young Latino athletes and a major U.S. university. His recruitment of a steady stream of Mexico's finest juniors, such as Francisco Contreras, Rafael Osuna, Joaquin Loyo-Mayo, Marcelo Lara and Raul Ramirez, earned Toley the title, "The Father of Mexican Tennis." Toley's teams won ten national championships, including the first four-peat between 1966-1969.

Between 1980 and 2002, Dick Leach, one of Toley's former top players, returned to campus as coach. Dick also produced numerous winning teams and top players, including his sons Rick and Jon Leach, Robert Van't Hof, Eric Amend, Matt Anger, Scott Melville, Luke Jensen, Tim Pawsat, Brian MacPhie, Byron Black, Wayne Black, Andrew Park, Cecil Mamiit and Prakash Amritraj. Leach's teams also won four national championships.

Since 2003, Peter Smith has been the head coach at USC. Smith's teams have won five national championships over a 14-year period, including the second USC four-peat between 2009-2012. Smith has produced many outstanding players including Robert Farah, Kaes Van't Hof, Daniel Nguyen, Ray Sarmiento, Emilio Gomez, Roberto Quiroz, Yannick Hanfmann, Max de Vroome, Steve Johnson and Brandon Holt.

In the pages that follow, you'll read about highlights of the most memorable matches and teams of each period and reminiscences from numerous players and coaches. As noted earlier, the Appendices provide even more detailed information about team members and their achievements. While many ascended to highly successful professional careers, this book focuses primarily on their time playing for USC. In the last section of the book discusses how I became involved with this project and why I consider myself to be one of the most fortunate Division III tennis players of all time.

1

Origins

The preponderance of evidence regarding the origins of tennis suggests the game began in 12th Century France, although some suggest that the Egyptians, Greeks and Romans played crude versions of the sport. Monks and members of the Court could be heard bellowing *"tenez"* (ten-ay) inside dimly lit French monasteries and royal chambers. The term *tenez* derives from the French verb *tenir* meaning to receive or take. Shouting *tenez* indicated that a server was about to hit a ball to a receiver. This early version of tennis was known as *Jeu de Paume*, or game of the palm, since players used bare hands, and later gloves, to hit a cork ball covered in woolen fabric back and forth. By the 16th Century, *Jeu de Paume* evolved into Court Tennis (also called "real tennis" or "royal tennis") with wooden paddles replacing gloved hands. In turn, those wooden paddles transformed into rackets strung with twisted fibers made from sheep, goat or cattle intestines, sometimes referred to as catgut (the term probably abbreviated from cattle-gut). Court tennis was played in an enclosed area and is still somewhat popular in parts of Europe.

In the early 1870's, Major Walter C. Wingfield, a Welsh inventor and former soldier enamored with tennis, saw a business opportunity to bring the sport to the masses. To make the game which he called *Sphairistike* (an ancient Greek term meaning "skill at playing with a ball" and pronounced, "shair-rist-ik-ee"), more accessible, Wingfield assembled a portable kit that came in a three foot box containing poles, netting, court markers, four racquets, a mallet to hammer net stakes, and a brush for marking the court. The price of the set, including a six-page pamphlet of rules, was five guineas or about $25. A court could be marked out on any flat stretch of grass. As a major innovation, Winfield also included a bag of German-made, hollow balls created using Charles Goodyear's invention of vulcanized rubber. These new cloth-covered balls could bounce on any surface.

Those who found Sphairistike unpronounceable simply called it "Sticky." The game was appealing and began to catch on in England. Legend has it that the future Prime Minister of England, Alfred Balfour, an accomplished tennis player and friend of Wingfield's, coined the term "lawn tennis." Wingfield shaped his court like an hourglass, and used a more complicated scoring system than that used today. The All England Lawn Tennis and Croquet Club made some changes to Wingfield's system, including using a rectangular court and a simplified method of scoring. By 1877, the club had wrested control of the game, and announced the first Wimbledon Championship. Wingfield's contribution to the sport was pushed aside, and he passed away in relative obscurity in 1912, never having achieved his goals of wealth and fame.

It has not been definitively established where the very first tennis match was played in America. Several sites have been suggested, including Camp Reynolds on Angel Island in

San Francisco, Camp Apache in the Arizona territory and East Point, Nahant on the Massachusetts peninsula. Regardless, the game became popular at each of these locations sometime in 1874, with players using Wingfield's kits.

As with many innovations and trends, college students were some of the first to become enamored with the game. In April 1883, representatives from Amherst College and Brown University met at Trinity College in Hartford, Connecticut to form the Intercollegiate Lawn Tennis Association. A constitution was drafted with Yale, Harvard, and Williams being the first to join the association, followed closely by Lehigh, Princeton, Columbia, and the University of Pennsylvania. That year, the first intercollegiate championship took place in Hartford, with Harvard winning both the singles and doubles titles. For the next 38 years, the original founding members of the Lawn Tennis Association, led almost exclusively by Ivy League and other East Coast schools, won all of the singles and doubles championships.

By 1881, a year after the University of Southern California was founded, lawn tennis reached California. Due to the arid climate, constructing grass courts was problematic, and thus, the vast majority of tennis courts were built using asphalt or cement. The first tennis courts on a college campus in California were built at the California State Normal School, which was founded in San Francisco in 1862, later moving to San Jose in 1871. At the time, Normal Schools—or teachers' colleges—were proliferating across the U.S. In 1882, The California Normal School was established in Los Angeles on W. 5th Street, the current site of the Central Library of the Los Angeles Public Library System. The school operated under the control of San Jose State University until 1919 when it merged with the University of California, Berkeley and renamed the

Southern Branch of the University of California. In 1929, the Southern Branch was relocated to Westwood, California, becoming the University of California, Los Angeles (UCLA). Today, the school's former location on N. Vermont Avenue in East Los Angeles is the site of Los Angeles City College (LACC).

Records from 1893 indicate that the Normal School in San Jose had an active all-female tennis club that likely influenced the creation of a similar club at the Los Angeles Branch. In 1896, documents from the Los Angeles Branch mention the newly developed Peculiar Hill Tennis Club, so named since it was built on the undulating terrain surrounding 5th and Grand Avenues in downtown Los Angeles.

In December 1887, the Southern California Interscholastic Association (SCIA) was formed, consisting of seven institutions which were a mix of colleges and high schools: the Normal School, Throop (now Caltech), Los Angeles High School, Ventura High School, Santa Barbara High School, Pasadena High School, and San Jacinto High School. Football, basketball, baseball, track and field, and tennis were the dominant sports at these schools.

The first mention of a USC Tennis Association was noted in 1899 in *El Rodeo*, the USC yearbook, as George F. Bovard was being named President of the Board of Trustees at USC (He later served as the fourth President of USC from 1903 until 1921.) The Association was comprised of 13 members and led by President C.E.D. Ballou. Tennis quickly became popular, with the majority of players hailing from the Liberal Arts, Medicine, and Law Schools. USC held men's and women's singles, doubles, and mixed doubles tournaments under the auspices of the Tennis Association; however, tennis was considered a club sport. While *El Rodeo* did not publish from 1900 through 1907, due to a lack of funding, an early photo from 1908 shows three courts on campus labeled the "Old Tennis Club." The Club was located west of the Bovard Administration Building the current site of Associates Park. During those early years, the first notable tennis player for USC—Thomas C. Bundy— emerged.

Maurice McLoughlin, "The California Comet" (left), and Tom Bundy (right) at the Los Angeles Tennis Club, circa 1927

Tom Bundy was the son of successful real estate developer Nathan Pearl Bundy and his wife, Harriet. The Bundys had six children, and were among the earliest residents of Santa Monica. Tom joined the Tennis Association and began playing at USC in 1902. While at USC, Bundy played intramural matches against both students and faculty. He was a superior tennis player and, after he graduated, won Ojai's

All Comers Tournament in 1911 and the Southern California Tennis Association (SCTA) Championship in 1913. He went on to become a three-time men's doubles champion with Maurice ("The California Comet") McLoughlin at the U.S. National Championships (later the U.S. Open) between 1912 and 1914, and a two-time member of the U.S. Davis Cup Team.

In 1912, Bundy married U.S. National and Wimbledon champion May Sutton. May was one of the four Sutton sisters who were famous in tennis circles for their athletic ability. Born in England, she grew up in Pasadena. In 1904, at age 18, and while still a student at Pasadena High School, she won the U.S. National women's singles title, holding the record as the youngest winner until 1979 when 16-year-old Tracy Austin won the title. May was also chosen as the Rose Queen in 1908. In 1956, she was the first female to be inducted into the International Tennis Hall of Fame. Although they separated in 1923, and eventually divorced in 1940, Tom and May's tennis genes carried on into the next generation. Their daughter, Dorothy "Dodo" Bundy Cheney, was the first woman to win the Australian Championships in 1938 and was a member of the 1937, 1938 and 1939 winning U.S. Wightman Cup teams. She also won the U.S. Indoor, Clay, and Hard Court Doubles Championships in 1941, 1944, and 1954, respectively. Dodo played into her 90s, earning 394 USTA national titles, including a final one at the USTA women's 90 Hard Court doubles in 2012, before passing away at age 98. One of her favorite stories occurred when she was 73 years old and playing an exhibition with a ten-year-old prodigy named Venus Williams. After the match, May was quoted as saying; "She just wiped me off the court."

As a Santa Monica realtor and civic leader, Tom Bundy (for whom Bundy Drive in Brentwood is named) is credited with the growth of Los Angeles and surrounding communities and developed the Miracle Mile on Wilshire Boulevard. Most significantly related to USC tennis, Bundy co-founded the renowned Los Angeles Tennis Club (LATC) at 5851 Clinton Street in Hancock Park with Captain G. Alan Hancock and several other notable Angelenos in 1920, serving as president from 1920 to 1925. The LATC, also known as the "cradle of tennis," is considered one of the most influential tennis clubs in the nation and is hallowed ground for the stars that played there. The LATC hosted major events, including the Pacific Southwest tournament and several ties (elimination rounds) of the Davis Cup. Over its long history, the LATC was also home to the Southern California Tennis Association, run by tennis czar Perry T. Jones and secretary Doris Cooke, and served as the base for many of the greatest champions of the game, including Pancho Segura, Pancho Gonzalez, Gussie Moran, Bill Tilden, Ellsworth Vines, Pauline Betz, Jack Kramer, Budge Patty, Gene Mako, Bobby Riggs, Alex Olmedo, Dennis Ralston, Bill Johnston and Bob Lutz among others. Later, George Toley and Dick Leach coached their USC teams at the club.

As early as 1892, both Stanford and the University of California at Berkeley had formed intercollegiate teams. Each team consisted of six male players who played six singles and three doubles matches. In that year, the two schools played their first match, with Stanford winning 5-4. While the SCIA had been formed in 1887, USC was not a member. It wasn't until 1910 that the first university wide, co-ed tournament was held on campus to select a team to play Occidental College. The USC squad consisted of four men: Hal Paulin, Barrat Hanawalt, John Malcom and Arthur Lawrence, and two women: Misses Taft and Hurst. Despite a strong effort, the team lost to Occidental.

Over the next few years, USC's coed teams played other schools, including Throop University, Stanford and Occidental. Match play consisted of men's and women's singles and doubles and mixed doubles. Men competed in long trousers and long-sleeved shirts, while women wore corsets, floor-length skirts, ruffled blouses and broad brimmed hats. All players dressed in white clothing since it reflected the heat, hid perspiration and was consistent with the high dress standards and decorum of the game. In 1911, a standout player named Henry Grady Clardy was a team member. Mr. Clardy's legacy lives on through his great grandson, Nick Crystal, who captained the Trojan team in 2016-2017.

In 1912, *El Rodeo* reported that USC had finally formed a varsity tennis team, although tennis was still relegated to minor sport status. The team took its first "northern trip" to play Stanford, with whom they would have an enduring rivalry. The team consisted of Harold Huntington, Kenneth Newell, G. Brumley Oxnam, Mr. Dixon, Ray Morrow, Frank Chaffee, Lily Kincade and Maida Wellborne. USC won the closely contested match. The following year, the Trojans suffered humiliating losses at the hands of Berkeley's very strong varsity and freshman teams.

Tennis activity at the university was still divided between intramural tournaments, team tryouts for varsity positions and matches with other universities. In 1913, USC took first place in the Southern California Intercollegiate competitions. The team continued to improve when William G. Bonelli became president of the USC Tennis Club. Also in 1913, "Varsity Monograms" (the precursors to Varsity Letters) were first granted to USC tennis players. The monograms could be sewn onto sweaters and blazers—including those in Cardinal and Gold—the school colors adopted by USC in 1895.

Gene Mako at the LATC wearing a USC Varsity Monogram, circa 1933

During the 1914 season, *El Rodeo* reported the formation of separate women's and men's teams. Jesse Grieve, a star player with a big serve and strong groundstrokes, captained the women's team, while Eugene Warren led the men. The women had a great season, soundly beating Stanford and Berkeley. That year Stanford did not play USC and Occidental and Pomona couldn't put together enough players to field teams, leaving the men with only one match against the University of California. While the team was frustrated with the lack of competitive play, they beat Berkeley and avenged their previous year's losses.

USC entered the 1915 season with high hopes as the men were fielding one of their strongest teams, consisting of captain and top player Harold Huntington, Eugene Warren, Kenneth Newell and Ray Morrow. Other standout players of this period were Ronald Stannard, Ralph Sindorf and Robert Nathan. Despite having a superior team, their hopes for a winning season were dashed when, during the first week of the semester, Huntington announced that he was leaving school to take up the "simple life." The simple life was a social movement in America begun by John Wannamaker in 1860, whose central tenets were to live a life that was self-sacrificing, spiritual and less materialistic. With Huntington's departure, the Trojans finished with a mediocre season.

In February of 1916, a talented young man named Leon Godshall played on USC's team against Hollywood Junior College (later absorbed by the University of California Southern Branch). While Godshall, who played No. 1 singles, easily won his match in straight sets, USC ended up tying with Hollywood Junior College, 3-3 (four singles and two doubles matches were played at the time). The Godshall name would later become fully enshrined in USC tennis history when Leon's younger brother, Harold L. Godshall, joined the team in 1922 and later become its head coach.

In March of 1916, the U.S. joined Allied Forces to fight in World War I. While tennis activity decreased during the war, both the women's and men's tennis clubs continued to play. Across the country, the 1917 U.S. National Championship—officially renamed the National Patriotic Tournament—took place at the West Side Tennis Club in Forest Hills, New York. Robert Lindley Murray, a Stanford graduate, won the tournament. No prizes were awarded that year, with all proceeds donated to the American Red Cross.

A year later, in March of 1917, USC tennis received a significant boost when the university held an East-West tournament on campus. A special asphalt court, surrounded by gallery seating, was built on Bovard Field close to Jefferson Boulevard to commemorate the event. A number of international players, including William Johnston, the eventual 1923-1924 Wimbledon singles champion, May Sutton, the 1904 U.S. and 1905-1907 Wimbledon champion, Maurice McLoughlin and Tom Bundy played for the West. George Church, Harold Throckmorton, Frederick Alexander and Miss Molla Bjurstedt represented the East. A much-hyped match was a mixed doubles pairing with Tom Bundy and May Sutton for the West squaring off against George Church and Molla Bjurstedt for the East. While the West overcame the East in tournament play, Church and Bjurstedt surprised everyone by beating Bundy and Sutton 6-2, 6-0.

In 1918, USC continued to play a mix of institutions, including Hollywood Junior College and Throop, which changed its name to California Institute of Technology in 1920. Ralph Sindorf, the former Hollywood High star considered the best player at USC, teamed with Leon Godshall to score a major victory over California. Sindorf later made headlines of another sort when he publically sued real estate agent W.E. Conrad for $100,000 for "stealing his wife's affections." Conrad and actress Helen Sindorf denied the accusations. A trial took place several months later, with the jury needing only 45 minutes to decide in Sindorf's favor. The victory was somewhat anticlimactic when Sindorf was told that the financial settlement would only be $5,000. While tame by today's standards, the case was considered scandalous at the time.

Members of the 1914 USC men's tennis team, Harold Huntington, Eugene Warren, Ray Morrow (Captain) and Kenneth Newell

Over the next few years, college tennis increased in popularity, with West Coast teams becoming increasingly competitive. In 1919, the University of California formed what they called the Southern Branch of their university. In 1920, the first athletic competition, a baseball game between the Southern Branch and USC, took place. The Southern Branch Cubs whipped the Trojans 5-2, and the rivalry between USC and what would become UCLA began. That both universities were located in the same city—only 13 miles apart—helped to fuel the desire for supremacy. So deeply rooted was this rivalry that years later, at the start of the 2001-2002 season, the two teams agreed to formalize it with the inauguration of the Crosstown Cup in which USC and UCLA compete against one another in 19 sports. Each sport counts for ten points. All ten points are awarded to the winner of the most head-to-head contests in each sport (if both schools win an equal amount of matchups in a season, the points are evenly split.) After the 2016-2017 season, USC led UCLA 10-6.

Until 1921, the Ivy League and other East Coast teams had won every singles and doubles intercollegiate championship, but the pendulum began its swing to west coast dominance when Philip Neer of Stanford broke the streak by winning the singles championship. In 1922, Neer and teammate James Davies won the doubles championship. From that time to the present, only one Ivy League team ever won a national title again, when Princeton's John Van Ryn and Kenneth Appel won the doubles tournament in 1927.

In 1922, the varsity team was comprised of Paul Greene, Stanley Welch, Joe Skleners, Charles Olerich Leo Freese and Ed Berry. The racket wielders took their first major trip back east to play many top schools, including Michigan, Annapolis, Columbia, Princeton, Williams, Amherst and George Washington. Welch and Greene were one of the top doubles teams in the nation and won every match. H.R. Lee, a member of the Physical Education Department, was listed as the team's advisor. Overall, the team had a successful season winning the Southwestern Championship.

In that same year, SC's freshman class yielded one of the strongest teams in the nation, especially after recruiting

Harold Lincoln Hall Godshall. Born in 1903, Godshall had an illustrious junior tennis history: he was the Southern California boy's champ at 11; junior men's champion at 15; winner of the national junior doubles title at 17 with Bob Allen in 1920; the Southern California Open champion for several years, and won the Southern California doubles title with four different partners. In 1923, USC also had a winning season.

In January 1924, an editorial in the *Daily Trojan* bemoaned the university's lack of support for tennis and tried to appeal to USC students to follow the sport. The editorial stated, "… there is a reason why measures should be taken to improve tennis morale about the campus. Consider the dusty, sandy courts; lack of funds to send a two-man team north to meet Stanford and California. These are two glaring reasons why you as a student hear so little about the USC tennis teams."

It wasn't until October, however, that members of the men's tennis club were galvanized into pushing for more support from the university's administration. Tennis was booming all across the country, with teams forming in the Midwest, and those on the east coast gaining more and more momentum. Tennis at USC still had no real following from the student body or administration, so the Men's Tennis Club took it upon themselves to open the doors to anyone on campus who wanted to play—including faculty members. This move helped to break the insularity of the club, which previously had consisted only of varsity and freshmen team players. The club decided to sponsor campus-wide tournaments in order to determine who should play on the team, thus attracting attention by showcasing their top players. In a bold move, the club pushed the university to build three "first class courts" on campus given the poor, non-competitive facilities as noted in the aforementioned *Daily Trojan* editorial. Ironically, the poor facilities may have helped build strong teams. Coaches would seek alternate locations for their players to practice, often landing at many of the best tennis clubs in Los Angeles (such as the LATC). USC players were able to play against many top tennis professionals seeking respite from the tour. No doubt these opportunities improved the skills of the Trojan athletes.

Members of the 1924 team included Howard White, Joe Call, Earle Cullingham, Harold Williamson, Harold Godshall and George Parmelee. Parmelee went on to win the Southern California Intercollegiate Championship that year. Godshall, a sophomore, also made a name for himself in an inspired match in the 1924 Southern California Championship against national champion Bill Tilden at the Los Angeles Tennis Club. After losing the first set 6-3, Godshall was down 4-2 in the second. With the crowd behind him, Harold broke Tilden's serve and the crowd went wild. Tilden, obviously shaken by Godshall's play, complained vociferously to the referee, saying no applause should occur during the point as it was distracting him. Tilden's obnoxious gamesmanship rattled Godshall, who promptly lost the next three games and the match 6-3, 6-3. Godshall did have some success in mixed doubles, pairing with May Sutton to win the 1925 Midwick Country Club Championship in Alhambra, California.

As a result of the team selection process initiated in the previous year, the 1925 team was determined by an All-University tennis tournament. Led by Howard ("Honest John") White, the team consisted of Mal Robinson, Robert Mucks, Stew Robinson, Earl Cunningham, Howard Murphy and Jack Fazakerley, and was touted by *El Rodeo* as the "most powerful squad" to date. In their first year, they defeated every college in Southern California, including the University of California,

Southern Branch Cubs. The Trojans ended the season by beating the University of Arizona to win the Southwest Championship. The match play format at the time consisted of six singles and three doubles matches, with doubles played after singles matches were completed.

In 1925, tennis courts began cropping up in other parts of Los Angeles. Just across the street from USC, the City of Los Angeles built eight hard courts in Exposition Park at the corner of S. Hoover and W. Martin Luther King Drive. These courts, which no longer exist, would play a major role in nurturing many top ranked players, including locals Pancho Gonzalez and Manual Arts High School student Bobby Perez.

Harold Godshall was an integral part of the team for the four years he played at SC. He didn't dominate the team as expected, since he was focused on his studies. He graduated in 1925 with a degree from the College of Commerce and went to work as an insurance broker at Rule & Sons, Inc. in Los Angeles. While still a broker, Harold also played tennis professionally— but mostly in local tournaments. He also gave a number of tennis exhibitions in the Los Angeles area.

In 1926, fresh off wins over Caltech, Loyola and Pomona, the team finally got what they desired when the university spent $30,000 to construct three new tennis courts near Hoover and Jefferson Boulevards. The "Hoover Street" courts provided the boost that the team sorely needed after so many years of playing on substandard courts. The courts survived for many years, but were eventually torn down in 1992 to make way for the construction of Leavey Library.

2

Harold Godshall:
The Forgotten Coach

In 1927, two years after he graduated, Harold Godshall returned to campus to coach the team. During the 1927-1928 season, Godshall's first team won 50 percent of the dual matches against tough teams from Stanford, California and UCLA.

Godshall was an amiable man with a relaxed style. He was relatively tall at 6 foot 2 inches and thin with a receding hairline. The *Daily Trojan* described him as "a popular coach who deserves a great deal of credit for the year's success." Probably his biggest strength was his ability to corral extremely talented players—given his reputation and the growing stature of the team. For the first time in USC tennis history, the players had a very accomplished player as their coach. Godshall coached successful teams with players Eva Miller, Kenny Faulkner, Theron Wilson, Francis Hardy, Bob Bagley, Red Kerr,

Bob Gates, Stan Stele, Roy McGinnis, Jack Herbs, Ray Swain, Harold Barr and Bill Kelley.

In his autobiography *The Golden Age of College Tennis*, George Toley, who played under Godshall, noted that Godshall did not coach the players and rarely attended practices. He even let the players determine the starting lineup. While few records exist regarding Godshall, an interview in *El Rodeo* noted that the Godshall coaching philosophy seemed to be that, if he recruited

Harold Godshall stretching for a low forehand, circa 1928

top players, he didn't have to spend time teaching them how to play the game. Since the tennis budget was still very limited, and coaching tennis was a part time job, Godshall persisted as a practicing insurance agent even while he was running the team. He also spent additional time studying aviation at Lockheed Martin with the dream of someday going into the aviation insurance business.

Thanks to the push by the Men's Tennis Club, interest in tennis increased on the USC campus and, in the 1929-1930 season, a record number of players tried out for the team. The Trojans had decisive victories over Santa Ana Junior College and Cal Tech. But USC wasn't the only school where tennis was becoming a popular sport. College tennis teams continued to expand across the country and matches became more and more exciting as USC's teams faced stiffer and stiffer competition. Within a few years, USC was taking on the top teams from universities such as California, Stanford, UCLA and Arizona, all of whom had become members of the Pacific Coast Conference. In 1930, college tennis saw a big change when matches were changed from the best-of-three sets to the best-of-five. The five-set format remained in place until 1980 when matches returned to best-of-three sets.

A critical turning point for the team occurred in 1931, when tennis was deemed a major sport at USC. This meant that, unlike club or intramural sports, the team would receive a budget and other university support and, in turn, would follow university standards as well as those of the governing body of the particular sport. In addition, earning a spot on a major sports team was prestigious. Over his seven-year tenure, Godshall had been successful in attracting many top players who could compete with the best. The 1931 team consisted of Captain Art Flum, as well as star player Jack DeLara, who went on to win

11 out of 12 matches that season. Flum was well known for his heavy topspin forehand, a stroke that stood out in an era where most players hit the ball flat. The team also included Harold Barr, Theron Wilson, Roy Stoebe, Bob Crane and James Stocks. The team played two matches each against California, Stanford, UCLA, and St. Mary's. The team also played in the Pacific Coast intercollegiate championship and the Ojai Valley tournament.

One way that Godshall was able to continue to develop the skills of his players was to make use of his connections at various tennis clubs in Los Angeles, including the Los Angeles Tennis Club, and the Beverly Hills Tennis Club (started by Fred Perry and Ellsworth Vines). Each of the head professionals at these clubs had affiliations with USC, giving players the opportunity to play against the top touring pros.

It is a testament to Godshall's ability to recruit and retain top players that he was able build a strong team during one of the worst economic downturns in American history. Even though The Great Depression of the 1930s devastated the U.S. economy, it actually led to an enormous boom in tennis activity in Southern California.

While there were many private tennis clubs, including those in Mt. Washington, Alhambra and Los Angeles, the Southern California Tennis Association (SCTA) decided to expand their tennis activities, most likely as a way to create something positive for local communities. According to LATC tennis historian Pat Yeomans, the SCTA organized local exhibitions at the college and high school levels in Pasadena, Eagle Rock, Glendale, Pomona, Burbank and Montebello. Starting in 1931, players of all ages played in 19 junior and 107 regular tournaments on 56 municipal courts built by the City of Los Angeles to support the SCTA initiatives. Playing on the courts was free and provided relief to many seeking solace from the harshness of the Depression. As a result, tennis became the second-most popular sport next to softball. The SCTA also worked in tandem with other municipal groups and with the City of Los Angeles to build 56 new public courts.

One of the most influential individuals of this period was Perry T. Jones, who produced an incredible array of superstar tennis players over a 15-year period at the Los Angeles Tennis Club. Jones had been a successful junior tennis player who had acquired a deep love of the game. He employed what he called "the factory system," designed to have local coaches and players identify top young talent that he would recruit and put through a systematic process of training and grooming at the LATC. He viewed his students as "products" of this system. Jones was known to be all-controlling, extremely difficult and even sometimes bigoted when it came to sponsoring players. If you ran afoul of Jones, you were doomed. He decided who could train at LATC, what tournaments they could enter and even how they dressed. Viewed by many as a tyrant, he was nevertheless instrumental in player development in Los Angeles and the United States.

Annette Buck, past director of adult and senior tennis for the SCTA for over 30 years who knew Jones, described him as someone who got things done and did a great deal for Southern California tennis; however he was "a prissy man who fussed over his appearance and other people's behavior." Former SC Coach Dick Leach concurred and described Jones's personal style, "Perry T. used to wear a bow tie and suspenders. We didn't know why, but he hiked his pants up so high above his waist that he could reach over his shoulder and pull out a comb from his back pocket!" Jones also demanded that his players conform to his grooming standards. Ed Atkinson who was National Doubles Champion with Alex Olmedo in 1958

"The Czar of Tennis," Perry T. Jones, at the Los Angeles Tennis Club, circa 1945

recalls, "Bobby Delgado and I were set to play doubles on an out-of-town tour to several major tournaments including the national 18-and-under juniors. At the last minute, Jones called me in and said that I couldn't go on the trip. When I asked why he told me that my hair was too long. I was really upset, as we were all packed and ready to go. I decided that I had to do something fast, so I ran to the back of the LATC and jumped the fence to get to a local barber I knew. He cut my hair very quickly and I ran back the club. Jones was unfazed. He looked at me and said, 'OK, now you can go.' The man was a dictator!" Despite Jones' personal peculiarities, he was both respected and feared.

Atkinson continued, "At the time, all of the Grand Slam tournaments were played on grass, except for the French. We didn't have too many grass courts in LA, as they were hard to maintain. So, to be competitive at these tournaments, Jones decided to have his players train on cement courts. Cement was the closest surface to grass in those days. In colder parts of the country cement wasn't popular, as it would crack during the winter. Thus, the players from LA were well prepared for these major tournaments, and tournament directors wanted LATC players in the draw since they did well. This gave Jones a huge amount of power. He could pick and choose who to send to these tournaments, and players had to toe the line if they wanted to be selected to play."

In 1930, Jones became the first secretary of the Southern California Tennis Association, headquartered at the LATC, where he served for over thirty years. He passed away in 1970 at age 80.

Jones helped groom a number of players, but nine stand out: Ellsworth Vines, Jack Kramer, Richard (Pancho) Gonzalez, Gene Mako, Bobby Riggs, Ted Schroeder, Budge Patty, Bob Falkenburg and Joseph Hunt. All have been inducted into the International Tennis Hall of Fame in Newport, Rhode Island. Initially five of those players, Vines, Mako, Falkenburg, Schroeder, and Hunt, went to USC.

"I remember my brother played against Ellsworth Vines at La Pintoresca Park at the corner of Fair Oaks and Washington Boulevard in Pasadena," recalled long-time Pasadenan Denise (Fildew) Walker. "My older brother, Dick Fildew, (who went on to become a superior court judge in LA), was a good player, but Vines was truly something else," Born in 1911 in Pasadena, Vines was indeed something else. He was an extraordinary athlete who excelled in every sport he attempted, winning accolades in basketball, table tennis and even croquet. Vines picked up a racket when he was 15—very late by prodigy standards—and began playing at the public courts at Brookside Park near the Rose Bowl. Within a couple of years, he was under the tutelage of Mercer Beasley at the LATC.

Elly Vines was always playing one sport or another and would rarely sit still. His son, Ellsworth Vines III, speculated that his father, "… needed an out. He was very frustrated. His own father left him and his mother and brother when he was six years old. He helped raise his brother who was three years younger, while helping to support the family financially." Sports provided him the necessary release from all of the pressure he faced as he continued to sacrifice for his family throughout college.

By all accounts, Vines was a formidable tennis player. Both Jack Kramer and Don Budge called him the best player they ever saw. Kramer states in his autobiography that "When Elly was on, you'd be lucky to get your racket on the ball once you served it." And Vines' serve and forehand were legendary. Fred Perry described Vines as, "…truly a meteoric flash across the sky of tennis." His son recounted how, in a tournament at the Los Angeles Tennis Club, a referee said to Vines, "Go ahead and serve, Mr. Vines," to which Vines replied, "I already did!"

According to Kramer, Vines hit his forehand and serve very hard and very flat. While he could serve and volley, he preferred to play from the backcourt. In his autobiography, *The Game: 40 Years in Tennis*, Kramer describes Vines' power and grace, writing "And here is Ellsworth Vines, 6'2½" tall, 155 pounds, dressed like Fred Astaire and hitting shots like Babe Ruth."

Fred Perry, Douglas Fairbanks and Ellsworth Vines at the Pacific Southwest Tournament, LATC, 1931. Vines won the match in five sets.

Vines had an unusual tennis history at USC. He enrolled in 1931 and majored in commerce. By all accounts, Vines fully intended to play tennis for USC; however, due to a technicality of his transfer from a junior college, he was ineligible for a scholarship during his first semester. Paying tuition out of his savings depleted most of his money. As noted by Pat Yeomans, the Vines family was strapped for funds and he left the university during the second semester of his freshman year to get a job selling insurance. He returned to USC on a basketball scholarship and played on that team during his sophomore year, but left again for financial reasons before the tennis season started — this time for good.

Under these circumstances, it is easy to see why there has been confusion over whether Vines actually played tennis for USC. An article in the *LA Times* in 1930 headlined "Trojan Star Given Honor" stated that Vines was the No. 1 ranked player in Southern California. This was certainly true, but his top ranking was based on his winning record nationally. Even though Vines is named in *El Rodeo* in 1931 as being a top player at USC, and was a Trojan, he actually never played on the tennis team.

After leaving USC, Vines played on the circuit, winning the U.S. Nationals (now the U.S. Open) in 1931 and repeating in 1932, the same year he won Wimbledon, earning him the cover of *Time* magazine in August. He was the No. 1 player in the world in 1932, 1935, 1936, and 1937. And, in 1934, he was the fourth athlete to appear on the front of a Wheaties box. Vines retired from competitive tennis in 1951 at age 40.

Vines married in 1934 and signed an endorsement deal with Wilson Sporting Goods. After his run on the circuit (strictly for amateurs in those years), Vines turned professional and in 1939, played Don Budge 39 times and won 22 of those matches. But this wasn't the end of Vines' athletic career. His interest in multiple sports had led him to learn how to play golf. In 1942, just as he was turning 31, he became a professional golfer. His natural athleticism and determination led him to a PGA title at the Massachusetts Open in 1946 and a third-place finish at the PGA Championship in 1951. In 1959, he retired from professional golf and taught at the Tamarisk Country Club among others. Later in the 1980s, he became Vice

President of Golf Operations at the La Quinta Country Club in Palm Springs. In 1962, he was inducted into the International Tennis Association's (ITA) Hall of Fame. During his career, Vines hobnobbed with many celebrities, including Frank Sinatra, Zeppo Marx, Danny Thomas and Red Skelton—all of whom lived in the Rancho Mirage area of Riverside County, California.

An amusing postscript to Vines' story is discussed in *The Real Adventures of Dennis the Menace*, written by Vines' adopted son, Ellsworth Vines III. In this whimsical book, Ellsworth III makes the case that Hank Ketchum, who wrote the original Dennis the Menace comic strip, modeled the father-son relationship not only on his own son, Dennis, but also on Ellsworth III's childhood antics. Apparently, Ellsworth Vines III was a truly precocious child who annoyed all of his famous neighbors, most notably Frank Sinatra. Since many found it hard to believe that Ketchum based "Dennis" on Elly's son, Ellsworth III states that Dennis' characterization in the strip— blond hair, unruly cowlick and freckles looked just like him, and not Ketchum's own son, Dennis. Without a doubt there is significance resemblance to the Dennis of the strip and Ellsworth Vines III.

In the early 1930s, the team continued to improve, with Jack DeLara emerging as a star player. DeLara won the National Clay Court title and was an inspiration to the team. He and James "Slick" Stocks were one of the best doubles teams of the period. Other members during the '30s included Bob Little, who transferred from Pasadena Junior College, Jesse Millman, Cliff Johnson, Hal Steiner, Bob Chadil, Roy Lindsay, Phil Wooledge and Phil Castlen. While the team had a losing season in 1933, their hopes were pinned to the following season when freshman newcomer Gene Mako would be eligible for the varsity.

Tennis on campus garnered even more interest in 1934 when a very distinguished visiting faculty member took to the courts. Arnold Schoenberg was a highly-lauded, Viennese-born composer and music theorist—and avid tennis fan—who began teaching at USC in part to escape the tyranny of Nazi Germany. On many occasions, after the music composition class that he taught in Mudd Hall, Schoenberg would challenge his students to a game of tennis. Every student had to play with him. His wife was very anxious about him playing and thought that he would overly exert himself, especially since he was an ardent smoker. She admonished his students not to make him run very much.

As anticipated, Coach Godshall had great success with his 1934 team, going undefeated for the season. Captain Phil Castlen led the team to victory in the Pacific Coast Championship for the first time in their history. Players Phil Wooledge, Vernon John, Bob Rowley, Jess Millman, Les Harris and Kenny Hughes all contributed, but the star of the team was sophomore Gene Mako who played first singles. The team trounced Redlands, Occidental and Caltech and defeated UCLA, Stanford and California. Mako upset the reigning national champion singles champion Jack Tidball of UCLA 6-1, 7-5 to win the prestigious Ojai tournament. In October of 1934 during his sophomore year, Mako stunned a bewildered Fred Perry, at the time the world's No. 1 tennis player, by beating him 6-0, 6-2 at the Ambassador Hotel in Los Angeles.

Born in Hungary in 1916 to Georgina and Bartholomew, Mako was a gifted athlete and a man of many talents. The family moved first to Buenos Aires, Argentina for three years to avoid the war, and then, when Mako was 7, settled in Los Angeles. Bartholomew Mako was a prolific artist whose concrete sculptures are located all over Los Angeles, including at Burbank City Hall, St. Sophia's Greek Orthodox Catholic Church and Hoover Elementary. Perhaps his most famous works, completed in 1931, are several very large stone friezes that appear at the Memorial Gateway to Exposition Park to commemorate the tenth International Olympiad, held in the Coliseum in 1932. His life and work is memorialized in a book written by his son and published in 2006 called *Bartholomew Mako: A Hungarian Master*.

Like his father, young Gene was an extremely skilled artist and avid soccer player who started playing tennis at the Harvard Mini Park in Glendale, California when he was 12. He just picked up a racket and started swinging. He spent a lot of time hanging around the Griffith Park courts waiting for a match. Between the ages of 13 and 17, he amassed 75 trophies and while playing at the LATC caught the attention of gatekeeper Perry T. Jones.

Gene lettered for four years at Glendale High School in Los Angeles and graduated in 1932. As Pat Lancaster, the Athletic Director at Glendale, told Charles Rich of the *LA Times*, "He was another of those exceptional athletes to come out of the Glendale area at the time." In 1932 and 1934, he won the national boy's singles title. Mako patterned his game after his hero, Ellsworth Vines, and developed a big serve and powerful overhead. In 1933, he faced Vines in the final of the Ojai Valley Championships, losing 6-2, 3-6, 6-0.

Gene Mako, the NCAA singles champion in 1934 and
the doubles champion in 1934 with Phillip Castlen

Mako entered USC in 1933 at age 17, and lettered in
tennis in 1934, 1936, and 1937. In 1934, he won the NCAA singles
title and the doubles title too with Phillip Caslin. Mako did not
play for the team in 1935, briefly leaving school to play for the
U.S. Davis Cup team. While the USC team consisted of strong
players like Chuck Carr, Phil Wooledge, Jack Knemeyer, Boyd
Georgi and Bob Rowley, Mako's absence left them struggling
in some matches. Nevertheless, they had a winning 7-2 season.
In a handwritten note at the end of the '35 season, Godshall
lamented, "Gene Mako, enrolled in USC, (for the 1936 school

year) will probably again forsake intercollegiate tennis for Davis Cup team. Can you blame him?" Fortunately, in 1936, Mako returned to the squad, joined by top players Vernon John, Louis Wetherell and Jack Creamer.

To kick off the 1936 season, the Los Angeles Tennis Club issued a friendly challenge to the Trojans for a non-conference match. The LATC planned on bringing in a ringer, Francis X. Shields, the top-ranked player in the world in 1933 (and the grandfather of actress Brooke Shields) to play Mako, but unfortunately, Shields was unable to attend. Instead, a 16-year-old player named Joe Hunt stepped in to take the place of Shields. While Hunt lost to Mako 6-2, 6-0, Joe's career was about to launch.

In 1936, an accident altered the course of Gene Mako's future in tennis. At a London tournament, he lunged for a ball that was out of reach and heard something pop in his upper body. Mako had felt an intense soreness in his upper chest before, but this time he tore the major muscles near his shoulder. The doctors told him that his tennis playing days were over.

In time, the muscles healed but Mako had lost the ability to hit serves and overheads with any sort of power. After the 1937 season, he dropped out of USC, but wasn't ready to give up the sport. Perry T. Jones was still interested and paired Mako with champion Don Budge to play a demonstration doubles match at the Exhibition Hall of the Palace of Fine Arts in San Francisco. Budge was known as having one of the most complete games in tennis, with a huge serve and forehand and a thundering backhand. With a relatively weak serve, Mako relied on his incredible speed to get to the net and put away sharp volleys. Together the two men were almost unstoppable and they easily defeated most opponents. The two got to the final of seven major tournaments, winning four of them—two Wimbledon titles (1937-1938) and two at the U.S. Championships in 1936 and 1938. Mako also won the U.S. national mixed doubles title with Alice Marble in 1936. Said Mako, "It's interesting that my best tennis was played after the doctors said that I would never play again because of what I had done to my arm." Don Eisenberg, who played with Mako in the late 1960's, recalled, "Mako could still play excellent doubles and could more than hold his own with many of the current USC players. Because of his shoulder injury, he hit a very unusual serve. He would throw the ball high and slice it from the side so that it was very low and slow. The ball stayed so low that it was hard to hit back. It frustrated many of us."

It was in 1937, however, that Mako was involved with one of the most dramatic team matches of all time when the U.S. played Germany in Davis Cup. Mako was teamed with Budge and, despite injuries, managed to win their doubles match against the formidable team of Henner Henkel and Gottfried von Cramm. In four grueling sets, Budge and Mako helped set the stage for one of the most famous Davis Cup matches in history between von Cramm and Budge. Considered by many to be one of the greatest tennis matches ever played, Budge, the world's No. 1 player, faced the German von Cramm, ranked No. 2 in the world. Germany and the United States were tied at two matches each. The winner of the match, which was played at Wimbledon, would face Great Britain in the Davis Cup Challenge Round for the championship. At the time, the Davis Cup was considered the most prestigious tennis tournament in the world, even more so than the four Grand Slam tournaments. While Budge prevailed in five sets and the U.S. beat Germany, he revealed many years later that von Cramm had received a phone call directly from Adolf Hitler just before the match. Some dispute that the phone call ever took place, but Budge stated that at the start of the match, von Cramm, played, "like a man possessed." The United States went on to beat Great Britain 4-1 to win the Davis Cup.

Mako and Budge were rivals as well as teammates. The next year, when Budge was playing in the final of the U.S. Championships in Forest Hills to try and clinch the first-ever Grand Slam in 1938, it was Mako who he had to beat in the final. Budge, however, was in top form and won the match 6-3, 6-8, 6-2, 6-1, to complete his sweep of the Australian, French, U.S. and Wimbledon titles during the year.

In 1939, Mako had to serve a one-year suspension for an amateur tennis rule violation. As world-renowned players, he and Budge were asked to play an exhibition match in Australia. Mako denied ever asking for money and laughed off the reports. He did say, however, that he and Budge accepted 20 Australian pounds each, and said that they would have played the exhibition regardless of whether they were paid. Mako was suspended nevertheless, and spent the year working at a broadcast radio station. Despite the suspension, Mako was inducted into the Glendale Hall of Fame in 1969.

Mako's later career had the gloss of Hollywood glamour, with him proving to be as adept at the arts and entertainment business as he was at tennis. In 1941, he married 25-year-old Laura(Lari) Mae Church. She recalls that "Playwright Charles Macarthur, who was married to Helen Hayes, arranged a blind date with Gene. We were married in Manhattan in 1941 after a five-month courtship." Macarthur gave the bride away, and Oscar winning actor Paul Lukas was Mako's best man.

After serving in the Navy during World War II, Mako continued to play competitive tennis on the pro tour, but it was no longer his main career. Never one to sit still, he used his considerable talents to go into several different types of businesses. He was an accomplished pianist and composed and published two songs. He even acted in two movies. In 1948, with his tennis career winding down, Mako, a talented portrait artist, established Gene Mako Galleries on Burnside Avenue in Los Angeles, and became a successful art dealer. In addition to his art gallery, Mako decided to go into the tennis court construction business, making concrete and asphalt tennis courts. He was able to get his famous tennis buddies to endorse the courts in his advertising. Alex Olmedo, another famous Trojan tennis player, actually has a court in his backyard with a plaque indicating that it was Gene Mako's company that built it.

In 1973, Mako was inducted into the International Tennis Hall of Fame, and in 1999 he was inducted into the USC Hall of Fame. In 2004, St. Mary's College in Moraga, California acquired the Mako collection of over 700 pieces of art. On June 14, 2013, Gene contracted pneumonia and passed away at Cedars-Sinai Medical Center in Los Angeles. He was 97 years old.

His wife Laura, who had graduated from the New York School of Interior Design, had established herself as a much sought after Beverly Hills interior designer with a client list that included Betty and Gerald Ford, Bob and Delores Hope, Danny Kaye, Jimmy Stewart, Gregory Peck and Henry and Ginny Mancini. Laura described Gene as a very attractive man with a great sense of humor, extremely kind and giving—a man of many talents. After Gene's death, Laura moved back to her home state of Maryland, and in 2016 celebrated her 100th birthday.

Jack Kramer congratulates Joe Hunt who fell to the ground cramping after hitting the winning shot at the U.S. Nationals in 1943

The influence of Ellsworth Vines and Gene Mako on young tennis players reached from the USC team to the pro ranks. One such example was Jack Kramer. The son of a railway worker, Jack was born in 1921 and grew up San Bernardino. By 1937, Kramer was working out with Vines and enrolled at USC on a tennis scholarship. He left after only one semester upsetting his father. Jack enrolled at Rollins College in Winter Park, Florida, playing for the 1941 and 1942 seasons, but left before graduation. Like Vines, Kramer was another great Trojan who never played on the team, going on to become one of the greatest tennis players of all time, winning the U.S. singles title twice in 1946 and 1947, as well as numerous major doubles titles and Davis Cup matches. An International Tennis Hall of Famer, Kramer became one of the game's biggest professional tennis promoters starting in 1952 and helped form the Association of Tennis Professionals (ATP) in 1972. In 1962, he and renowned coach Vic Braden founded the Jack Kramer Tennis Club in Rolling Hills Estates, California. Many top players spent a great deal of time there including Vines, Pancho Segura, Tracy Austin, Lindsay Davenport and Pete Sampras.

Kramer may have left USC in 1937, but thanks to Harold Godshall's skill for recruiting top talent, it wasn't long before USC was blessed with another great player, Joseph Rafael Hunt. Joe Hunt was a truly gifted tennis player and one of Perry T. Jones protégés. In 1937, he enrolled at USC where he played for two years, earning the spot as the No. 1 player on the 1938 team. With a lineup that included Captain Lewis Wetherell, who was the National Public Parks Champion, Ken Bartelt, Karl "Bunny" Hasse, Leon Everett and John Nelson, the team had an undefeated season.

During that year, Hunt fell in love with a top female tennis player named Jacque Virgil. The two were inseparable. In 1939, he decided to transfer to the Naval Academy in Annapolis where he played on the team. When Hunt announced that he was leaving for Annapolis, Jacque was distraught. It's hard to know for sure what her motivation was, but shortly after he left, Jacque married Hunt's USC teammate Lawrence Nelson. Pat Yeomans noted that in October 1942, Joe and Jacque found themselves at the same tournament in Coronado, and Jacque was rooming with Perry Jones' niece Betty Brown. Betty was asked by friends to keep Joe and Jacque apart, but she was unsuccessful, and after their meeting Jacque decided to divorce Lawrence. The day after the divorce was final, Joe and Jacque married.

Hunt was a skilled serve and volleyer with fluid groundstrokes. In 1943, he reached the singles final at the U.S. Championships at Forest Hills, beating one of the toughest players of the period, Bill Talbert, en route. Hunt's opponent in the final was none other than top dog Jack Kramer. Both players faced extremely hot and humid conditions on that day. Kramer had been battling a very bad case of the flu and lost 19 pounds over the course of the tournament. Hunt was also not prepared for the temperature and became dehydrated, leading to cramps in his legs. At match point in his favor, Hunt hit a shot to Kramer's forehand and then fell to the ground. Kramer's forehand went long and Hunt won the match. Since Hunt couldn't move, Kramer crossed the net and sat down with Joe to congratulate him – an iconic moment in tennis history. As noted by Bud Collins, Kramer joked later that, "If I could have lasted a point more, I might have been champ on a default." Hunt went on to achieve the No. 1 ranking in the world and induction into the International Tennis Hall of Fame, but unfortunately his career—and his life—ended very shortly thereafter. As Pancho Segura noted in his induction speech for Hunt in the International Tennis Hall of Fame, "He was a very good-looking man with a body like Charles Atlas . . . He drew women to his matches. He would have been good for tennis. He was a credit to the game." Kramer's brother, Jack, later described Hunt as "...sort of the James Dean of tennis."

On February 2, 1945, Lieutenant Joseph Hunt was performing gunnery practice in a Grumman Hellcat fighter plane about 19 miles off the Daytona Beach, Florida coast when his plane went out of control. Joe plunged 4,000 feet to his death in the ocean and his body was never found. He was only a couple of weeks away from his 25th birthday. To this day, no one is sure what caused the crash. In 2014, Hunt was honored at The Ojai Tennis Tournament, and on September 1, 2014, 69 years after his death, he was feted at the U.S. Open for his achievements and military service.

In early 2014, a picker was doing her rounds at the garage sales in Beverly Hills and purchased, among other things, an ornate silver tennis trophy mentioning The Ojai Tennis Tournament. The tennis trophy sold quickly on eBay for $96. The buyer was a tennis fan, who knew Steve Pratt, the media director of the Ojai, and called him. Pratt did some digging and found that Joe Hunt, the name inscribed on the trophy, had won the 1938 singles division. Through Facebook and Google searches, a Joseph T. Hunt was located. This Joseph T. Hunt was the great-nephew of Joe Hunt, and also grew up playing tennis, starting first at Seattle University and then transferring to the University of Redlands. He recalled playing in 1982 at USC against Trojan Antony Emerson. "We were no match for USC, but it was a thrill to play in their stadium and on the campus where my great uncle played," he said.

When he was ten, Joe T. Hunt was rummaging around his maternal grandmother's carport on Beverly Glen Boulevard in Los Angeles and discovered large plastic tubs filled with trophies and scrapbooks. "I began to scramble through the tubs and found an intriguing photo of a very handsome, blonde, young man being presented with a trophy by none other than Bob Hope," he said. The blonde man was his great-uncle, Joseph R. Hunt. The trophies were eventually divided up among Joe's family. But the trophies given to Joe T.'s father were stolen in a home robbery, and those in the care of his aunt had been given away. Joe T., on the other hand, cherished the trophies he had been given. "Finding those trophies and photos led me on a lifelong obsession with understanding and preserving the legacy of my great-uncle Joe."

Remarkably, the trophy was found about eight miles from where Joe T. Hunt's grandmother had lived. Was this one of the trophies that was stolen from his father's home or perhaps one that was thrown out by his aunt? It turns out that it was neither. The Hunt family believed that when their grandmother's home was sold, the new owner found more old trophies and either kept or disposed of them. One of those trophies turned up at the garage sale.

"I now have in my possession the companion trophy from that same 1938 Ojai tournament in which my grand uncle Joe had also won the doubles title," said Joe T. "Both sit side by side on my mantle."

Shortly before Joe R. Hunt had left for the Naval Academy in 1939, another Godshall recruit, a young player named George Toley, transferred to USC from the University of Miami where Gardnar Mulloy, a multiple Grand Slam tournament winner and future International Hall of Famer, had recruited him. Toley was attracted to Miami since the school was on its way to making a name in tennis. Bobby Riggs had also enrolled at Miami a year before Toley, but did not like being in school. Riggs did not attend classes and dropped out after a month. Later, Miami would increase its visibility when Pancho Segura would go on to win three NCAA singles titles (1943-1945) for the school.

While at Miami, George received word that his mother had taken ill, so he returned to Los Angeles. Fortunately his mother recovered fully, but Toley decided to stay in LA, stating in his autobiography, "...I enrolled there (at USC) in the fall of 1938, changing the course of my life." Little did he know that his decision would be the one of key turning points in USC—and college tennis—history.

Coach Harold Godshall was a passionate tennis advocate. In 1938, Godshall did 13 live radio broadcasts with Bob Allen on KFWB, interviewing well-known tennis personalities in order to promote the sport. In a letter to *American Lawn Tennis, Inc.* dated November 13, 1939, he summarized the future prospects of the USC team and made some noteworthy revelations that were indicative of his prowess as a recruiter. He noted that Ted Schroeder, the national junior champion, Ronald Lubin, the national public parks champions, George Toley, a transfer from Miami whom he expected to be "the most consistent man on the team," Bill Reedy of Beverly Hills (Tracy Austin Holt's uncle), and Charles Mattman would all be joining the team. Godshall noted that Reedy was unable to play in his freshman year due to an acute case of appendicitis. Godshall was also very enthusiastic about his freshmen prospects, Jack Kramer, Ted Olewine and Arthur Marx, the son of famous actor Groucho Marx.

In 1940, there were many excellent players on the team, including Ted Schroeder, Bill Reedy, Ron Lubin, George Toley and Captain Ken Bartelt with Toley and Schroeder capturing the intercollegiate doubles title. Another young man named Bobby Carrothers, who had won the national junior championship in 1940, joined the freshman team. By all accounts, Carrothers was an incredibly gifted player with legends like Vic Seixas saying that his game "was a level above the rest of us." Tragically, his true potential was never realized. On his way home from USC in his freshman year, he was killed in an automobile accident. Jack Kramer noted in an interview with the *New York Times* in 2009 that, "Had he lived, in my opinion, he would have been the best of his time."

Ted Olewine won the NCAA doubles title in 1941 with Charles Mattman

The 1940 team was considered the best in the nation, with Ted Schroeder playing No. 2 behind Toley, followed by Ken Bartlett, Marvin Carlock, Myron McNamara and Bill Reedy. USC drubbed UCLA during that season 8-1, but did not fare well in either of the NCAA singles or doubles tournaments. Toley's tennis continued to improve and he scored a major victory later that year over Gene Mako in the 1941 Atlantic Coast Championships.

Ted Schroeder was born and raised in Newark, New Jersey and, like many other top players, was nurtured by Perry

T. Jones at the LATC. Schroeder played at USC for his first two years and then transferred to Stanford. Despite their teamwork on the court, there was a definite rivalry between Schroeder and Toley. In his book, *The Golden Age of College Tennis*, Toley mentions that the two of them did not get along, and that he wasn't unhappy to see him leave. Bobby Riggs once described Schroeder as "the most spectacular, most aggressive player I've ever seen. His power overhead stuns you." Schroeder went on to win Wimbledon and the U.S. singles titles and was the No. 1 ranked American in 1942. Schroeder was nicknamed "Lucky Ted" because of his five-set victories. Schroeder and Jack Kramer were very good friends and Kramer unsuccessfully spent a lot of time trying to convince Schroeder to turn pro. In 1942, Schroeder enlisted in the Navy as a fighter pilot and was discharged in 1945. He was inducted into the International Tennis Hall of Fame in 1966, and he passed away from cancer in 2006.

In 1941, the team consisting of Reedy, Toley, Bartelt, Charles Mattman and Captain Marvin Carlock won the Pacific Coast Conference title, beating every team in sight. Schroeder had decided to transfer to Stanford, leaving a big hole in the team. Fortunately, sophomore Ted Olewine stepped up to play No. 1 singles. Olewine was a star and already ranked 18th on the national tennis roster, making him the highest ranked U.S. collegiate player. That year, Olewine also won the Ojai intercollegiate singles crown.

Godshall's efforts were critical in building a strong foundation for USC men's tennis. He was highly successful recruiting players, but did not live long enough to reap the full benefits of his work. Tragically in August 1941, just before the 1942 season began, and after 14 years of coaching at USC, Godshall was struck and killed by a drunk driver while crossing Wilshire Boulevard. He was 37 years old. A jury found that both

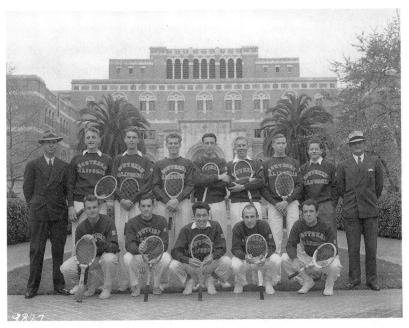

The 1941 team outside of Doheny Library – Front Row: Ted Olewine, Fred Roth, Ronald Lubin, Captain Marvin Carlock, Bill Reedy
Back Row: Coach Harold Godshall, Richard Odeman, Gordon Nelson, Charles Mattman, George Toley, Frank Jorgensen, Don Sweet, Manager Harry Peetris, and Willis O. Hunter, Director of Athletics

Godshall and the driver were negligent, leading Godshall's family to ask for leniency for the driver.

Unfortunately, in the annals of USC men's tennis history, Harold Godshall has been largely forgotten. This has occurred in part because tennis was transitioning from a minor to a major sport at USC when Godshall was the coach. Further, while singles and doubles championships were played, no team championship existed until 1946. Thus, while individual players and doubles teams were celebrated, coaches, who worked part time, went largely unrecognized. Godshall did have a significant impact on the Trojan tennis team, recruiting many great players, and having some major successes, laying the foundation for what was to come. After his death, several others would step in to fill the coaching void, two of whom would get the credit for winning USC's early national titles.

3

Transitions, Disruptions, and the First National Championships

The tragic death of Harold Godshall dealt a major blow to USC's tennis program. Over the next 12 years, four different individuals would step in to lead the team: interim coach George Toley, Arnold Eddy, William Moyle and Lou Wheeler. Despite the difference in coaching styles and the rapid turnover of the coaching staff, USC continued to recruit a number of extremely talented players, including Bob and Tom Falkenburg, John and Gil Shea and Bobby Perez. While many of these players grew up playing locally, USC had developed a name for itself as one of the leading places to play on the West Coast.

Very shortly after Godshall died, athletic director Willis (Bill) Hunter asked assistant professor of administration John McDiarmid to become the new coach. McDiarmid was an excellent player who played at Texas Christian University and at one time was ranked ninth in the nation. He had notched a win over Toley in a tournament in Cincinnati in the late 1930s. The *Daily Trojan* reported that McDiarmid began to organize practices in the late fall of 1941. However, McDiarmid's specialization in government spending was needed and he was called to Washington D.C. to consult. He left the university in late December before the 1942 season began. Toley, still a member of the team and its No. 1 ranked player, was asked to step in as interim coach.

Toley had a full plate. He had just married his girlfriend Miriam, was managing and teaching at the Beverly Hills Tennis Club and taking a full load of classes at USC. But Toley, always a team player, agreed to take the job. With a strong team led by Captain Bill Reedy, star player Ted Olewine, Don Sweet and Henry Zertuche, Toley's team had a successful 8-3 season. Olewine, in particular, had a great year. He beat Ted Schroeder, the former Trojan who played for Stanford, twice in three sets— once in a dual meet and the other at the Ojai Valley Tournament. Olewine would die just four years later in June of 1946, at the age of 25, after contracting Hodgkin's disease while serving as a marine lieutenant in the Pacific. Olewine was part of the 28th regiment that raised the flag on Iwo Jima in 1945.

Toley only coached for the one season before he left school to join the war effort, enlisting in the Army Air Corps stationed in Texas, where he trained airmen in a wide variety of physical and safety drills, including how to correctly land a parachute. With Toley's departure, the tennis team once again needed a coach. Arnold Eddy, who was the Athletic Director and Dean of Students, had to determine who the next coach would be. In his memoir, *Troyditionally Yours – Recollections Mostly about Sports 1920's, 1930's, and 1940's,* Eddy recalled what happened; "Two weeks before our big match with California, I went to a scheduled workout and said, 'Boys, keep up your practicing. Sooner or later I'll have a coach for you.' The next morning I was greeted by Ted Olewine, our team captain and already a tennis 'great' with this remark, 'After you left yesterday, we selected a coach.' My answer was, 'Good, tell me who and I'll call him.' To which he replied, 'That won't be necessary. I'm looking at him." I was stunned, but managed to say, 'Ted, I've never owned a tennis racquet in my life." He laughed and replied, 'You have six ranked players…no one can teach us much at this late date. All we need is someone with a big foot who is not afraid to use it.'"

Eddy served as coach in the undefeated seasons of 1943 and 1944. The team consisted of Ted Olewine, Al Davenport, Jack Collins, Bob Kimbrell, Jack Tiel, Earl Cochell, Chuck Peters, Straight Clark, S. Claude (SC) Voges and Choi Smith. Practices and matches were still held on the Hoover Street courts, despite their deteriorating condition. Due to war conditions, the team traveled little and played most of its matches at home. SC Voges remembered Eddy as "…a very charming man and a top administrator. I concur that Arnold knew little about tennis. For instance, he thought we played with two balls!" A self-taught player who grew up in Englewood, California, Voges desperately wanted to be a Trojan after attending his first football game in 1931 at age six. He saw his dream come true when he joined the team in 1943 and proudly wore the USC colors until his death in 2017. On the 1943 Trojan team, he considered himself a doubles specialist, partnering at third doubles with Keith Robert. "Keith and I hardly ever lost. I didn't have a big serve, but I used what I had and mastered a half dozen shots," said Voges. "I played the deuce court on return of serve and the two shots that were really effective for me were a chip crosscourt return to the server's feet when he came in, and a deep lob on return of serve right down the line. Both worked well against net rushers." Voges played for one season and then, like many others, was drafted for two years as a naval aviator.

The undefeated "Eddymen" even bested an all-star team from the Exposition Park Tennis Club. Like many of the other major public courts in the United States, Exposition Park had a series of age group ladders, local and regional tournaments and a national championship. The most prominent player to come out of Exposition Park was Pancho Gonzalez, a "court rat" by his own admission, who was always at the park looking for a match.

In 1944, Bob Kimbrell emerged as a star, winning the Southern California Intercollegiate singles title as well as the doubles title with teammate Fred May. Eddy continued to coach the team until 1945, losing twice to UCLA in dual meets for the first time in thirteen years. Those losses were a harbinger of seasons to come. In 1997, Eddy was inducted into the USC Athletic Hall of Fame for his contributions to the school.

It was Eddy, in his role as athletic director, who teamed up with David X. Marks, to develop the David X. Marks Foundation which today funds over 50 annual athletic scholarships at USC. David Marks was a well-known philanthropist who founded the Los Angeles Civic Light Opera, among other institutions, but he also had some tennis experience. James Eddy, now the director of the Foundation and Arnold's son, recalled that Marks played with Arthur Ashe from time to time at the LATC. Another famous family member, Joshua Marks, David's brother, was the architect and builder of Grauman's Egyptian and Chinese Theaters, two of the most famous landmarks in Hollywood. It was Joshua Marks who came up with the idea to put stars in the sidewalks of Hollywood Boulevard to honor members of the motion picture industry.

At the close of the war in 1946, USC, like many other schools, experienced a resurgence of students enrolling in or coming back to college as a result of the GI Bill, which provided tuition and living expenses benefits for veterans. The Trojans 1946 team was one of the most talented teams ever assembled and included Bob and Tom Falkenburg, Bobby Perez and John Shea. Other team members included John Flietz, Keith Roberts, Arnie Saul, Dick Odman, Jack Tunnell and Gene Feigenbaum. Bill Moyle, an instructor from the athletic department, was tapped to take over the team until a full-time coach could be hired. But with such a powerhouse of players, there perhaps wasn't much need for traditional coaching. In fact, Voges, who had returned from the navy to rejoin the team, doesn't recall ever even seeing Moyle, claiming, "I don't know much about him and we didn't have any interactions."

In 1946, the team was undefeated. Most notably, the Trojans vanquished the Bruins 7-2 in a dual meet to take back the Pacific Coast Conference Championship. That same year, most likely prompted by the nationwide rebirth of tennis, the NCAA, an organization that had been in existence since 1906, held its first National Team Championship at the Vandy Christie Tennis Center in Evanston, Illinois. At the time any team in the country could enter the tournament. The scoring system was as follows: four singles players and two doubles teams constituted a team. All four singles players and both doubles teams entered the draw. Every time a singles player or a doubles team won a match they received a point. At the end of the tournament, the team that had accumulated the most points won the national championship.

Tom Falkenburg, Coach Bill Moyle and Bob Falkenburg at USC. Bob Falkenburg was National Singles Champion, 1946 and National Doubles Champion (with Tom Falkenburg), 1946

On USC's team, Bob and Tom Falkenburg, Bobby Perez and John Shea played singles, with the Falkenburgs and Perez and Shea playing doubles. The Falkenburgs and Shea made it to the third round, but unfortunately Perez lost in the first round to Roger Downs, a star at Illinois. Nevertheless, USC was victorious, winning the first NCAA team title by beating William & Mary, 9 points to 6. Bob Falkenburg also had a great individual season, winning the NCAA singles title by beating William & Mary's Gardner Larned 7-5, 6-2, 6-1 and teaming with his brother Tom to overcome the team of Larned and Bernard "Tut" Bartzen 7-5, 2-6, 6-3, 5-7, 7-5. Bartzen would go on to become one of the top-ten ranking players in the world. Ohioan Jon Gurian, who played under Bartzen when he coached at Texas Christian University in the mid-70s, recalled that Bartzen's philosophy was rooted in consistency and playing "plain vanilla" tennis—avoid low percentage shots and don't make any unforced errors.

Bob, Tom and Eugenia "Jinx" Falkenburg were the children of Eugene (Genie) and Marguerite (Mickey) Falkenburg. Genie was a very successful Westinghouse engineer, whose work took him to Spain, Chile and Brazil. Mickey was an accomplished tennis player who won several tournaments as a young girl in Santiago, and then the state tennis championship in São Paulo when she was 16. The children spent most of their early lives in Brazil, until the family moved to Chile, and then back to Los Angeles in 1935.

Almost as soon as they arrived back in Los Angeles, the Falkenburgs became members at the LATC. Bob attended Fairfax High School and in 1942 won the National Interscholastic singles title as well and the doubles title with younger brother, Tom.

In her autobiography *Jinx*, Eugenia stated that her mother nicknamed her Jinx "as it seemed to her a natural contraction from Eugenia." Jinx's tennis career was cut short when Sam Goldwyn discovered her while both were watching the Pacific Southwest tournament at the LATC. The 5'7" brunette became a "Goldwyn Girl," leading to a career as a fashion model and movie star in the 1930s and 1940s. In 1941, she was the highest paid model in the United States, and was considered by many as the first American supermodel. Jinx starred behind Rita Hayworth and Gene Kelly in the 1944 film *Cover Girl*. A crowd favorite, she entertained the troops during WWII through the USO, and was commemorated on a USO stamp. Said John Shea, "Jinx used to come to all of our varsity matches at the LATC. She was very beautiful, had a sparkling personality and was an excellent tennis player."

After graduating, Bob Falkenburg defeated Aussie John Bromwich in five tough sets, 7-5, 0-6, 6-2, 3-6, 7-5, to win the singles title at Wimbledon in 1948. Falkenburg held off three match points to come back and win the fifth set with two aces in a row. The crowd, who heavily favored Bromwich, was stunned by the upset. Falkenburg was ranked as high as No. 7 in the world and ended up adding a U.S. and Wimbledon doubles title to his career resume. In the 1950s, he married Mayrink Veiga Machado, a Brazilian woman, and moved to Rio de Janeiro where he opened up Falkenburg Ice Creams, Ltd. (Sorveteria) serving soft vanilla ice cream. In 1952, his friends encouraged him to expand and "Bob's" was created. The restaurant served burgers, shakes and hot dogs to customers in Copacabana in Rio. His single location turned into 600 restaurants, including locations in Chile, Portugal and Angola. In 1970, the Bob and Mayrink Falkenburgs moved back to Los Angeles and retired in Santa Barbara. The "Bob's" restaurant chain was acquired by Libby of Brazil and then later by Nestlé.

Hollywood cover girl Jinx Falkenburg (and sister of Bob and Tom Falkenburg) with John Shea in La Jolla, 1943

Tom Falkenburg's life did not go as smoothly

as his brother and sister's. In January 1947, he married socialite Beatrice Allred. Within three weeks of their marriage, Beatrice, in a fit of jealousy, attempted suicide by drinking iodine. Fortunately, on the brink of death, she had the foresight to swallow a mixture of flour and eggs—which neutralized the poison—and she survived.

In 1949, Tom and Beatrice moved to Mississippi, where her family lived, and Tom played on the professional tour until 1961. Over the course of his career, he won three professional titles, all in Mississippi, but he never made it into the major leagues like his brother.

In 1965, *The Lewiston Evening Journal* reported that Tom Falkenburg was arrested in connection with a bank robbery that occurred on February 25th, just north of Jackson, Mississippi. The paper noted that, "The FBI accused the handsome, 6'3" athlete who had affected a lisp and a limp, of robbing a bank wearing a ski mask and taking $4,080 at gunpoint...." Incredibly, on March 27th, while out on bail, Tom engaged in a second robbery, this time fleeing with over $14,000. Tom was sentenced to two concurrent 15-year terms in the Lewisburg Penitentiary in Pennsylvania and fined $5,000. At Lewisburg, Tom's incarceration overlapped with infamous Teamster boss Jimmy Hoffa. In an article about Hoffa in the *Press and Sun Bulletin*, Falkenburg was also mentioned: "In the prison gymnasium...a tall young man booms a tennis ball against a wall volleying endlessly with himself. He is Tom Falkenburg, NCAA Doubles Champion with his brother in 1946. Lewisburg has two tennis courts and Falkenburg is the prison tennis pro, racket stringer, and all-round aide in the recreation department."

While Tom's family was stunned by this bizarre turn of events, some of his friends and neighbors were not surprised. It was rumored that Tom had been arrested previously in

England, although the reason was unclear. Some noted that he and his family were living well beyond their means, and that Tom had accumulated high gambling debts, speculating that he had robbed the banks to pay off these debts.

Tom was paroled in the early 1970s. It appears that his sentence was commuted by nine years—most likely for good behavior although no records are available about the exact date of his release. In February 1971, the Falkenburg brothers played in a senior doubles tournament at the South Florida Open Tennis Championships. Tom Falkenburg later opened the Buttonwood Tennis Club in Stuart, Florida in 1983. He continued to play in senior tournaments, making headlines again in 1986 when he developed a prototype racket that was shaped like a parallelogram. He claimed that the shape created a larger sweet spot than an oval racket. Tom Falkenburg passed away in Florida in 2005.

Another member of the championship 1946 team was Robert (Bobby) Perez. As a kid growing up in Los Angeles, Perez used to go to Exposition Park, just down the street from USC, to play pickup football games. One day, an older boy took him aside, told him he was too small to play football and handed him a tennis racket. Paula Dichara, Perez's daughter, said that the young man who gave him the racket was a Mexican named Tom Fears, who went on to become a tight end for the LA Rams (1948-1956), Head Coach of the New Orleans Saints and an inductee into the Pro Football Hall of Fame.

Perez grew up in South Los Angeles in a GI tract home on West Gage Avenue—just a few miles from USC—and attended nearby Manual Arts High School. After being honorably discharged from the U.S. Navy in December 1945, Perez then enrolled at USC on a four-year tennis scholarship at the beginning of 1946. Journalist Joe Jares, writing about Perez,

Bobby Perez and wife Helen Pastall surrounded by their many trophies. Perez played on the 1946 Championship Team and was the first major Latino player at USC

noted that his first nickname was "The Stump" since he was only 5'6" and had a stocky build. But a few years later when he was winning and leaner, "he got tagged with a more elegant moniker, 'The Puma.'" Considered the first major Latino to play at USC, Perez grew up hitting tennis balls at the Exposition Courts where he befriended Richard (Pancho) Gonzalez. The two became fast friends. Gil Shea, who played with both Gonzalez and Perez, recalls, "Bobby Perez was a great guy.

I knew him very well. He was very likable and had a good temperament."

During his USC career, Perez played No. 2 singles and No. 2 doubles. He also helped Coach George Toley recruit a long line of top players from Mexico, including Rafael Osuna, Joaquin Loyo-Mayo and Raul Ramirez as well as Peruvian Alex Olmedo. After graduation, Perez played for five years in the pros and went on to become a Vice President and General Sales Manager at CBS in 1969. In 1976, he returned to California and was ranked No. 1 in singles and doubles in the senior division. After he retired from CBS in the late 1980s, Perez moved to Irvine, California, and became a volunteer assistant coach at UC Irvine.

Perez married Helen Pastall, a top U.S. tennis player, in 1948 when she was 19. The two of them were a formidable tennis-playing couple. From 1946-1955, Helen was consistently ranked in the top ten of women players in the U.S. She beat every top player at one time or another including Darlene Hard, Gussie Moran, Dorothy Bundy Cheney, Louise Brough, Maureen Connolly and Althea Gibson. A bad back—and taking time off to raise children—halted her career until she resumed as a senior player in 1985. Her husband was once quoted as saying that Helen "ran like a deer and fought like a gored bull." Helen passed away in December 2005 after a 20-year struggle with cancer, and Bobby died peacefully in 2015.

In 1947 and 1948, sophomore SC Voges became USC's team manager. "I remember Bill Hunter, the athletic director, calling me into his office and saying, 'Do you have any ideas about how we can compete with the Bill Ackerman (the first tennis coach at UCLA) and the Bruin team? They are coming on strong and putting a lot of resources into their tennis program and we have to be able to compete.'"

The Pacific Coast Conference had passed a ruling that, in order to play intercollegiate matches, a team had to have six home courts. "In those days, the three courts on campus were terrible," Voges said. "The Hoover Street Courts were wedged between two homes near the old band shack around 34th Street about a block from the Shrine Auditorium. We had the worst courts on any campus. They were in poor shape, no bleachers, not even a drinking fountain." Voges told Hunter that the LATC had 17 courts and that he would approach George Toley, who was now the head pro there, to see if he could persuade the LATC Board to let the Trojans practice at the club. Voges had a preliminary meeting and Toley seemed to be amenable.

A short time later in 1947, Bill Hunter and Clark Cornell, who was a member of the LATC and president of the Trojan Club, approached Toley formally. Pat Yeomans, the tennis historian at the LATC, reported that Toley convinced the LATC to allow USC use of the courts for a fee of $250 a month, guaranteeing daily access. Most of the world's major pros passed through the LATC at one time or another during the year, earning the club the moniker the "cradle of tennis." "The UCLA alums who were members at the LATC weren't very happy," said Voges. "They knew that this would give us a huge advantage over UCLA." The very next season, all USC team matches were played at the LATC. The new location proved to be USC's single biggest advantage, paving the way for many years of dominance of the sport. No other team in the country had the kind of access to, and opportunities to compete against, the top professionals in the country. The Trojans continued to practice at LATC for the next 25 years, until the David X. Marks Stadium dedicated in 1972.

On February 10, 1947, Bill Hunter announced that Lou Wheeler would assume the head coaching job, replacing Bill Moyle. Wheeler, a USC varsity basketball player (1925-1927) was a good tennis player as well. Don Eisenberg, who took lessons from George Toley when he was young, and subsequently lettered for USC between 1950-1952, said, "My dad introduced me to Lou Wheeler, as they used to play together at Griffith Park. Coach Wheeler said that coaching tennis was still only a part-time job so he also kept his full time position as a math teacher at Marshall High School in LA."

Wheeler was walking into a tough situation: the Falkenburgs had graduated and John Shea had been called up by the Air Force. Fortunately, Bobby Perez, Keith Roberts, Jack Teal, John Kerr, Straight Clark, Arnie Saul, Jean Feigenbaum and Jack Tunnell still presented a powerful lineup and, in 1947, USC won the Pacific Coast Conference Southern Division (consisting of Stanford, UCLA, USC and University of California, Berkeley) title for the ninth time since 1932.

One of the most memorable matches of the 1947 season occurred when No. 1 player Straight Clark faced Santa Monica City College star Glenn Bassett. The match was tightly contested but Clark held on to win 6-2, 3-6, 6-4. The next year, Bassett transferred to UCLA where he would go on to become a revered coach, winning seven national titles and coaching such legends as Jimmy Connors and Billy Martin over a 27-year-run. That year, William & Mary beat Rice for the NCAA team title and their top player Gardnar Larned took the singles title. Bob Match and Sam Curtis of Rice won the doubles title.

In 1948, USC was expecting another strong season. Perez played No. 1 singles, backed up by Arnold Saul, Jack Tunnell and Jean Feigenbaum. With Wheeler in the coaching spot, the Trojans continued to build their reputation, beating

Occidental, Arizona, Pepperdine, Los Angeles City College and Glendale College. Of most significance, they pounded northern rival Stanford 9-0. Another welcome benefit was that John Shea returned from military service and re-enrolled at USC. His younger brother Gil came with him.

The Shea brothers grew up about a mile from the Los Angeles Tennis Club and attended John Burroughs High School. "We loved tennis and started playing when John was 11 and I was nine," Gil said. "We never took any real lessons growing up. When we were teenagers, one of our friends invited us to a party at the LATC. My dad was smart. He steered us into tennis rather than football. There were just too many injuries in football, even back then, and tennis was so much fun. The LATC was our second home. It was cheap. There were no restrictions as to who could join the club. It didn't matter if you were Jewish or black, you could play there. We liked that."

Playing at the club was very inexpensive at the time as the war reduced memberships and thus dues had been lowered to entice more people to join. "John and I both wanted to go to USC," Gil said. "Our dad was a Cal guy, so in the beginning he wasn't too happy, but he softened up over time. We went to USC because they offered a great variety of subjects. I studied business and John studied engineering as he wanted to work for my dad's company. John was an excellent player but his mind was really on engineering. I was more focused on tennis and was very happy to receive a tennis scholarship from SC."

Gil Shea, known as a strong serve and volleyer, circa 1948

Interviewed at a youthful looking 88 years of age, the 6'1" athletically built Gil Shea was quick to laugh and got very animated when he talked about two things—his stint in the service and his time at USC. "First, I have to say that I love USC," he said. "There's no place like it. At the time the level of competition was great. I played at the LATC, but also at Exposition Park. Pancho Gonzalez and I became good friends and we worked out three or four days a week. The courts were better than the ones on campus. I must have played Pancho a hundred times. He had a big serve. I can only remember one time when I took a set off him. He was a very competitive guy. He got so mad when I beat him that he busted up his racket. After he saw me laughing so hard he finally stopped!"

"Lew Hoad was one of the great Aussie players," Gill continued. "The Aussies were so good in those days and Lew was a wonderful guy. I played a lot with him at LATC. He had the greatest American twist serve. That twist was most effective on hard courts because you got a big jump. You didn't get that kind of a jump on grass. I also had a big twist serve, which was effective because back then most of the guys hit a slice. My main strategy was serve and volley. When Hoad won his first Wimbledon in 1956, he came to me and said, 'Gil, I know you like my Ford and I'll sell it to you for $500. I don't need the damn thing as I am turning pro and I'm gonna make a lot of money.' I told him that the price was too low. He said he didn't care; he just wanted to get rid of it as he was going on tour. So I bought it. What a bargain!

"During that time we all seem to get along well. Lou Wheeler was our coach. He wasn't a real tennis player, but he was smart and just left us all alone. He knew we were playing every day and that we were all good players. He didn't want to interfere. I also knew George Toley well. He was a fantastic coach and was always at the club. I don't think I ever saw him play though."

Gil had gone through three years at USC from '48 to '50, when he received a letter telling him that he had a week to report for duty at Fort Ord in Monterey, California. The Korean War was raging. He became a private in the army, serving from 1951 to 1952. "They didn't give you a choice as to where you could serve and I only played a little tennis in the army," He said. Gil, of course, was being modest. In 1952, he was the U.S. Army Champion.

"After 16 weeks of basic training we had to wait to see if we would be called up," he said. "Every morning, we lined up. If they called your number, you had to fly overseas to fight. One day I realized I only had six months left. I went to the head sergeant and said, 'I've got less than six months to go so you can't call me up now as there's not enough time.' He looked at me and said, 'You son of a bitch. I'm gonna come down there and kill you.' I looked at him and said, 'C'mon…' He stood up but was really overweight and out of shape and I looked at him and laughed. He stared at me and yelled, 'Get the hell out of here.'" In 1953, the war ended, and Gil returned to campus for his senior year.

"One of the things I remember best was the great rivalry we had against UCLA," he said. "Bill Ackerman was the coach then. We always geared up for those matches just as the players do today. We played one match at home and one at UCLA every season. It's the greatest rivalry in college tennis. Herb Flam, a great player at UCLA, was my good friend. But when Herbie and I faced each other on the court, we had battles like you can't believe. We were about even with winning and losing!"

Gil's older brother, John Shea, had started playing in 1946 alongside the Falkenburg brothers and Bobby Perez on the winning NCAA team, and then, like so many young men at the time, was called up to join the Air Force.

"We had a great team," John said. "Even though Bobby was small, he was very fast and had a strong return of serve. This is what made him a great doubles player. Bob Falkenburg was a strong serve and volley guy and at 6'3" his serve was really huge. He also had extremely quick reflexes. Tom Falkenburg also had a very big serve."

When John returned from the army, he rejoined the team in practices at the LATC. But the LATC was known for more than tennis in those days. "Many nights we would gather with other members at the club and there were so many guys who had returned from the army with money to burn," John said. "So we all started gambling. Every night there were groups of people huddled around tables playing poker and backgammon for money. At the center of a lot of this was Bobby Riggs, a really fun guy. Riggs wasn't a great poker or backgammon player but was very good at betting on sports. Even though we played for table stakes I remember coming home with $4,500 one night!"

Ed Atkinson, who played a decade later for USC, remembered two other ruses that Riggs would pull with unsuspecting victims, "Bobby would find someone at the club who didn't know him well," Atkinson said. "His first bet was to say to that person, 'I will bet you $100 that I can take a deck of cards and throw every one of them into that trash can over there without missing.' The victim would agree and then Bobby would pull out an unopened deck of cards from his pocket and throw the entire cellophane-wrapped deck into the trashcan." Another Riggs' "card trick" was to bet someone that he could throw a card into an air conditioning vent. The victim would think this was impossible and would take the bet. What the poor sucker didn't realize was that Riggs would practice this trick for hours at the club and could do it at will."

John said his most memorable USC match was in 1948 when he and Gil played against UCLA's Glenn Bassett and Robin "Lefty" Willner. "The team match was tied 4-4 and the winner of the doubles match would win the Pacific Coast

Conference title," he said. "The score was 8-6, 5-7 and we were down 5-4 in the third set with match point for UCLA with Gil serving. Gil hit a good serve to Lefty in the ad court. Willner hit a very strong return that landed right at Gil's feet. Gil popped up a half volley high and over the net. Lefty came running in fast. I figured it was all over and when I saw Lefty charging the net I turned my back to protect myself. Apparently, Lefty took a huge backswing on his forehand and clobbered the ball, but he was so excited that the ball hit the top of his racket and went out. We ended up winning the third set 8-6 and the match and the conference title."

At the NCAA tournament in 1948, Straight Clark had another great year, advancing to the fourth round by beating three seeded players before losing to Gardner Larned. William & Mary won their second national team title in a row, besting San Francisco. Harry Likas from the University of San Francisco won the singles title, with the doubles title going to Fred Kovaleski and Tut Bartzen from William & Mary. In 1949, the University of San Francisco won its first NCAA team title and Jack Tuero from Tulane took the singles title. James Brink and Fred Fisher from the University of Washington won the doubles title.

John Shea graduated in 1949 and immediately started a career in construction engineering. He has had a highly successful career and became Chairman of the Board of J.F. Shea Heavy Construction, Shea Homes and other enterprises. Gil Shea went on to play on the tour and was ranked as high as No. 4 in the U.S. in 1957. He said that his two wins over Wimbledon and U.S. singles champion Vic Seixas were probably his best victories. In 2013, Shea was inducted into the Southern California Tennis Hall of Fame.

The 1950 Trojan lineup included Earl Cochell, Gil Shea, Hugh Stewart, Jack Kerr, Ray Love, Bob Blackmore, Don Eisenberg and Chuck Stewart. Hugh Stewart, a top-ranked player, transferred to USC from Pasadena City College, having already won the national junior college doubles championship with Fred Houghton. Stewart was a tall man with a booming serve. "Hugh was an excellent volleyer and had a very strong forehand. If he got hold of a forehand he usually won the point," said Don Eisenburg. Going into the NCAA Championships, the team was undefeated with a 14-0 record, beating Cal, Stanford and UCLA twice. The odds seemed in favor of USC winning the national championship, until Cochell became ill and had to withdraw from both the semifinals in singles and doubles. A passionate competitor, Cochell was known to have a fierce temper. During a round of 16 match at the U.S. Championships in 1951 against Gardnar Mulloy, Cochell, after splitting the first two sets but down 4-1 in the third, decided to throw that set and save his energy to come out strong in the fourth set. When it became obvious to the crowd that he was throwing the set (he began to serve underhanded), they started to boo and heckle him. Cochell began to yell back. The chair umpire asked Cochell to "play tennis," at which point he attempted to climb the umpire's chair to grab the microphone. Cochell was pulled back before he could get the mike. At one point he hoisted his racket to the crowd as an extension of his middle finger. After he lost the fourth set to Mulloy, he confronted referee Ellsworth Davenport and used such abusive language that the U.S. Lawn Tennis Association (now the USTA) banned him from tennis for life. To this day he holds the distinction of being the only tennis player to have ever been sanctioned for life by the USTA. In 1962, he was reinstated, but by that point he was no longer competitive.

Hugh Stewart won the NCAA singles title in 1952 and the doubles title in 1951 with Earl Cochell.

Cochell's teammate Eisenberg was surprised by the news about him when the news of his famous tantrum came out. "In 1951, I played Ed in a Palm Springs tournament and I won the first set and had a chance in the second. He could have gone off and shown his temper then but I don't recall anything. I do remember that he was a character, would clown around a lot and had a good sense of humor. He would also would sing opera while he was walking between classes. After the Forest Hills incident, I never heard from him again."

Despite Cochell's withdrawals at the 1950 NCAAs, the Trojans amassed enough points to secure a second-place finish behind UCLA. This was a banner year for UCLA as Herbert Flam won the singles championship and then teamed with Gene Garrett to win the doubles title. This was the first of many championships for the Bruins fueling the long-standing rivalry that begun in 1920.

The next year, the 1951 Trojan team was intent on capturing the title that they felt was swept out from under them in 1950. Even with the loss of Gil Shea to the army, the team was very strong consisting of Earl Cochell, Hugh Stewart, Captain Jack Teal, Chuck Stewart, Bob Fullerton, Ray Love and Jack Kerr. The Trojans did endure and captured their second NCAA team title, handily beating the University of Cincinnati 8 points to 7. Tony Trabert, the Bearcats star player, beat Cochell in the singles final, but Hugh Stewart and Cochell won the doubles title. With that win, USC gained permanent possession of the Garland Bowl, a trophy donated by Charles S. Garland, a former Wimbledon doubles champion in 1920. Garland specified that the first team to accumulate 20 points in NCAA competition would retire the cup and USC had amassed 14 points prior to the 1951 championship. With the retirement of the Garland Bowl, the University of Texas placed into competition a new trophy, known as the Penick Bowl after Dr. D.A. Penick, the veteran Longhorn coach.

In 1952, Coach Lou Wheeler had high hopes for another NCAA title with a strong team consisting of Jacque (Jack) Grigry, Allen Cleveland, Hugh Stewart, Ray Love, Don Eisenberg and Jim Perley. In the six conference matches with UCLA, Stanford and California over that season, USC lost three of the six meetings, with Cal winning one of their two matches and the Bruins beating the Trojans twice. At the NCAAs, Hugh

Stewart came through to win the singles title while Clifton Mayne and Hugh Ditzler of Berkeley won the doubles title. Despite these strong showings by the Trojans and the Bears, it was UCLA, under coach J.D. Morgan, who ended up winning the team championship with USC tying for second place with Berkeley. Stewart went on to become a member of the U.S. Davis Cup team and was inducted into the Southern California Tennis Hall of Fame in 2011.

In 1953, Allen Call and Van Grant joined returning team members, including Gil Shea who came back from the Korean War to play his senior year. The NCAA Championships were held at Syracuse University and UCLA won their third national team title, and their second in a row, with Berkeley finishing as runner-up. The fourth-place finish for USC was seen as disappointing. Shea made it to the semifinals in singles only to lose to Ron Livingston from UCLA. Ham Richardson, Tulane's top player and later Rhodes Scholar, won the tournament. Shea teamed with Grigry only to lose to eventual doubles champions Bob Perry and Larry Huebner from UCLA in the semifinal.

With NCAA team titles in 1950, 1952 and 1953, UCLA was emerging as the dominant national tennis power under coach J.D. Morgan. The UCLA athletic department was allocating increasing resources to build up their program to lure more top players into their ranks. However, the tide would begin to turn when George Toley returned as the head coach of the Trojans in 1954.

4

George Toley: Architect of the Future

From the time he set foot on campus as a young tennis player in 1937 until his retirement as head coach in 1980, George Toley was emblematic of USC tennis. Born on April 23, 1916 to Yugoslavian parents Kate and Andrew, Toley grew up in Angelino Heights, close to Dodger Stadium. He attended Polytechnic High School in its original location in downtown Los Angeles, graduating later from Los Angeles High School.

Toley was a tall, striking man with a natural gift for the game. On a whim, he entered his first tennis competition in ninth grade, partnering with a high school buddy. With no tennis experience or formal instruction, the youngsters won the doubles title. While he was not part of the junior circuit, Perry T. Jones saw Toley's potential and took him under his wing at the Los Angeles Tennis Club. An enterprising young man, George supported himself by selling tennis balls and equipment and stringing rackets in a small shop that he converted from an old garage behind Los Angeles High. In the early '30s he remembered stringing a racket for Gene Mako.

In 1937, before arriving at USC, Toley played the Eastern circuit, scoring an impressive win over Jacques Brugnon—one of France's "Four Musketeers" (along with Jean Borotra, Henri Cochet and Rene Lacoste)—who dominated tennis from the mid-1920s to early 1930s winning a combined 20 major singles titles, 23 major doubles titles and six straight Davis Cup titles. Toley left the circuit to enroll at the University of Miami and transferred to USC for the 1939 season, to be close to his ailing mother. That year the team was considered the best in the nation, with Ted Schroeder playing No. 2, followed by Ken Bartlett, Marvin Carlock, Myron McNamara and Bill Reedy. USC drubbed UCLA during that season 8-1 but did not fare well in either of the NCAA singles or doubles tournaments. Toley's tennis continued to improve and he scored a major victory later that year over Gene Mako in 1941 at the Atlantic Coast Championships.

After he returned from the Army, Toley worked for his wife's uncle making cement blocks. In 1946, he was offered the job of tennis coach at the Marlborough School, an elite private girls' high school in Los Angeles. Within a few months, the head pro job opened up at the LATC. Los Angeles had become the epicenter of American tennis, with the LATC being the location where the best amateur and professional players congregated. Because Marlborough and the LATC were located only a mile apart in Hancock Park, George took both jobs. The LATC had 17 excellent courts, a great location and lots of amenities. It was also less than a mile from Paramount Studios, and boasted many movie stars among the its membership roster. While there had always been a relationship between the movie industry and USC, tennis served as another connector, one that linked the glamour of Hollywood to the stars of the sport.

Meanwhile at USC, Lou Wheeler stepped down as coach mid-season in 1954, and transitioned to become the supervisor of tennis activities, coaching the freshman team and assisting with the varsity until 1960. Wheeler then went on to become the coach at John Marshall High School in Los Angeles. USC continued to have outstanding players in Jacque Grigry, Allen Cleveland and Alan Call and ended up placing second in the Pacific Coast Conference. UCLA beat USC 15-10 to win the 1954 NCAA championship to complete a three-peat. Ham Richardson from Tulane won his second straight NCAA singles title with Robert Perry and Ronald Livingston from UCLA winning the doubles title.

With Wheeler stepping down, the USC alumni asked Toley to take over the Trojan squad. Toley's wife Miriam didn't want her husband to take the job, given his full plate, but he did so out of loyalty to the school. He said, "The pay was terrible. I think I got $600 a season, or at the most $900. In the later years, I was getting $30 an hour teaching at the club, and USC was paying me $22,000 a year."

Toley inherited some very good players from the previous year, including Alan Call, Allen Cleveland, Jacque Grigry, Richard Haskell and James Perley. Toley had been hearing about some talented Mexican players at Modesto Junior College about 90 miles east of San Francisco. Former Trojan player Bobby Perez from the 1946 championship team initially contacted one of Modesto's top players, Pancho Contreras, at Toley's request and, after a brief conversation with Toley, Contreras left Modesto for USC. Francisco (Pancho) Contreras was the third-ranked singles player in Mexico and a member of the Mexican Davis Cup team. Contreras had also won the national junior title in Mexico in 1952. A semester later, Joaquin Reyes, a friend of Contreras' and another recruit from Modesto, joined the team. Thus began George Toley's legacy of recruiting great Mexican national tennis players.

Pancho Contreras and Joaquin Reyes, winners of the 1955 NCAA doubles title

Jacque Grigry was also an excellent player and considered by many as the best player in the country, although his personal reputation was sometimes called into question. In May 1955, Grigry was profiled in an article in the *Daily Trojan* in which he was described as talented, but arrogant, with his bravado not matching his poor playing performance at the start of the year. During the interview, Grigry revealed that he had a bad case of bursitis in his knee and was unable to attend practices and could play only in dual matches. After the NCAAs, he became a teaching pro. In 1959, he played Manuel Santana in an infamous second-round match at Wimbledon. Ed Atkinson recalled that Grigry brought beer onto the court. In the fifth set, he ran out of alcohol and requested, and received, more beer because he was cramping. He lost 6-1 in the final set.

In 1955, the Trojans won their third NCAA team title at Chapel Hill, North Carolina with a five-point margin over runner-up Texas 12-7. The 1955 Trojan win ended UCLA's three-year stranglehold on the title. With intense coaching by Toley, Contreras and Reyes, USC's No. 2 doubles team behind Jacque Grigry and Peruvian Alex Olmedo, ended up winning the NCAA doubles title. According to Ed Atkinson, Contreras and Reyes were terrific athletes but they didn't really know how to play doubles together—they were out of position and didn't play the net well. However, they were so motivated to win that despite Contreras spraining his ankle in the fourth set the duo still beat Sammy Giammalva and John Hernandez of Texas on clay 15-13 in the fifth set—quite a feat.

In the 1955 NCAA singles championship, Tulane's Jose (Pepe) Aguero from Brazil beat the University of Washington's William (Bill) Quillian in four sets. Quillian went on to coach at UW until his untimely death from leukemia in 1973 at age 39. The tennis stadium at UW is named for him. That year, Tulane's star, Ham Richardson, was supposed to play in the tournament but was deemed ineligible by the NCAA since he had played during his freshman year in violation of the rules.

In a 1956 editorial in the *Daily Trojan*, sports writer Jim Morad predicted that the Trojans would win the NCAA title again—given how the team was shaping up. Both Contreras and Reyes were returning and Toley also recruited Yves Le Maitre, the runner-up in the Mexican national doubles championship, and Alex Olmedo. Ernie Follico and South Pasadenan Jim Wilson rounded out the team. Toley continued to form the foundation of what was to become one of the strongest connections between Mexican and South American athletes and any university in the United States.

In March of 1956, the Trojans played a dual match against a tough team of USC alumni with Coach Toley playing for the alumni. Proving that he still had the skills, Toley lost in three hard-fought sets against Joaquin Reyes. Toley got his revenge, however, teaming with Jack Kerr to beat Reyes and Follico in straight sets.

At the 1956 NCAAs at Kalamazoo, Michigan, Olmedo won the singles title, and then teamed up with Contreras to win the doubles title. However, UCLA won the team title, edging out the Trojans by just one match victory 15-14. Reyes also played one of the best matches of his career, defeating defending champion Jose Aguero of Tulane in the singles tournament. After graduation, Contreras, who Toley described as a "brilliant kid," went on to very successful career as an executive at Coca-Cola, Eastern Airlines, and later, as a sports commentator for Televisa Television.

Alex Olmedo came to Los Angeles from Arequipa, Peru in early 1954 when Stanley Singer, who was an American coach living in Lima, noticed him. He had just won the Peruvian national championship, and Singer sent the 18-year-old to California to play and to learn English. Olmedo spent about a year practicing in parks around Los Angeles and playing in local tournaments.

While at USC, "The Chief" Alex Olmedo won two NCAA singles and doubles titles. He won both the NCAA singles and doubles titles in 1956, winning the doubles title with Francisco Contreras, and swept both titles again in 1958, winning the doubles title with Ed Atkinson.

Many people assumed Perry T. Jones would take Olmedo under his wing, but Jones resisted because Olmedo was not in school. Some speculated that because Jones didn't "discover" Olmedo, and had not groomed him like his other protégés, that he was reluctant to take him on. Eventually Jones came around because he needed a young star to keep his reputation as the czar of young American tennis alive, especially after Pancho

Gonzales had left his fold. Perhaps Jones thought that Olmedo just might be the kid who could get him on top again.

After a year in Los Angeles, Olmedo's visa was about to expire. He was considering moving to Mexico. Fortuitously, he ran into George Toley on the eve of his departure and explained his situation. Both Toley and Lou Wheeler counseled that he could stay in California if he was enrolled in college and helped him apply for a student visa. Said Olmedo, "I wasn't really considering going to school, but George got me into Modesto Junior College and so I went." Olmedo played at Modesto for one year and following year transferred to USC and majored in business. At USC, his teammates called him "The Chief" — or *El Cacique* (in Peruvian) — because of his Incan ancestry.

Toley worked Olmedo hard every day and saw him make big gains on his serve and court strategy. His game improved so rapidly that in his sophomore year in 1956 he became the NCAA singles champion, beating Jack Frost of Stanford in the final. He then teamed with Pancho Contreras to win the doubles title, beating Mike Franks and John Lesch of UCLA. In 1956, at the Pacific Southwest tournament, Olmedo beat Lew Hoad 7-5, 4-6, 6-4 in the third round. Hoad had just fallen one match shy of winning a Grand Slam, having won the Australian, French, Wimbledon titles, losing to Ken Rosewall in the U.S. singles final.

Olmedo, however, said his greatest match was against Ashley Cooper in the 1958 Davis Cup in Brisbane. Australia had won the Davis Cup three years in a row, and Cooper was the No. 1 ranked player in the world. With the U.S. up two matches to one, Olmedo upset Cooper 6-3, 4-6, 6-4, 8-6 to clinch the title for the United States. Right after the win, an ebullient Olmedo gushed, "It is the most thrilling moment of my life," while Jones, who was the U.S. Davis Cup captain, stated, "I've said it before and I'll say it again, he's the greatest amateur in the world today."

Alex won the Australian and Wimbledon singles titles in 1959 to add to his U.S. doubles title in 1958. To win Wimbledon in 1959, he beat Rod Laver in straight sets 6-4, 6-3, 6-4 in the final. "Alex was in top shape and very fast," said Laver of Olmedo 58 years after his final-round loss. "I recall that he moved like a cat on the court. I think he played some of his best tennis that day."

After he retired from the tour, Olmedo spent the next 37 years as the head pro at the Beverly Hills Hotel. He greeted everyone with his signature phrase, "Hey baby, how are you?" He taught Presidents—Ronald Reagan and George Bush, Sr.— and major Hollywood figures like Katherine Hepburn, Charlton Heston, Glen Campbell, Kenny Rogers, Sumner Redstone and Lorne Michaels. One of his most memorable students was Tina Louise, the actress who played Ginger on *Gilligan's Island* who ran around the court carrying an umbrella so that her fair skin wouldn't burn. Another famous student, *Godfather* author Mario Puzo, was so taken with Olmedo that he acknowledged him in his book *The Godfather Papers*. Puzo wrote, "The Beverly Hills Hotel is for me the best hotel in the world. It is a rambling three-story affair surrounded by gardens, its own bungalows, swimming pool and the famous Polo Lounge. The tennis pro Alex Olmedo called me Champ. Of course he called everyone Champ. Still…"

But even though Olmedo hobnobbed with hundreds of celebrities, one of his most prized possessions is a photograph on his mantle showing him with Ken Rosewall and Pancho Segura. "These are some of the greatest players who played the sport," Olmedo said. "They were both extremely talented and smart, but above all else they were true gentlemen." These remarks are telling, because from time to time some critics took umbrage with what they perceived as Alex's inconsistent on-court temperament. He could beat the best players in the world and then lose to a local public parks player. Behind several of these stories, though, are events in which Olmedo felt disrespected by officials and other players and these incidents infuriated him. Alex Olmedo was, and still is, a true gentleman—just like the guys in his prized photo—and he wanted to be treated the same way as he treated others. Olmedo was inducted into the International Tennis Hall of Fame in 1987, the USC Athletic Hall of Fame in 1997 and the Southern California Tennis Association Hall of Fame in 2000. He was George Toley's first great champion.

Over the course of the next few years, the USC sports program went through a rocky period. In 1956, the USC football staff used slush funds to pay football players in violation of Pacific Coast Conference rules. UCLA, the University of California at Berkeley and the University of Washington also engaged in similar activities. Somewhat inexplicably, the PCC handed down sanctions not only to the football teams, but to other sports as well—including tennis. These sanctions kept the USC tennis team out of contention for the NCAA Championships, although the team could play in dual meets.

In 1957, Olmedo, LeMaitre and Follico returned and George Toley recruited Ed Atkinson, Jim Buck, Greg Grant and Gordon Davis, a top player who transferred in from Santa Monica City College. Jim Buck, who transferred to USC as a junior recalled, "I transferred to USC from Compton Junior College (now part of El Camino College) in February 1957. We played all of the dual and conference matches but were banned from playing the NCAAs. This was a tough penalty for violations by one of our other teams." The sanctions did open the door for other teams and for the first time the University of Michigan won the NCAA team title beating runner-up Tulane 10-9. Barry MacKay from Michigan won the singles title and Crawford Henry and Ronald Holmberg from Tulane took the doubles championship.

Once sanctions were lifted, 1958 proved to be another banner year for the Trojan squad. Under Jim Buck's leadership as captain, the team consisted of returning top players Olmedo, Atkinson and Gordon Davis. Toley added Eduardo Guzman and Martin Schiller. Delgado was the national junior doubles champion with Ed Atkinson, and runner-up in singles. The freshman team was also very strong with the recruitment of Bobby Delgado and future Trojan coach Dick Leach. Olmedo won the national singles title again in 1958, beating Stanford's

Ed Atkinson won the NCAA doubles title in 1956 with Alex Olmedo

Jon Douglas in four sets. Douglas, a great athlete, became Stanford's first All-American in tennis, and was a member of the Davis Cup team later in 1961 and 1962. He was also Stanford's starting quarterback in 1957.

Olmedo then teamed with up Ed Atkinson to beat Douglas and David Nelson of Stanford in straight sets to win his second NCAA doubles title. USC also won its fourth NCAA team title edging out Stanford 13-9 in points. Ed Atkinson recalled, "You have to realize that since there was no professional tennis in those days, college tennis was great. The level of play was incredible."

In 1958, Perry Jones became the captain of the U.S. Davis Cup team and selected Olmedo for the squad. The selection was not without controversy, but because Peru did not have a Davis Cup team and Olmedo had been a U.S. resident for more than three years, Jones argued that Olmedo qualified.

Sixty-one years after that NCAA title, Alex Olmedo is an affable, striking 81-year-old with a broad smile. He is still very fit and trim, thanks no doubt to the full set of weights and workout equipment that sits on his back porch just a few steps away from a glistening pool. The weights are old style—the ones that have a hard plastic coating encasing them. Olmedo uses them every day. Behind the pool sits a beautifully appointed tennis court—built for him by friend Gene Mako—where Olmedo still gives lessons and imparts the wisdom earned over seven decades of tennis: "I'm not a big fan of the heavy topspin that players use today," Olmedo said. "I can still hit a flat ball at 80 miles per hour even at my age. A badly hit topspin forehand really sets you up to fail. If the ball lands short, your opponent will kill it. In my mind, guys like Connors and McEnroe were doing it right."

"Here's another question for you," he continued. "Why does the server have such an advantage? Apart from starting the point, the key reason is that he can control the center of the court. He can pull the receiver off the court in either direction and be in the dominant position."

The 1959 USC team was severely weakened when Olmedo, Atkinson, Buck and Davis graduated. Team captain Buck later returned to USC as the volunteer assistant coach of

USC's women's tennis team for ten seasons. Jim's wife, Annette, a graduate of USC, worked for over 30 years for the Southern California Tennis Association.

The team may have lost some of their power players, but prospects for the season still looked strong with Greg Grant, Dick Leach, Howard Lee and former marine and reigning National Public Parks singles champion Allen Tong as the team's top players. Their hopes were dashed, however, when the staff of the football team was accused of once again violating NCAA recruiting rules by paying transportation fees for USC football recruits. As a result, several USC teams, including tennis, were again penalized and not allowed to play in national championship matches. Thus, USC was unable to defend its national title. In an article in the *Daily Trojan*, university officials claimed that they had evidence that completely refuted the NCAA's claims, but the NCAA refused to grant them an audience. As a result, the charges stood. Ultimately, this series of events led to the demise of the Pacific Coast Conference on June 30, 1959. The Pacific Coast Conference was replaced on July 1, 1959 with the Athletic Association of Western Universities (AAWU) with USC, UCLA, Berkeley, Washington and Stanford as charter members. In 1968, the conference was renamed the Pacific-8, and subsequently the Pacific-10 in 1978 and the Pacific-12 in 2011.

In an unusual turn of events, for the first time in NCAA tennis history, two schools—Notre Dame and Tulane—tied for the national team title each amassing eight points. Whitney Reed of San Jose State was the singles champion and Crawford Henry and Ronald Holmberg won their second doubles title, the first occurring in 1957.

Members of the USC team sit at the 1958 NCAA Champions table to celebrate Perry T. Jones as Captain of the 1958 Davis Cup Team at the Beverly Hills Hotel: Left to Right: Martin Schiller (JV), Jim Buck, Gordon Davis, Greg Grant, Alex Olmedo (key member of the Davis Cup squad), Howard Lee (freshman), Dick Leach (freshman), Ed Atkinson, and Coach George Toley

UCLA returned as a contender for the national title in 1960 after a three-year probation was lifted for NCAA violations. For their return, UCLA fielded a very strong team that included Larry Nagler and Allen Fox. Nagler was a versatile athletic who also played basketball under John Wooden for two years before joining the tennis team. Nagler upset defending champ Reed from San Jose State in a grueling five-set match to take the singles title. He then teamed with Allen Fox—who would ultimately go on to a stellar career as one of the top players in the U.S.— to win the doubles titles, beating USC's Greg Grant and Bobby Delgado in straight sets in the final. UCLA won the team title dominating USC by 18-8 points.

Howard Lee and Bob Whitehall joined the USC team in 1960, but there was another significant addition to the Men of Troy. Rafael Osuna, one of Toley's greatest recruits, first arrived on the USC campus, but was ineligible to play as a freshman.

Toley had been hearing about Osuna for quite some time from former Mexican players Francisco Contreras, Yves Lemaitre and Eduardo Guzman. Like Ellsworth Vines in the 1930s, Rafael Osuna's athletic abilities went far beyond the tennis court. At age nine he entered his first table tennis tournament and made it to the quarterfinals, losing in five sets to the Mexican national champion. He was so small that he had to stand on a box to see above the table. A few years later, he won the national table tennis championship in doubles. A gifted basketball player, he also played in the national basketball league in Mexico. By that time he had grown to be six feet tall.

Osuna's debut at USC in 1961 came at an opportune time— just after all of the NCAA sanctions had been lifted. Toley rebuilt every aspect of Osuna's game, making him battle the ball machine daily. While incredibly fast, with great hand-eye coordination, Osuna needed to focus on his footwork, technique and physical conditioning. Toley found him to be a hard worker who desperately wanted to improve. "Rafe did everything I told him, never questioned me," Toley said.

Rafael Osuna won the NCAA singles title in 1962 and the
NCAA doubles title in 1961, 1962 and 1963

Toley was particularly amused that Osuna like to use
head fakes just as he was about to hit a volley, but soon he was
broken of this habit. Toley also knew that Osuna had the raw
talent to be a world champion, at one point saying, "He moves on
the tennis court like a god!" To beat the heat, Osuna decided to
shave off his full head of hair earning him the nickname *El Pélon*
or The Bald. While not particularly glamorous, the nickname
stuck. At the NCAAs, USC lost the national team championship
to UCLA by one point (17-16), with UCLA's Allen Fox winning

the singles title. However Osuna and Ramsey Earnhart, the No. 1 seeds, won the doubles title, beating Bill Hoogs and Jim McManus from Berkeley in the final.

For the next three years—between 1962-1964—USC would dominate the national tennis scene. In addition to already having an incredibly strong team, they were bolstered considerably in 1962 by a young man from Bakersfield named Dennis Ralston. The team was extremely talented and swept the NCAAs, with Osuna winning the NCAA singles title beating Northwestern's Marty Riessen 2-6, 6-4, 6-4, 6-2 in the final. He then teamed with Earnhart as in the previous year to clobber Miami's Rod Mandelstam and John Karabasz 6-2, 6-2, 6-4 for their second consecutive doubles title. USC amassed 22 points, the most-ever accumulated by a team, to beat UCLA for their fifth national championship 22-12.

Osuna's career pinnacle came when he won the 1963 U.S. singles title at Forest Hills, defeating Riessen in the quarterfinals in an NCAA final re-match, top-seed Chuck McKinley in the semifinals and Frank Froehling in the final. He also garnered three major doubles titles – the 1960 and 1962 U.S. doubles titles with Ralston and Antonio Palafox, respectively, and Wimbledon doubles in 1963 also with Palafox. In 1962, Osuna, Palafox, Pancho Contreras and Mario Llamas helped lead Mexico all the way to the Davis Cup final, where they lost to Australia.

Tennis historian Bud Collins stated that Osuna and Palafox were true innovators in doubles, crediting the duo with inventing the "I-formation" in which one player crouches down at the net in the middle of the court when his partner is serving. The net man springs up as soon as the serve is hit and then has the option of moving to the left or right, or staying in position.

This formation keeps the receiving team off balance since they don't know in which direction the net man is going to move.

Rafael Belmar Osuna, Osuna's nephew, who later played under Dick Leach, was only an infant at the tail end of his uncle's career but does remember hearing the roar of the crowd when his uncle played the Davis Cup in Mexico. It inspired him to become a tennis player. Belmar recalled hearing that his uncle Rafe was "the fastest man who ever set foot on a court. Legend has it that he could catch a drop shot in the air. But, ironically, he was constantly late for everything and drove at a snail's pace." Osuna also loved kids, and whenever he played a tournament he always found a way to get any kid who wanted to attend the match to come in free.

Osuna is the only Mexican national tennis player to be ranked No. 1 in the world (in 1963 by the International Tennis Federation), and he played on the Mexican Davis Cup team for 11 years beginning in 1960. In 1968, he won a Gold Medal in singles at the demonstration tournament at the Olympics in Mexico City and teamed with Vincent Zarazua to also win the doubles. Tragically, Osuna's brilliant career was cut short when he was only 30 years old. On June 4, 1969, he was on Mexicana Airlines flight 704, which was flying over a part of the Sierra Madre range, when the pilot encountered dense fog and penetrating rain. Unable to see well enough to land, the plane crashed into a 500-foot vertical wall called Monk's Mountains, killing all 79 people on the flight. One Mexican official said, "I cannot believe it. I don't know what to say. He can never be replaced." Eduardo Martinez Lanz, a close friend of Osuna's and Toley's said, "George would lend Rafe—and only Rafe—his beautiful 1957 classic Salmon Thunderbird. I think that George thought of Rafe as a son. One of the saddest moments George and I shared was learning about the death of Rafael in 1969."

The Rafael Osuna Sportsmanship Award was established in 1969. This award, the Intercollegiate Tennis Association's most enduring honor recognizes, "A Division I player who displays sportsmanship, character, excellent academics and has had outstanding tennis playing accomplishments." To date, six Trojans have won the award, including Joaquin Loyo-Mayo (1969), John Andrews (1974), Roger Knapp (1982), Byron Black (1989), Kaes Van't Hof (2008) and Daniel Nguyen (2012). Elena Osuna de Belmar has also honored her brother's legacy with the publication of her comprehensive Spanish language book *Sonata en Set Mayor*.

Coach George Toley with Tony Novelo at Estero Beach, Ensenada, Mexico

Osuna was also indirectly responsible for another famous Mexican recruit to USC tennis. On a vacation trip to Ensenada, in Baja, California in the early 1960's, the Toleys stayed at the Estero Beach Resort where they had a chance meeting with Tony Novelo, the resort manager. Novelo was a tennis enthusiast who followed USC tennis closely. When he heard that *the* George Toley, Rafael Osuna's coach, was staying at his resort, he became very excited. The Novelo family became lifelong friends with the Toleys. Two of the Novelos' children later played at USC: Lupita, a standout player on the women's team in the late 1980's and a future Olympian for Mexico, and her brother Marco, a two-time letter winner in the early 1980's who went on to become the Mayor of Ensenada. It was through the Novelos that George Toley met Raul Ramirez, Sr. whose son, Raul Ramirez, would later come to USC and become another of its most famous players. This connection further deepened George Toley's relationship to Mexican tennis and USC tennis players would regularly go to Ensenada to participate in events. The Los Rosas Resort & Spa, owned by the Novelo family, houses a professional tennis stadium that is dedicated to George Toley.

Dennis Ralston, Osuna's USC doubles partner in 1962, was a tennis prodigy. According to the Ralston family, Dennis took to tennis when he was an infant. His father gave him a cut down racket, and when other kids were playing in a sandbox, he was out hitting balls against the wall. At nine, his parents put him on a bus by himself so that he could make the trek from Bakersfield to the LATC where he met Perry Jones. Jones recounted the story to Jack Olsen of *Sports Illustrated*, "His eyes barely came up to the counter, and right next to him was the biggest valise you ever saw. He looked up at me and said,

'I'm Dennis.' I had no idea who he was but the Ralstons were awfully smart with Dennis because they didn't baby him."

One day, Aussie great Ken Rosewall came through Los Angeles on the way to Wimbledon to visit Jones. Rosewall told Jones that he only had a few hours in LA and wanted to hit with someone. Jones told Rosewall that the only person available was a 16-year-old boy who wouldn't give him much of a game. Rosewall agreed to hit with him. Jones recalled, "I took Dennis out to court No. 2 and he beat the heck out of Rosewall. Beat him, beat him, beat his ears back! Rosewall wasn't concentrating and just trying to loosen up, but he never expected a 16-year-old with that collection of strokes and so much finesse."

In 1960, Rafael Osuna was a freshman at USC and Ralston was a senior at Bakersfield High School. The two met at the Ojai tennis tournament and clicked immediately.

Three weeks later, Ralston signed with USC and George Toley asked him if he wanted to play doubles at Wimbledon with Osuna. Even though Ralston was still in high school, he had already distinguished himself and was ranked in the top ten in the United States. Friends from his hometown financed Ralston's trip. Said Ralston, "Rafe and I became friends very

Dennis Ralston won both the NCAA singles and doubles titles in 1963 and 1964 quickly. Even though we were kind of thrown together, we respected each other and played very well together." When the pair arrived in England, they discovered that they had not secured a berth in the tournament as they were led to believe, but instead had to play several other tournaments such as Manchester before they could be considered for the main draw. As Ralston said, "There were no real 'qualifiers' per se but we did have to make a good showing before tournament officials allowed us into the main draw. Luckily Rafe and I did that." Thus, it could be argued that they were the first men's team to ever win that tournament as "qualifiers." It wasn't until 2005 that South African Wesley Moodie and Australian Stephen Huss won the doubles title at Wimbledon beating Bob and Mike Bryan in the final as the first duo to win at the All England Club as modern-day qualifiers, having to win matches in a qualifying tournament to gain entry into the main draw.

Fortunately, the duo played very well with Ralston bombing serves and Osuna crushing volleys at the net. Entering the tournament unseeded, they ended up beating Mike Davies and Bobby Wilson of Great Britain in the Wimbledon final 7-5, 6-3, 10-8. On their way to victory, they also beat second seeds Rod Laver and Bob Mark, one of the best teams in the world, in the semifinal in five sets. At the end of the match, the crowd gave the two Trojans a standing ovation.

Said Ralston, "After finally qualifying for the main draw we were told to report to Locker Room B. Now Locker Room B is for all of the newcomers to the tournament. The big stars were in all in Locker Room A. After we won a few rounds, the tournament officials came to us and asked if we wanted to move to Locker Room A. We said, 'No thanks, we are happy here.' We played Laver and Bob Mark and won 11-9 in the fifth. We had to play Davies and Wilson in the final and played very well. We won in straight sets. I think we were one of the few teams to ever win Wimbledon out of Locker Room B! We sent George a telegram that said, 'We Won!'"

Growing up playing at the Bakersfield Racquet Club, Ralston worked his way up the club ladders. He had very strong groundstrokes and a particularly good forehand. His serve was extremely accurate and he volleyed very well. But Dennis always thought he would follow in the footsteps of other Bakersfield kids and go to UCLA. What changed his decision was his recruiting trip to the Bruin campus. At the time of his visit, UCLA had top tennis players Allen Fox and Larry Nagler on the team. During his recruiting trip, he watched while Coach J.D. Morgan barked orders at his players and decided on the spot that he didn't have a future as a Bruin. So he enrolled at USC. "George Toley had such a relaxed style of recruiting," Ralston said. "He was soft-spoken and low-key. When I finally arrived at USC, I asked George why he didn't put any pressure on me to come, and he smiled and said, 'I always knew you would join us.'

"Toley had that sense about him," Ralston continued. "It was the best decision I ever made. When I enrolled in January 1961, I was very happy to become part of the USC family that included players like Alex Olmedo, Rafe, Dick Leach and Bobby Delgado."

The 1963 USC team has been called the greatest college tennis team of all time. The team had a perfect 12-0 season. "Back then, we were kids, we were doing our best to play well," Ralston said. "We knew we were pretty good. Chuck Rombeau was the captain. We had so many great players on that team - Tom Edlefsen, Bill Bond, Rafael Osuna, Ramsey Earnhart, Leon Meyberg and Timothy Carr. Edlefsen, Bond, Ralston, Osuna and Earnhart were all inducted into the Intercollegiate Tennis

Association Men's Collegiate Hall of Fame. We played as a team and no one thought they were better than anyone else."

Ralston won the 1963 NCAA singles title beating Marty Riessen of Northwestern in a four-set final at Princeton. He and Osuna joined forces to beat their teammates Bill Bond and Ramsey Earnhart in a very close five-set final 9-7, 4-6, 7-9, 6-3, 6-1. USC won its sixth NCAA title, once again beating UCLA 27-19 in points.

"While the '63 team was great, the '64 team was just as good in my mind," Ralston said. "Bond, Rombeau, Meyberg and I all came back and David Blankenship, Jerry Cromwell, Dave Ranney and Horst Ritter joined us. George made sure we all got along. I felt that we were playing for the team and for USC. The team wanted to smash UCLA all the time. We beat them 9-0 when they had Arthur Ashe and Charlie Pasarell!"

In 1964, Tom Edlefsen made headlines by scoring a major upset over reigning French and Australian champion Roy Emerson at the U.S. National Indoors in Salisbury, Maryland. Allison Danzig, reporting for the *New York Times* wrote, "Tom Edlefsen, a long-legged undergraduate from the University of Southern California who ranks ninth nationally, put on an astonishingly fine exhibition to defeat Emerson. Hitting with murderous fury with both forehands and backhands that stopped Emerson in his tracks time and again on flat and overspin drives, the blond Californian won 6-4, 6-8, 6-3." Edlefsen went on to beat Arthur Ashe before succumbing to his USC teammate Ralston in straight sets in the semifinal. Unfortunately, Ralston lost in a marathon five-set match to Chuck McKinley of Trinity.

When asked about his most memorable singles and doubles collegiate matches, Ralston said, "In 1964, we were one point behind UCLA in the NCAA team tournament in East

Lansing, Michigan, and I had to win my singles match against Arthur Ashe. I beat Ashe in straight sets, and then won against Northwestern's Marty Reissen—also in straight sets—to win my second straight NCAA title. Bill Bond and I then had to play Ashe and Charlie Pasarell in the doubles final and won 6-2, 6-3, 6-4. This also gave us the team victory 26-25 over UCLA. It was our third national team title in a row.

"Even though we won the team title, we couldn't enjoy it. We finished the tournament on Saturday and then had to fly directly to Wimbledon as we were scheduled to play on Monday. At Wimbledon, they don't care what you were doing before the tournament; you just have to be on the court at your scheduled time. My wife, Linda, was frantic, as she knew that we had to run back to our hotel room, pack our bags and go to the airport. But unbeknownst to us, Coach Toley and Linda had loaded up the station wagon while we were playing. As things were extremely hectic, I didn't question what had happened but just jumped into the car and sped to Detroit to catch the plane to London. It was only 25 years later at George's tribute party that he admitted that he hadn't seen a single point in our doubles match with Arthur and Charlie, but was busy packing up our stuff in the hotel! When I asked him why he did this, he said, 'You guys had to make it to the airport and I knew you were going to win!' George had confidence in his players. He didn't say too much to us when we were playing. He was always calm."

Ralston continued, "Rafe and I remained good friends. We roomed together at USC and then got a house close to the LA Tennis Club. I even played against him in Davis Cup. Neither of us liked flying and shied away from it. It was heartbreaking when his plane went down. We were all stunned and completely distraught.

"In 2009, I came out to The Ojai tournament and Peter Smith asked me to say something to the team. I greatly admire Peter for a number of reasons but particularly because I think that he knows how important it is to keep his players and teams linked to the past. We have such a strong tennis tradition at USC and I am so proud to have been inducted into the USC Athletic Hall of Fame. Stan Smith was first and I was second."

Ralston won five major doubles titles and was instrumental in beating Australia in the 1963 Davis Cup Final with teammate Chuck McKinley. He also captained the Davis Cup squad in 1972 vanquishing Romania for the title. He was a member of the "Handsome Eight," who were a major part of the beginnings of men's professional tennis. The Handsome Eight (or as some wags referred to it: "The Handsome Seven plus Tony Roche") were a group of eight top amateur tennis players who turned pro and changed the nature of men's professional tennis. In late 1967, as the "Open Tennis" era began—in which amateur and professional players could compete in the same tournaments—the Eight signed with the World Championship Tennis (WCT) organization under businessman and promoter David Dixon (also responsible for the Louisiana Superdome and the New Orleans Saints) and backed by Texas oilman Lamar Hunt. The group consisted of Nikola "Niki" Pilić, Earl "Butch" Buchholz, Dennis Ralston, Pierre Bathes, Cliff Drysdale, Roger Taylor, John Newcombe and Tony Roche. A rival group, known as the National Tennis League, consisted of Rod Laver, Ken Rosewall, Pancho Gonzales, Andres Gimeno, Fred Stolle and Roy Emerson. The WCT and the NTL were constantly at odds over who would play particular tournaments. Ultimately, the NTL was absorbed by the WCT, but conflicts still persisted with the International Lawn Tennis Federation (ILTF). In 1972, players decided to form the Association of Tennis Professionals

(ATP). The WCT ended in 1989, and in 1990, the ATP assumed the running of the men's professional tennis tour, being renamed the ATP World Tour.

All of the years of playing had done great damage to Ralston's knee and leg. In 2010, after close to 30 knee surgeries and other injuries that ultimately affected his left foot, he went under the knife and had the leg amputated from the knee down. As a result of all of the surgeries, Ralston also developed an addiction to painkillers that lasted ten years, but finally, at the urging of his family, he finally checked himself into the Betty Ford Clinic to get clean. Ralston still coaches tennis and is drug free. His amputation has made his understanding of the game that much sharper. "I now coach a wheelchair player and it is one of the most gratifying things I have done in my life."

In 1965, the Trojans were looking for a four-peat victory at the NCAAs. But their quest was denied due to several key factors. First, Ralston and Osuna both graduated, leaving Tom Edlefsen as the No. 1 player. Since he was unable to play in the tournament due to academic ineligibility, it was a severe blow to the team's chances. Kent Schick, Jerry Cromwell and sophomore John Tidball lost in the first, second and third rounds, respectively. Horst Ritter advanced to the quarterfinals, but was beaten by Bruin Ian Crookenden in straight sets. In doubles, Schick and Tidball lost in the second round, while Cromwell and Ritter lost to UCLA's Dave Reed and Dave Sanderlin in the quarterfinals. Things might also have been different if USC had been able to bring a talented freshman recruit named Stan Smith into the lineup, but at the time freshmen could not play on the varsity.

Second, the Bruins were led by senior Arthur Ashe, the first prominent African American to enter the top ranks of collegiate (and then professional) tennis. He joined the UCLA squad in 1962 and improved significantly each year but had not had the success that he wanted. As a senior under head coach J.D. Morgan, Ashe, who had watched the Trojans beat the Bruins for three years in a row to win the national title, was primed to win the team title for the Bruins. In front of a huge home crowd on the UCLA campus, Ashe won the singles title, demolishing Miami's Mike Belkin, 6-4, 6-1, 6-1 in the final. George Toley was quoted as saying, "Ashe wins or loses every match. Nobody really beats him in that sense." Ashe then teamed with New Zealander Ian Crookenden to beat their Bruin teammates Reed and Sanderlin in straight sets to win the doubles title. With these and several other major wins, the Bruins took the team title over the University of Miami 31-13 in points. The Trojans placed sixth with ten points, one of their worst finishes.

Ashe graduated in 1966 with a degree in business administration. He went on to win 33 career titles, including the U.S. Open in 1968 and Wimbledon in 1975. He played on the U.S. Davis Cup team for a decade, helping his team win five titles, and was inducted into the International Tennis Hall of Fame in 1985. In the late 1980's Ashe contracted H.I.V., apparently from a blood transfusion during emergency brain surgery. He died tragically in 1993 due to AIDS-related pneumonia.

Between 1960 and 1965, USC and UCLA had each won three national titles. The dominance of these two teams in the national college tennis arena was no doubt frustrating for just about every other university in the nation. The USC-UCLA logjam was difficult to break because both teams were always vying with each other for the best talent and young players were clamoring to join either squad. One school would end up dominating the other for next few years and then another powerhouse would enter the fray.

5

The First Four-Peat

With the departure of stars Rafael Osuna and Dennis Ralston, UCLA's victory at the 1965 NCAA Championships and the continued pressure from archrival coach J.D. Morgan, George Toley wanted to regain the upper hand on the college tennis landscape. Beginning in 1966, through a series of fortuitous events, another tennis dynasty was in the making at USC. The Trojans would also make collegiate tennis history by being the first team to claim an NCAA team championship four-peat.

Toley's instinct for talent brought together Stan Smith and Bob Lutz, one of the greatest doubles teams of all time. At 6'4", Stan Smith was one of the tallest players in the game. Bud Collins called him, the "Leaning Tower of Pasadena," while Romanian Ilie Nastase referred to him as "Godzilla." In 1963, when he was 17, at the Davis Cup match between the U.S. and Mexico at the LATC, the official in charge of selecting ball boys told Stan that he was ungainly and his stature might distract the players. Of note, two of the players in that match were Dennis Ralston and Rafael Osuna, former USC teammates now representing the U.S. and Mexico, respectively, and playing against each other in an American Zone match. Ralston ended up beating Osuna in straight sets to lead the United States to victory.

Born on December 14, 1946, Smith grew up in the lower Hastings Ranch area of Pasadena, California. He attended Pasadena High School and played basketball and tennis. His former high school basketball coach George Terzian said of Smith, "He was an accomplished off guard who was deadly from 15 feet and closer...he played with us until his junior year, when he played California Interscholastic Federation tennis full-time."

Smith honed his tennis skills at the Altadena Town and Country Club and also played a few miles away at the Arcadia and Sierra Madre Parks. His athletic prowess most likely came from his father Ken Smith, who coached basketball, swimming, golf and tennis at Pasadena City College. As Smith's game progressed, he began playing at the LATC where Perry T. Jones saw his talent and convinced him to focus on tennis.

"I wanted to get a tennis scholarship to go to college," Smith said. "The Pasadena Foothill Tennis Patrons, and particularly entertainers Linda Hayes and Lou Crosby (whose daughter was Cathy Lee Crosby), who had supported me for some time, really wanted me to go to USC but Coach Toley did not recruit me at first. Nevertheless, I really felt that USC was the place for me and I really liked George Toley. I knew that he had taken some very talented players like Alex Olmedo, Rafael Osuna and Dennis Ralston and molded them into champions.

Stan Smith won the NCAA singles title in 1968 and the NCAA doubles title with Bob Lutz in 1967 and 1968

It wasn't until June that I got the word that I had a scholarship at USC for the 1964-1965 academic year."

One possible reason that Toley might have overlooked Smith was that he was considering offering a scholarship to Ray Moore, a talented South African player. But the South African government preempted any plans that Toley might have had with Moore when they decided to sponsor him on the pro tour. If Moore had gone to USC, Stan Smith might have gone to UCLA—and USC tennis history would have been written very differently.

The outcome was perfect for Smith since he wasn't excited about going to UCLA. Stan told Tom Hoffarth of the *Los Angeles Daily News,* "J.D. Morgan was a great salesman and recruiter...but he wasn't a 'tennis guy.' He spent a lot of time telling me how much money he raised for facilities." Smith knew that USC's facilities couldn't compare to UCLA's, but since the team practiced at the LATC, he would have opportunities to play with top professional players on great courts in a highly motivating environment. "Overall, for me, George Toley was the best college coach in my time."

Rafael Osuna had been instrumental in getting Joaquin Loyo-Mayo a tennis scholarship at USC and he joined the USC team in 1965 with Smith. While at USC, Loyo-Mayo was also able to fulfill one of his dreams by training with his idol, Pancho Gonzales. While he was relatively small at 5'6", his speed and agility on the court more than made up for his stature. He was once quoted as saying, "(Rod) Laver and (Ken) Rosewall aren't very tall either. I don't think my height will hurt me." Since he and Smith were ineligible to play on the varsity squad as freshmen, they spent a lot of time hitting with one another. Smith credits his ability to play lefties like Rod Laver and Tony Roche with the time he spent practicing with Loyo-Mayo.

Smith and Tom Edlefsen, a talented player known for his big serve and accurate groundstrokes, led a very strong 1966 team. Later, in 1967, Edlefsen contracted Guillain-Barré syndrome from a vaccination for smallpox. He recovered from total paralysis and continued to play until the early 1970s. He achieved a career high of No. 94 in 1974. The rest of the team consisted of Dave Ranney, Jerry Cromwell, Robert Eisenberg (Don Eisenberg's younger brother), Horst Ritter and Jim Hobson. The team had a banner year, going undefeated with a 17-0 record and winning the Athletic Association of Western Universities Conference title.

At the NCAA Championships at the University of Miami, Smith lost a tough 6-4, 3-6, 2-6, 6-3, 6-1 decision to UCLA's Charlie Pasarell in the singles final and Edlefsen also lost to Pasarell in the semifinals. Smith and Edlefsen, who had beaten Pasarell and Crookenden earlier in the season, lost to the Bruin pair 10-8, 6-4 in an upset, giving the Bruins the doubles title. Despite both losses, the Trojans edged out UCLA 27 to 23 points to win the team title. George Toley had won his sixth national title and was named collegiate coach of the year. At the end of the year, J.D. Morgan retired from UCLA after 17 years as head coach of the Bruins, passing the torch to new coach Glenn Bassett. Morgan continued as UCLA athletic director until his retirement in 1979. He passed away from heart disease in 1980 at the age of 61.

Joaquin Loyo-Mayo won the NCAA singles and doubles title in 1969

Bob Lutz: NCAA singles champion in 1967; NCAA doubles champion in 1967 and 1968 with Stan Smith

Smith returned in 1967 as the No. 1 player on the team along with Joaquin Loyo-Mayo, Jim Hobson, Dave Ranney, John Tidball, Robert Eisenberg and Larry Davidson. Bob Lutz also joined the squad, transferring from Stanford.

Lutz was born on August 29, 1947 in Lancaster, Pennsylvania. His father, Walter Lutz, played high school tennis at Rocky Creek High School in Cleveland. When Lutz was two, his family moved to Alhambra, California and later to the Pacific Palisades. At nine, he started playing tennis in Santa Monica, working out with his sister, Judy, after baseball practice. He met tennis pro Ray Casey and started taking lessons. Casey was a former top player at Berkeley and a doubles finalist at Wimbledon in 1925 whose claim to fame was that, in the Eastbourne tournament in England in 1925, he beat Patrick Wheatley 6-0 in 9 minutes—the fastest recorded set ever played in a tournament match.

"I played junior tennis at Lincoln Park," said Lutz. "When I first started out, I got hammered for the first year but then slowly started winning. By age 11, I was No. 1 in Southern California. My coach Ray Casey was a gruff old Irishman with a huge serve. He wasn't very talkative and only saw me play once the entire time he coached me. He taught me the Continental forehand and my only regret was that I wish he had emphasized an Eastern forehand grip. I went back to him all the time so that he could correct any problems. At USC I followed George Toley's advice with strategy, but continued to use Ray as my technical coach."

Everyone assumed that Lutz would go to USC, but he had other ideas. "In August 1965, I beat Steve Avoyer to win the national junior championships at Kalamazoo and that really got me noticed. I started at Stanford in the fall of 1965 with a full scholarship." At the time, however, Stanford didn't have as strong a team as UCLA or USC, so I contacted George Toley and asked if I could transfer. I left Stanford, enrolled at USC and started playing in spring 1967." That year, the team's record was 12-2 during the regular season and they won the AAWU Conference title once again. At the NCAA Championships at the University of Southern Illinois at Carbondale, top-seeded Smith lost in the quarterfinals to No. 5 seed Gary Rose of UCLA. Lutz faced Jaime Fillol of Miami in the final.

"I clearly remember that final against Jaime Fillol," said Lutz. "It is probably my most memorable match. George Toley talked about that one for years."

Lutz started out dominating Fillol by winning 15 games in a row and taking a 6-0, 6-0, 3-0 lead. The day before, Fillol, complaining about stiff knees, did some deep knee bends to loosen things up. In so doing, he tore the cartilage in one of his knees. Midway through the third set, Fillol rallied to win the third set and then took a commanding 4-1 lead in the fourth. Toley then told Lutz, "Bob, I want you to throw this set. But I want you to do it this way: hit out on every ball. Don't worry about losing the set, but try to keep the point going as long as you can so you can hit a lot of balls and get your timing back." Lutz did exactly as Toley instructed, got back into a rhythm and won the final set 6-2.

After the match, Toley said, "Lutz's game is his consistency and movement. He was particularly consistent today. If there were a record for the fewest errors in two sets I'm sure Bob would have broken it today. I doubt if there were 15 errors in the first 15 games." Quipped Lutz, "I had to win. How was I going to go back to the LATC and tell everyone that I won the first 15 games but lost the match?" As a bit of trivia, Lutz was the first player to win the NCAA singles title with a metal racket—the Spalding Smasher. Lutz's Smasher, as well as the Wilson T-2000s that Loyo-Mayo used to win the NCAA singles title in 1969, and the one used by Jimmy Connors (UCLA) in 1971, are housed at the University of Georgia's Intercollegiate Tennis Hall of Fame in Athens, Georgia.

Lutz also garnered the NCAA doubles title when he and Smith defeated teammates Loyo-Mayo and Hobson 6-2, 9-7 with both teams agreeing only to play best two out of three, rather and three out of five sets. Toley garnered his seventh team title—the second in a row—beating runner-up UCLA 28-23.

As with Smith's story, USC tennis history most likely would have taken a different turn if Lutz had stayed at Stanford. The following year, Dick Gould, who would become one of the most accomplished tennis coaches in collegiate history, left Foothill Junior College in Los Altos Hills, California and took over as head coach of Stanford's team. Some have speculated that Gould was hired in part because of Lutz's departure to USC. After a rocky start in his first two years, Gould had enormous success, recruiting Roscoe Tanner, Alex "Sandy" Mayer, Jim Delaney and Chico Hagey in the early 1970's. Gould went on to build a dynasty at Stanford and no doubt Lutz would have been a building block for his early teams.

The seeds of the Lutz-Smith doubles reign at USC began as early as 1964. "Perry T. told us that we had to play together," Lutz said. "Initially I wanted to play with Roy Barth (who later went on to become an All-American at UCLA), but if you wanted your expenses paid by the SCTA you had to do what Perry said. Stan and I didn't click right away. It took us a year. We were different people with different personalities. Stan was a very good singles player but didn't know much about doubles. I had played a lot of doubles at Lincoln Park and the LATC and knew about positioning and tactics. Stan and I got beat a lot in the first year but by the second year we really clicked. In our partnership, I played the ad side and Stan the deuce side. I liked playing the ad side and facing the pressure. The ads, in and out, all happen on that side." Lutz is also widely acknowledged as having one of the best backhand returns of serve in the history of the game.

What accounted for their success? Smith likened a doubles team to a marriage and believed that you had to accept your partner's strengths and weaknesses and not get down on him. "You really have to get along," Lutz said. "A lot of good teams have broken up because one player thought he was better than the other. My two best matches with Stan were winning the doubles finals in 1967 and 1968. I don't think that Stan and I lost a doubles match at USC." Later in their careers, Lutz and Smith would amass a phenomenal record of 37 doubles titles, including five major wins at the 1970 Australian Open and four U.S. Open wins in 1968, 1974, 1978 and 1980. They are considered one of the top ten doubles teams of all time.

While Lutz was a very serious tennis player, he also had a wild streak and always had a twinkle in his eye. "George was easy to get along with, but I put him through hell," said Lutz. "He was soft spoken and mild mannered, but you didn't want to rile him up since he could get very mad. I do remember one instance when I had a quick, easy win in my singles match. During that time we played doubles after the singles. I had a friend who was going to meet George Taylor and me between the singles and doubles matches to have a couple of beers. We lost track of time telling each other stories and having a great time. When we realized the time, we ran back to the courts, but had been defaulted. As you can imagine, Coach blew his stack.

"In another instance, I got into a betting match with Bobby Riggs. Riggs loved to gamble. He decided that we should play golf and tennis for money. We started out with golf and he gave me a stroke a hole. Riggs ate me up in golf and I was out $250. When we played tennis, I played the singles court but had to give him the doubles alleys and I only got one serve per point. I won 7-5 and so we were even, but he was mad about it. A little later, I was traveling up north and staying at the Tiburon Lodge. I got a call from Bobby. He wanted to keep the competition going so we decided to bet just on tennis. After a couple of days I was up $500. The next day we moved down to Carmel to play golf and tennis. It rained in the morning and I decided to go back to LA. I arrived home to a message from Riggs saying that the rain has eased up and why wasn't I around. He told me that because I took off we were square! I met him a year later and he had plenty of money but never paid me. That was Riggs. On another occasion, Ray Moore and I played backgammon all night at the LATC. We got locked in at the club and had to climb out of the window and jump down from the second floor."

The 1968 team consisted of Stan Smith, Bob Lutz, Tom Leonard, Steve Avoyer, Larry Davidson, Bob Eisenberg, Gary Tarna and James York, with Joaquin Loyo-Mayo being redshirted. Avoyer had clear reasons for wanting to come to USC. In August 1966, Avoyer had won the USTA National Boys' 18s Championships in Kalamazoo, Michigan—where they had been held since 1943, with the winner receiving an invitation to play in the main draw of U.S. Open. Said Avoyer, "USC had Stan Smith, the 1964 (Kalamazoo) champion and Bob Lutz, who beat me in the final there in 1965. I thought that if I went to USC, we would have the 1964 (Smith), 1965 (Lutz) and the 1966 junior champion all on the same team. In addition, Tom Leonard, who was known for his huge serve and sharp volleys, had committed to coming to USC and I thought that made the line-up even more compelling." Leonard went on to be ranked as high as No. 36 in the world with wins over Bjorn Borg, Jimmy Connors, Ilie Nastase, Arthur Ashe, John Newcombe and Roy Emerson among others. He retired from the pro tour in 1979. Avoyer stopped playing tennis on the last day of the 1970 NCAA Championships in Salt Lake City. He had broken his left hand during a freak accident playing softball with his fraternity brothers and missed his entire senior season, playing the NCAAs with his hand heavily wrapped. Unsurprisingly, he was not at one hundred percent and lost in the quarterfinals to Roscoe Tanner.

The Trojans had a strong regular season with a 15-1-1 record and won the first Pac-8 title. At the NCAA Championships in San Antonio, both Lutz and Smith sailed smoothly through the tournament only to face each other in the final. Lutz, who was the defending champion, succumbed to Smith in four sets 3-6, 6-1, 6-0, 6-2. Smith and Lutz then took on UCLA's Steve Tidball and Roy Barth in the doubles final, winning 6-1, 7-5. USC accumulated 31 points to win the NCAA team title over Rice (23 points). It was the third team title in a row for the Trojans and gave George Toley his eighth team victory. Later in December, Lutz and Smith defeated Australia's John Alexander and Ray Ruffels 6-4, 6-4, 6-2, and together with singles wins from Arthur Ashe and Clark Graebner, won the Davis Cup title for the U.S. for the first time in five years. This was the last year that only amateur players were eligible to play for their countries in Davis Cup competition. "Stan and I took fall semester off because we had so many Davis Cup matches that fall and we had to show up two weeks in advance to train and prepare," said Lutz. "Playing Davis Cup gave us both a lot of confidence that helped us immensely in all of our subsequent college matches."

Stan Smith and Bob Lutz playing Australia's John Alexander and Ray Ruffels in Davis Cup match, 1968

Smith and Lutz with Davis Cup Captain, Donald Dell

The 1969 Trojan team included Marcelo Lara from Mexico City, a doubles specialist who later in his career lost to Jimmy Connors in a three-hour, five-set battle (6-2, 6-1, 3-6, 4-6, 7-5) during the Davis Cup tie with Mexico. Connors characterized the match as "a real dog fight." Lara would continue to play on the pro tour until 1978. Joaquin Loyo-Mayo and James York returned to the team as did Steve Avoyer and Bob Lutz (at this time ranked No. 1 in the nation). Rounding out the team were George Taylor and Brazilian Fernando Gentil, grandson of U.S. ambassador to South Vietnam Ellsworth Bunker. Gentil played on the professional tennis tour and on the Brazilian Davis Cup team in 1976.

Stan Smith graduated and moved into the pro ranks, where he would face one of the most dramatic moments in his career. In October of 1972, Smith played for United States against Romania in the Davis Cup final in Bucharest, with fellow Trojan Dennis Ralston serving as the U.S. captain. Earlier in September, the horrific massacre of Israeli athletics by Palestinian terrorists at the Munich Olympics had set the world on edge. Tensions ran high as the Romanians were sympathetic with the Palestinians and the U.S. had two Jewish players on their roster, Harold Solomon and Brian Gottfried.

The Americans were warned that the Romanians would engage in all sorts of antics but they pressed on nevertheless. Erik Van Dillen, who played on the 1970 Trojan team, paired with Smith to beat Ilie Nastase and Ion Tiriac in straight sets to give the U.S. the lead two matches to one. Earlier, Smith had beaten Nastase in straight sets and Tiriac had bested American Tom Gorman in five sets. In the fourth match, Smith overcame Tiriac, despite the Romanian trying every trick he could think of to thwart Smith. The U.S. ended up winning 3-2 despite Tom Gorman's loss to Nastase in the final match.

In 1974, Stan Smith married Margie Gengler, the captain of the women's tennis team at Princeton. In his playing career, Smith won 39 singles and 62 doubles titles, including two major singles titles, the U.S. Open in 1971, Wimbledon in 1972, and five major doubles titles, four U.S. Open titles and one Australian Open title, all with Bob Lutz. In 1972, he was the No. 1 player in the world. Today he is a co-owner of the Smith Stearns Tennis Academy and President of the International Tennis Hall of Fame. He is famously one of the first American tennis players to land an endorsement deal for tennis shoes. By 2016, over 22 million pairs of Adidas Stan Smith tennis shoes had been sold. According to Smith, "They have come out with hundreds of versions of colors and materials and limited editions but still keep the old standard of white with green, blue or red on the heel."

Unlike UCLA, USC didn't have organized practices in the fall at this time but the team organized training on their own at the Los Angeles Tennis Club. Coaching was still considered a part-time job until 1972 when Marks Stadium was dedicated on USC's campus. "Coach was also busy with his other teaching jobs," said George Taylor, the Southern California Intercollegiates finalist in 1969. "None of us blamed him, given that he only made $12,000 for coaching the team."

"During the spring season we practiced three days a week on Monday, Tuesday, and Thursday," said Taylor. "I do remember that, during the first week of the season, Coach made us go to a field close to LATC where he put us through a boot camp. We had to do sit-ups until we puked. Our practices were at the LATC, and we played all of our matches on the backcourts, too. So while we had amazing tennis teams, no one from USC ever came to see our matches and very few people associated us with USC tennis."

The Trojans had another strong finish in 1969, going 17-2 for the season and placing second to UCLA in the Pac-8. While USC had beaten UCLA earlier, they were edged out in the last dual meet of the season when Bruins Tito and Elio Alvarez beat Lutz and Avoyer 6-4, 6-3 to win the match 5-4 and take the Pac-8 title.

Going into the NCAAs that year, held on clay at Princeton, USC knew that they would face stiff competition from both UCLA and Trinity. From 1956-1974, under the guidance of head tennis coach Clarence Mabry, Trinity had one of the top teams in the country. Stars like Chuck McKinley, Dick Stockton, Butch Buchholz and Brian Gottfried all played for Trinity, located in San Antonio, Texas. The biggest surprise of the 1969 tournament came from Trojan Joaquin Loyo-Mayo, who had also taken over the top position on the Mexican Davis Cup team after the death of Rafael Osuna. He won the NCAA singles title by beating Mike Estep of Rice 6-1, 6-2, 6-3, and then teamed with his Mexican Davis Cup teammate Marcelo Lara to edge out Trojan brethren Bob Lutz and Steve Avoyer 7-5, 6-4, 12-10 to win the NCAA doubles title. USC racked up a total of 35 points in the tournament to take their fourth consecutive team title, with UCLA placing second with 23 points, followed by Trinity with 22. Trinity would finish second for the next two years before winning the team title in 1972.

USC was the first team to win four straight NCAA team titles. Apart from the talent and drive of individual team members, George Toley's superior coaching was evident, particularly in how he was able to identify opponents' weaknesses and then show his players how to exploit them relentlessly. It would be twenty-six years before Stanford, under Dick Gould's leadership, achieved the second four-peat (1995-

1999), followed a decade later by Peter Smith's teams winning the third four-peat for USC (2009-2012).

"During our win of the first four-peat 1966-1969, I was on three of those teams and Stan was on three as well," said Lutz. "From 1962-1964, we also won three titles in a row. Arthur Ashe and Charlie Pasarell won the title for the Bruins in 1965, and if they hadn't done that we would have won eight in a row. Further, Stan couldn't play in 1965 because he was a freshman. Despite the high level of competition, I was close friends with Ashe and Pasarell. And I was also good friends with Roy Barth, my nemesis in the juniors."

Rival Stanford Coach Dick Gould has long admired George Toley. "I watched George Toley coach his USC players at Ojai as a So Cal Jr. player, and then as a player at Stanford," he said. "If we won one point out of nine, it was a moral victory for the team in those days. I marveled at how George Toley handled his players. When I got the Stanford coaching position, I really appreciated how well he coached. In my first year in 1967, we lost to USC 9-0—twice—and in my first four years, our record against the Toley-coached Trojans was 0-9. George was always very cordial to me as a young coach starting out and that's something I have never forgotten."

During the first "Open Era" staging of the U.S. Open in 1968, in which amateurs and professionals could play together, Lutz and Smith won doubles titles but as amateurs and couldn't take the prize money. In the spring of 1970, Lutz turned pro and signed with Lamar Hunt's World Championship Tennis tour. Those who signed contracts with Hunt lost their eligibility to play in Grand Slam events such as Wimbledon and the U.S. Open. By 1974, these disputes were resolved and Lutz and Smith won their second (of four) U.S. Open doubles titles. "Since I was already playing against many professionals while

I was a student at USC, the transition to the pros wasn't such a big jump," Lutz said. "The competition wasn't as fierce as it is today either."

Lutz went on to have a stellar professional career, winning 43 doubles and nine singles titles and became a teaching pro in San Clemente. Dana Bozeman, who was mentored by and later worked with Lutz for 30 years marveled at the tennis IQ of the 1967 NCAA singles champion. "Bob has a very deep knowledge of the game and had every shot in the book," said Bozeman. "He knows everything about doubles tactics and how to out-maneuver his opponents. He was always very strong physically and in his 40s could still beat players half his age."

In 1970, the Trojans continued to recruit outstanding players, but on the west coast two major competitors were gaining ground. Glenn Bassett, the former co-captain of UCLA's 1950 NCAA Championship team, was in his third year as head coach of the Bruins. Bassett would go on to coach the Bruins for 27 years, beginning in 1967 and ending in 1993. His teams would win seven NCAA Championships. He is the only person to win an NCAA title as a player (1950), assistant coach, and head coach. Before returning to UCLA, Bassett was the head coach at Santa Monica High School where he notched a 142-2 record. Three hundred and fifty miles to the north, Dick Gould was quietly building what would become a powerhouse program at Stanford. Apart from being a talented coach, Gould was an extremely savvy recruiter. Both UCLA and Stanford teams were poised to unseat the Trojans from their dominant position in college tennis.

In 1970, Steve Avoyer, Fernando Gentil, George Taylor and Tom Leonard all returned to the team. Toley felt the loss of Bob Lutz and Joaquin Loyo-Mayo, but had recruited some outstanding players in Erik Van Dillen, Michael Machette, Dick Bohrnstedt, Dave Borelli and Neil Bessent. Another significant change was that in 1970 freshman could finally play on the varsity.

"In April 1968, Coach George Toley approached me at the Dudley Cup Interscholastic tennis tournament held at Lincoln Park and told me that he had one scholarship to offer for the following year since Stan Smith was graduating," said Bohrnstedt. "I was also considering UCLA, Stanford, Trinity and Houston. I accepted without hesitation, even though I had never seen the campus. We practiced at the LATC, and other USC alumni like Stan Smith, Alex Olmedo, Tom Edlefsen and Dick Leach were willing to practice with us. I would see Jack Kramer around the club regularly as well as Gene Mako and Pancho Gonzales. Don Budge was there a few times. Most of them would talk tennis with you and pass on valuable

knowledge if you asked. The LATC also served really good hamburgers and chocolate chip cookies in the coffee shop."

Erik van Dillen from San Mateo, California was a formidable player, winning the USTA Boys' 16 & 18 National Championship in singles and doubles at Kalamazoo. Van Dillen had a big topspin serve, crisp volleys and was very nimble on the court. He was also an accomplished

Dick Bohrnstedt in 1971

doubles player. In 1968 as a 17-year-old high school junior, he made his name by beating Charlie Pasarell, the No. 1 player in the United States, in five sets at the Longwood Cricket Club in Boston. Four years later, van Dillen would team with Stan Smith to win the Davis Cup for the U.S. in 1972, and get to the doubles final of Wimbledon with Smith. Unfortunately for USC, van Dillen left after his freshman year to play on the pro circuit. He went on to win 13 career titles in doubles and one in singles and achieved a career high singles ranking of No. 36 and No. 35 in doubles.

In 1970, USC had a successful 20-1 season, finishing second in the Pac-8 conference, but only placing sixth at the NCAAs. UCLA had put their stake in the ground, winning the team title with Trinity and Rice tying for second place. UCLA star Jeff Borowiak dominated Roscoe Tanner in straight sets in the singles final and Pat Cramer and Luis Garcia from the University of Miami won the doubles crown.

In 1971, everyone except van Dillen returned to the team. Toley continued to have success recruiting outstanding players: John Andrews from Fullerton, California, who was known for his crushing serve, and Sashi Menon, a top junior player from India, were his two biggest newcomers. Overall, the team won 17 matches, lost five, placed second in the Pac-8, and was fourth at the NCAAs.

Menon grew up in Pune, located about 120 miles southeast of Mumbai, India. His father loved tennis and taught him to play. While his dad pushed him hard, Menon was not sold on the game since all of his buddies preferred cricket or soccer. "I played on the Indian Junior Davis Cup team and also represented India at the Junior Wimbledon tournament in 1969," he said. "A few U.S. universities were very interested in me and I initially wanted to go to the University of Pennsylvania.

My friends told me to consider a California university because I would be more used to the climate, and since USC was the top school in tennis, I contacted George Toley who offered me a scholarship."

Menon arrived on campus in September of 1970 and was the first Indian tennis player at USC. He was known as a power hitter who was competitive with just about anyone when his game was on. In 1972, he scored wins over Alex Olmedo, Frew McMillan and Raul Ramirez. At USC, he was an All-American in 1971, 1973 and 1974, and won three doubles titles in his professional career.

Sashi Menon had some of the most powerful and consistent groundstrokes on the team, 1971

Menon remembered a dual match against UCLA in 1971 as one of the most fun memories while playing for the Trojans. "I was playing Argentinian Tito Vasquez in a key match," he said. "Tito was up a set and ahead 5-2 in the second. I was playing lousy, tight tennis. Tom Leonard, one of the best serve and volleyers on the team, started yelling, 'Come on Tonto!' (but of course I am not that kind of Indian) and the whole stadium burst out laughing—as did I. It helped me relax and I won the next five games in a row and the third set. This tied the match at 3-3, but unfortunately UCLA won two of the three doubles matches to beat us. At USC, I met an incredible group of guys and we all hit it off. In fact, we still get together every couple of months to eat Indian food and talk about the old days."

The 1971 college tennis season was historic. One of the greatest competitors to ever play the game, Jimmy Connors, enrolled at UCLA. Connors, a Midwesterner from Belleville, Illinois had moved to Rexford High School in Beverly Hills to work closely with Pancho Segura. In the dual meet between USC and UCLA, Tom Leonard squared off against Connors. Leonard's blistering serve won him the first set 7-5, but Connors came back by converting a number of break points with some stunning two-handed backhands, claiming the last two sets 6-4, 6-3. While playing Jeff Borowiak, Marcelo Lara, USC's No. 1 player fell, spraining his finger badly and had to default. The Trojans notched three strong singles wins as Bohrnstedt, Menon and Gentil all won their matches—with only Machette losing a very tough three-set match. In the doubles matches, UCLA's Connors and Jeff Austin beat Menon and Jim Hobson, USC's Leonard and Bohrnstedt beat Elio Alvarez and Modesto Vazquez, and UCLA's Borowiak and Ron Cornell beat Mike Machette and George Taylor to give UCLA the 5-4 win.

In the NCAA singles final, Connors, who had started the season as the No. 3 player on the Bruins roster, beat Stanford's top player Roscoe Tanner in four sets 6-3, 4-6, 6-4, 6-4 to become the first freshman to ever win the title. Borowiak and Haroon Rahim beat Trinity's Bob McKinley and Dick Stockton 7-6, 7-6 and UCLA won the team title for the second year in a row with 35 points. Trinity came in second with 27 and Rice and USC finished third and fourth, respectively, with 23 and 22 points.

According to George Taylor, Toley had spotted Connors at the LATC early on but decided not to recruit him. "George thought that Jimmy shouldn't stay back so much and that he needed to come to the net," said Taylor. "He also believed that Jimmy's serve wasn't strong enough." But UCLA must have felt differently, as they landed Connors.

Connors would play for only one season at UCLA. In early 1972, both Connors and Haroon Rahim announced that they would leave UCLA for the pro tour. Connors won eight major titles, including the U.S. Open five times and holds the men's record of 109 pro singles titles. Rahim became a top 50 player and was regarded as the best player ever from Pakistan.

On September 20, 1972, the David X. Marks Tennis Stadium was dedicated in an official ceremony. Constructed for $410,000, the stadium was designed to seat 1,000 people. To inaugurate the stadium, Bob Lutz, Stan Smith, Alex Olmedo and Dennis Ralston played an exhibition match. For the first time in USC tennis history, Trojan players had a first-rate facility that they could call their own and all USC matches and practices would then take place on campus. While SC players would no longer have the luxury of immediate access to the top professional players who came through the Los Angeles Tennis Club, Dave Borelli believed that having George Toley's undivided attention made them all better players. "We still had playing privileges at the LATC, so we got the best of both worlds," said Borelli.

In 1972, Mike Margolin, David Hochwald, Raul Ramirez and fellow Mexican Davis Cup partner Marcelo Lara, Dick Bohrnstedt, Sashi Menon, Mike Machette, John Andrews and Dave Borelli were on the team. The Trojans started the season at a disadvantage as Lara, their No. 2 player, had tendinitis in his wrist.

Newcomer Raul Ramirez was one of the best players to come out of Mexico since Rafael Osuna. "Rafe Osuna was the first pro I played with," said Ramirez, who started to play tennis at the age of 12 in Ensenada, Baja, California. "He brought George Toley to see me play in Ensenada. Later, I went to Toley's camp every summer for three years."

Ramirez enrolled in La Jolla High School and worked with well-known coach Russell J. Lanthorne. Robert Hagey, the patriarch of a prominent tennis family in La Jolla, saw Raul's potential and invited him to stay with his family for the 1970-1971 season. "Raul needed some high school credits to get his tennis scholarship to Southern Cal and he was a good player to practice with," said Chico Hagey, a future Stanford player. "We both worked out with my brother Ted under professional (and former Trojan) Bill Bond, who was a top ranking amateur some years ago."

Raul joined La Jolla High School, becoming part of one of the most impressive high school teams of all time. Between 1955 and 2016, the La Jolla High School Boy's Tennis Team won 42 California Interscholastic Federation (CIF) Section Championships. His teammates included future college stars Chico and Ted Hagey, John Holladay, Steve Mott, and Alex Hernandez. In an informal match, the 1971 La Jolla High School Vikings challenged USC at the LATC—and USC was in for a shock.

The Mexican Connection (left to right): Raul Ramirez, Sr., Stan Smith, Tony Novelo and 14-year-old Raul Ramirez at Estero Beach, Ensenada, Mexico in 1967

"I was playing No. 1 that day because Leonard and Lara weren't playing," said Bohrnstedt. "I lost to Ramirez in three close sets, but the kicker was that George was actually coaching Raul against me!"

With the match tied 4-4, La Jolla's third doubles team of Ted Hagey and Alex Hernandez were up 4-1, and at one point was serving for the third and deciding set. USC's John Andrews and Dave Borelli staved off a match point and clawed their way back, winning the third set 7-5, and winning the match—thus saving the Trojans from some embarrassment. During that season, La Jolla High also played UCLA and Stanford. The three universities were actively recruiting members of the La Jolla team and thought it would be instructive to see how good the Vikings really were. Every player from La Jolla went on to get scholarships to major DI schools: Chico Hagey went to Stanford and Ramirez and John Holladay enrolled at USC. Steve Mott went to UCLA and Ted Hagey and Alex Hernandez were recruited by Utah. Hernandez went on to become the captain of the Mexican Davis Cup Team.

Dave Borelli lived with Ramirez for the two years in an off-campus apartment complex called Portland Estates. "I was a pretty good student, so Coach Toley wanted me to help Raul in school," said Borelli. "Many athletes lived in that apartment building as well. Raul Sr. wanted to make sure we weren't hungry, so as director of fishing and canneries in Baja, California, he would send a private plane to Los Angeles carrying cases of tuna fish and abalone. We lived off that stuff. I ate so much abalone I can't even look at it today."

In 1974, Borelli returned to USC as the head coach of the women's tennis team. He would lead the Women of Troy to seven national team titles, five national singles titles and one national doubles title.

In his first year, Ramirez played No. 2 singles behind countryman Marcelo Lara, and the two also teamed up for doubles. Ramirez had one of the smoothest games in tennis, with great touch, finesse, quickness and anticipation. He also presented a very calm exterior and was frequently compared to Rafael Osuna. "Osuna didn't have a big game but he had a winning attitude—which is what I've tried to develop," said Ramirez. "He also told me never to get mad at myself, even if I'm playing badly. He said that all anybody remembers is whether you won, not whether you won and played a bad match."

In March of 1972, USC made a road trip to play two top teams: the Miami Hurricanes in Florida and the Trinity Tigers in Texas. Miami and Trinity sponsored the trip in an effort to promote college tennis. USC beat the Hurricanes convincingly 7-2, however Eddie Dibbs and Raz Reid beat Marcelo Lara and Raul Ramirez, USC's No. 1 and No. 2 players, in straight sets.

Against Trinity, the match pitted the No. 1-ranked Tigers against the No. 2 ranked Trojans. Trinity's top four players, Dick Stockton, Brian Gottfried, Bob McKinley and Paul Gerken were a formidable group, coached by Clarence Mabry. Even though Lara beat Stockton 6-1, 7-6, Ramirez whipped Gottfried, 7-6, 6-3 and John Andrews crushed John Burrmann 6-2, 6-1, USC still lost the match 6-3.

At the NCAAs, Trinity won their first team championship beating Stanford 36 points to 30. Trinity's top two players, Dick Stockton and Brian Gottfried, battled it out for the singles title with Stockton winning. Roscoe Tanner and Alex "Sandy" Mayer, took the doubles title for Stanford upsetting top-seeded Stockton and Bob McKinley of Trinity in three straight sets. UCLA placed third and USC was fourth in the team standings.

Raul Ramirez was a gifted athlete and had every shot in the book

Ramirez was a two-time All-American at USC in 1972 and 1973 but, according to Toley, was not interested in school. He left USC at the end of the 1973 season and became a professional. Raul was ranked as high as No. 4 in the world in 1976 and was ranked No. 1 in doubles. He won 19 singles titles and 60 doubles titles, including three major doubles titles at the 1975 and 1977 French Open and Wimbledon in 1976 with former Trinity rival Brian Gottfried. In Davis Cup, Ramirez won 36 matches, the second highest number of singles and doubles match wins for Mexico behind Rafael Osuna, who had won 42. Between the two players, however, Ramirez had the highest overall win-loss percentage of 63.88% (36-13) compared to Osuna's 45.24% (42-23) win-loss record.

For college tennis, 1972 was a year of change. Former Wilson Sporting Goods representative Bob Shafer received his first assignment for the company. "Soon after I started in 1972, the person in charge of tennis at Wilson had a heart attack and I was summoned to my boss' office," said Shafer. "He told me to drop everything and to go on the road to promote the next big thing—yellow tennis balls. I told him I didn't know much about tennis, except that tennis balls were white...and that these things were bright yellow. And he said, 'Yeah, that's the new product.'"

It was Lamar Hunt, the tireless promoter, who wanted to shake up the established order of tennis by instituting the tie-breaking system, having players wear colored clothing and encouraging fans to cheer at World Championship Tennis (WCT) events. Robert Langes, a manager at General Tire & Rubber, invented the yellow tennis ball after observing that white balls were hard to see indoors especially under fluorescent lighting. It wasn't long before Hunt and the WCT got on board. They exerted pressure on Wilson to promote the yellow balls because they would be easier to see on television. "But the players just hated them," Shafer said. "They told me they looked like grapefruits, that they didn't spin right and that they wobbled in the air on the toss—they came up with all kinds of excuses, and of course none of them were true."

Shafer was instructed to visit the major tennis tastemakers in Southern California, including George Toley at the LATC, Alex Olmedo at the Beverly Hills Hotel, Pancho Segura at the Beverly Hills Tennis Club, Fred Moll who ran the concession at Griffith Park, Arzy Kunz of Arzy's tennis shop in Beverly Hills and Shelby Jones at Westwood Sports to see what they thought of the balls. No one seemed to like them.

Shafer said he visited Toley first because he saw him as open-minded and an innovator. "I remember that he always walked around on the court with a tape recorder, making voice notes that he would review with players to improve their games," said Shafer. "I always thought this was the first use of technology on a tennis court."

Shafer asked Toley to let some of his players try the balls out. George called over two players who happened to be on the court and asked them to hit with the balls for ten minutes. When both players came off the court, Bob asked them what they thought. The players were very negative. The first said, "The balls fluffed up too much." The other complained that they were just too bright and appeared bigger than white balls. Bob took George aside and asked him if trusted the opinions of the two players. Toley looked at him laughing and said, "Well if Stan Smith and Bob Lutz don't like these balls you are in trouble!" The WCT's heavy promotion of the balls finally did get them accepted.

In 1973, British player Michael Wayman joined the USC team. John Andrews had a successful year, beating

Brian Teacher from UCLA to win the Southern California Intercollegiate tennis championship. USC placed second in the Pac-8, beating UCLA, but finished behind Stanford, who were now dominating college tennis along with USC and UCLA. However, a number of top freshman such as Victor Amaya, Eric Friedler, Freddie DeJesus from Michigan, George Hardie from Southern Methodist and Juan Diaz and Grey King from Florida were all rising contenders. Another bright hopeful, Vitas Gerulaitis, was set to play for Columbia as a freshman, but was disqualified from college play after leaving to play in the Masters tournament during the regular season—a violation of Eastern College Athletic Conference (ECAC) rules. Gerulaitis left Columbia shortly thereafter and turned professional. Another top player from Cincinnati Country Day High School, Henry Bunis took over the top singles spot. Gerulaitis went on to reach a career high of No. 3 in the world, winning the 1977 Australian Open and finishing runner-up at the 1979 U.S. Open and the French Open in 1980.

At the 1973 NCAAs at Princeton, Stanford's Sandy Mayer beat Ramirez in straight sets in the singles final and Mayer and Delaney beat North Carolina's Fred McNair and Richard McKee in four sets in the doubles final. Stanford won the NCAA team title with 33 points with USC coming in second with 28 points. UCLA placed third with 25 points. It was Stanford's first national title.

In 1974, Butch Walts, Hans Gildemeister, Peter Pearson, Ranie Martini and Richard Townsend joined the Trojan ranks. Pearson, who was considered a very talented player, was ranked higher than top Stanford recruits Gene Mayer and Nick Saviano in the USTA 16's rankings, and was a member of the Junior Davis Cup team. Very early in the school year, Pearson was accused of breaking into the other players' lockers and stealing rackets and clothes. Coach Toley actually found one of the stolen rackets in Pearson's dorm room. Shortly thereafter Pearson was asked to leave the team and did not play a single match for the Trojans. In 2009, Pearson was arrested in Santa Clara County on charges of robbing five banks in the area. Subsequently, he was sentenced to life in prison based on his prior convictions. Pearson claimed that he lived through a childhood that was "tense and full of fear." Later in his life, he developed a cocaine addiction, and claimed he was robbing banks to support that habit.

The No. 2 ranked junior in the nation in 1973, Butch Walts was born in Modesto, California. He stood at 6'4" and had a big serve and a formidable forehand. At 17, he was named to the U.S. Junior Davis Cup team and then later enrolled at USC. Said Walts, "I chose USC for a lot of reasons, but probably because of Coach Toley, even though I've worked with guys like Pancho Segura, Toley has a lot of patience . . . the guy is always right." Walts started at No. 5 as a freshman, but moved up to the No. 1 position the following year. Walts went on to a great professional career winning four singles and 15 doubles titles. He was ranked as high as No. 32 in singles and No. 23 in doubles. In 1981, he beat testicular cancer and returned to the pro tour and earned ATP Comeback Player of the Year honors.

Chilean Hans Gildemeister was another top-ranked junior who won the Junior Orange Bowl 14s in 1970 (14s) and 16s in 1972 using his signature two-handed groundstrokes and volleys on both sides. "I was very interested, initially, in the University of Michigan because Freddie DeJesus and Victor Amaya were there," said Gildemeister. "But I also knew that USC had a great coach in George Toley, and he had recruited a lot of Latin players. I was just about to sign with Michigan, when my brother Fritz decided to call Coach Toley to see if they had any interest. I ended up going to USC in 1973 when I was 17. They had a great team that included Andrews, Menon, Holladay and Walts. I enjoyed my time there, but don't think I ever played up to my potential.

"In my sophomore year, Coach tried to change my volley to a one hander and I think I only won one match that year. But the change paid off later. In May 1976, I beat Billy Martin at the NCAAs. I played for three years at USC, but left before graduating to go on the tour. I learned a tremendous amount from Coach Toley. He was technically excellent and taught me a great deal about teamwork. In the pros, my game really got better and I eventually made it into the top 40 on the ATP Tour in 1977. I attribute a lot of my success to how George Toley trained me. Overall, I won four singles and 23 doubles titles in the pros, and my highest ranking was No. 12 in singles and No. 5 in doubles." Following his pro career, Gildemeister founded the Hans Gildemeister Tennis Academy in Tampa, Florida.

In 1974, Stanford scored its second NCAA team title in a row when John Whitlinger beat teammate Chico Hagey in four sets in the NCAA singles final and Whitlinger and Delaney beat USC's John Andrews and Sashi Menon in the doubles final 6-4, 6-4, 4-6, 6-4. Stanford earned 30 points in the team tournament standings, five more than the runner-up Trojans. Stanford's win was even more impressive because Sandy Mayer, the defending NCAA singles champion, had left the team to join the professional ranks.

Stanford's Dick Gould said at this time was when the Stanford, UCLA and USC college tennis rivalry really started to heat up. "I'll never forget that, as we were entering the tennis boom and college fans were starting to grow and our old facility could no longer handle such crowds, I proposed a then-novel idea to Coaches Toley and Bassett," said Gould. "We always played the LA schools in Los Angeles the first weekend of April, and then again in Northern California during the third weekend in April. I loved this arrangement and I fought hard to retain it, as it meant that we would have a second chance at them both at home—and there is a big home court advantage in tennis—where our chances of a win were increased by the home crowd, which gave us tremendous momentum heading into the NCAA Championships. Stanford was also building fan support, especially after winning its first NCAA championship in 1973. So I asked both coaches if, for the 1974 season, they would be willing to play our match starting outdoors in the afternoon and then moving indoors in the evening. George and Glenn were willing to do this, and I was able to find a slightly used carpet from the old May Co. tournament in LA, and had it shipped to Stanford to cover the basketball court in the Pavilion. We worked hard at promoting this USC-UCLA weekend, and the match was even covered in person for *Sports Illustrated* by a former Trojan, Joe Jares.

"With Stanford barely prevailing in a very close 5-4 win in a dual meet at USC, the Trojans came to the Farm on Friday, April 17. It was also the first year of No-Ad Scoring. The afternoon matches were played in the stadium overflowing with nearly 1,000 fans. They began at noon with No. 3 through No. 6 singles, followed by No. 2 and 3 doubles. Doubles counted as one point per match and Stanford won all six afternoon matches to take an insurmountable 6-0 lead going into the evening matches beginning at 6:30 p.m. A documented 5,500 paying fans joined the Stanford Band as Sandy Mayer and Jim Delaney defeated John Andrews and Sashi Menon respectively at No. 1 and 2 singles, and then won the doubles for a 9-0 victory. The next night, over 7,000 fans were in attendance as Stanford defeated UCLA 7-2. For the next 15 years, Stanford

Bruce Manson won the NCAA doubles title in 1975 with
Butch Walts and in 1977 with Chris Lewis

would host these two teams with an evening indoor session at
Stanford. Only two coaches who understood the importance of
promoting college tennis would consent to do this, especially
since the team playing Stanford on Friday night would have
to travel to play Cal at 1:00 p.m. the next day. For this alone,
George Toley and Glenn Bassett earned my everlasting respect
and admiration."

Several very strong players joined the 1975 USC team,
including Chris Lewis, Bruce Manson, Tim O'Reilly, Mike

Newberry and Earl Prince. Toley coached Manson at the LA Tennis Club when he was a junior growing up in LA and had developed a close relationship with him, even before Manson decided to attend USC. Like many players before him, Manson learned more from Toley than just how to improve his game on the court. "He taught stroke techniques, strategy and a mental approach to the game," said Manson. "He was also a man of great integrity and principle. Those life lessons were not evident until after I retired from the professional game.

"My best match at USC was when Butch Walts and I beat Billy Martin and Brian Teacher in the finals of the NCAA doubles tournament in Corpus Christi to win the 1975 title 6-1, 6-4, 7-6," said Manson. "We had beaten defending champions John Whitlinger and Jim Delaney in the semis. I was a freshman and Butch was a sophomore. It was the first time a freshman had won the doubles title. On paper, we were never expected to come close to beating either of those teams and had lost to both during the regular season. Our games complemented each other's; he was a big hitter and I was steadier. He was right-handed and I was left-handed. We were also good friends and lived together. To be a good doubles team you need to believe in each other and enjoy that connection as players and friends. Winning that title is one of my great memories in tennis. I put it right up there with my best win in the pros, over Bjorn Borg when he was No. 1 in the world at the Congoleum Classic held at the Mission Hills Country Club, now the Indian Wells tournament, in 1979 in the first round. I had been a pro for only 18 months and was ranked No. 112. I got into the tournament when another player dropped out. I won 6-7, 7-5, 6-1. I made it to the third round and then lost to Tom Okker."

UCLA was blessed that year with another top freshman recruit named Billy Martin. Martin came from Evanston,

Illinois and was the nation's top recruit. In one of the biggest turnaround matches in NCAA history, Martin, seeded No. 1, was losing to George Hardie of SMU in the first two sets 6-0, 6-1 in the final. The *Pittsburgh Post Gazette* quoted Hardie, "I was looking at Billy and thinking that this could be the greatest lopsided victory in the history of the NCAAs." Imagine Hardie's surprise when Martin turned the tables, winning each of the next three sets 6-3. Martin was only the second person to win the NCAA singles title as a freshman. The first was Bruin Jimmy Connors.

Next, Martin teamed up with Brian Teacher in the doubles final, but lost to Trojans Walts and Manson. Martin had vowed that if he won the NCAAs he would turn pro—which he did following the tournament. UCLA won its 11th team title, besting Miami 27 points to 20. While having an excellent team, USC only placed third in the Pac-8 and seventh at the NCAAs. Billy Martin went into the pro ranks and was ranked as high as No. 32 in 1975. In 1993, he returned to UCLA as head coach.

"We were quite a bit weaker than UCLA and Stanford and struggled against them in the regular season," said Manson of the 1976 season. "But everything came together the week of the tournament, despite the fact that my partner Butch Walts had turned pro. Our team played well and UCLA and Stanford suffered some early upsets. We were able to take advantage of that. You just never know what can happen on any given day."

Another player who had started in 1975, Chris Lewis, came into his own in 1976. Lewis was a top-ten ranked junior in the United States. An excellent student, he had offers from USC, Stanford and Princeton to attend college. USC had offered him a full ride, Stanford a half-scholarship and Princeton did not offer him anything since it did not offer athletic scholarships. The weather at Princeton deterred him, so Lewis decided to go to USC because of the full scholarship and the opportunity to play for George Toley, who had been his coach at the LATC for several years.

"George was an incredible coach and a great human being," said Lewis. "He focused on tennis, but was more focused on what was right for you as a person. He cared about the whole package and not just about how well you played tennis. He wanted to make sure that your school and social life were going well, and that you were preparing for life, not just the next match. In many ways he was like a father figure who helped with all aspects of your life.

"As far as a being a coach, he was an incredible strategist and could dissect an opponent's strengths and weaknesses. As a result he could develop an effective strategy against almost any opponent. He wasn't so much into technique, although he could certainly help with that if you needed it. But for me it was all about strategy, playing the odds, playing smart and using your talents and strengths in the most productive ways. Very simply, he was still very sharp, and no other college coach that I knew had his understanding of the game and the ability to affect the outcome of a match by using strategy and a game plan."

By 1976, USC and UCLA had both won 11 NCAA team championships and the tournament was shaping up to be a real showdown. UCLA, the defending champions, were the odds-on favorite, but in the first round, star Bruin player Brian Teacher, who was nursing a shoulder injury, was upset by unseeded Gary Albertine of LSU in straight sets. No. 6 seed Bill Scanlon from Trinity ended up as the NCAA singles champion upsetting UCLA's Peter Fleming in a four-set final. Fleming and Ferdi Taygan defeated USC's Chris Lewis and Bruce Manson in the doubles final to clinch a tie for the Bruins with USC for the team title. A win for Lewis and Manson in the final would have given USC the team title outright.

"We had not expected to win the 1976 Championship because Stanford was in the lead during the tournament, but when a number of their players were upset all of a sudden we moved ahead with a great chance to win the whole thing," said Lewis. "If Bruce Manson and I had won the doubles final, we would have clinched the title outright, but we lost to Peter Fleming and Ferdi Taygan of UCLA in straight sets. We were very disappointed because we had beaten them on several occasions and felt we were in a good position to do so again."

Previously there had only been one other tie—Tulane and Notre Dame in 1959. Both teams had accumulated 21 points. Stanford finished third with 20 points.

"In those days, our team got along well and we never had issues," said Lewis of the 1976 team. "I wouldn't say we were all close. I think this is probably because we had different interests. For instance, Bruce wanted to go pro, Andy Lucchesi (who later became a male model) was mostly interested in co-eds, Mike Newberry was interested in art, and I was most interested in school. Bruce and I are still close and see each other quite often."

During the last four seasons that George Toley coached at USC, he continued to recruit many high caliber players, including Doug Adler, Jack Kruger, Earl Prince and Robert Van't Hof.

Van't Hof started playing tournaments at age ten with some success. As he entered the last year of the 16s, his game picked up significantly. He made the junior Davis Cup team, which consisted of the eight best players in the country. He continued playing well the next year, and was invited to play in all of the major international junior events. "It was a big thrill and an honor to play at Roland Garros, Wimbledon and Forest Hills," he said. "I ended up the year ranked No. 7 in the world. Not bad for a kid from Downey."

For Van't Hof, the opportunity to be coached by Toley played a key role in choosing USC.

"My parents liked coach George Toley, how successful he was and his personal demeanor," he said. "They also liked his style of coaching serve and volley players. Professor George Schick, a statistics professor and friend of the team, also sold them on the quality of education and that USC had an undergraduate business school."

The two matches Van't Hof remembers clearly were against John McEnroe in 1978. "We had just finished traveling to Wimbledon the summer before - that was the year McEnroe got to the semifinals as a junior and lost to Jimmy Connors in the men's draw," said Van't Hof. "Our first encounter was at USC. The stands were packed and I was pretty nervous. John was ranked No. 16 in the world on the ATP computer. In the first game I was serving and in those days we used No-Ad scoring and played nine-point tie-breakers. The game score was 3-3 and John hit the ball out, but I called it in! He eventually won the game. From that point on I lost 6-0, 6-0.

"Three weeks later we went up to Stanford to play. Our match was being played in the basketball arena—something that Dick Gould had set up. There were thousands of people in the stands and the Stanford band was playing. It was crazy. Boy, was I nervous. I lost the first three games, and I was hoping not to get double bagelled again. Luckily I made a match of it, losing 6-4 in the third set."

"I played on the team for four years," said Doug Adler. "I was a top 10-20 junior through the 18's. While Cal, Texas and others recruited me, it wasn't until later that I talked to George

Toley and he told me that he would put me on the squad and would see how I did. I was always a better doubles player than a singles player and moved between No. 3 and No. 2 doubles."

In 1977, the NCAA Championship changed its format from a points system to a dual-match tournament. Each team consisted of six singles players and three doubles teams. The teams would battle in a single elimination event with winning teams needing to win five out of nine points. Individual singles and doubles championships were also separated from team play. The University of Georgia graciously agreed to host the NCAA tournament at its new tennis stadium named for former tennis alum Henry Feild. The Trojans finished in third place in the Pac-8 and lost to Trinity 5-4 in the NCAA team tournament quarterfinals. Trinity went on to reach the final where it lost to Stanford 5-4.

Manson and Lewis both reached the NCAA semifinals. Manson lost to Tony Graham of UCLA and Lewis lost to eventual NCAA champion Matt Mitchell of Stanford.

"Although we were both very disappointed Bruce and I were able to pull it together and we came back to beat John Austin and Bruce Nichols of UCLA in four sets in the doubles final," said Lewis.

Against Toley's advice, Manson turned pro after the NCAAs, but returned in 1983 to finish at USC before going on to Wharton for an MBA.

In 1978, several new players joined Van't Hof, Doug Adler, Earl Prince, Marco Novelo(Tony's son from Mexico), and Fernando Van Oertzen from Brazil. These new additions to the USC team included top players Sean Brawley, Jim Agate, Billy Nealon, Jack Kruger and Roger Knapp. The Pac-8 was expanded to the Pac-10 with the addition of Arizona and Arizona State to the conference. It was, however, another disappointing season for the Trojans as they finished fourth in the conference and lost in the semifinals of the NCAAs to UCLA 7-2.

Coach Dick Gould of Stanford was well known as a top recruiter. Talking about his success, he says, "We were very successful in selling Stanford to players who were academically qualified. Once we got established—after about three to five years—I think I only lost one player who we admitted, and he was offered a full scholarship to another school. And if players enjoyed their experience here, got better while they were here and did well upon leaving for the tour, it is a pretty easy place to sell. I did feel that for whatever reason, our players always seemed to play their best at the NCAAs—our first two titles were with the old scoring method of four players scoring a point for each round they won. But once the "Team" tourney (best five out of nine points; six singles and three doubles) began in 1977, we reached the final championship match 17 times and won 15 of them. I am very proud of that."

In the summer of 1977 before John McEnroe enrolled at Stanford, he reached the semifinals at Wimbledon, losing to Jimmy Connors in four sets. Despite becoming a world-wide sensation, McEnroe still enrolled at Stanford in the fall.

In 1978, the Cardinal had a banner year and entered the NCAA tournament 20-0, its first undefeated season since 1943. McEnroe was certainly tested along the way, with one of his most memorable matches played against Eliot Teltscher, the top player from UCLA. Teltscher had lost 18 out 20 previous matches to McEnroe, but in this match on the Bruins home court at Westward, he jumped out to an early lead, winning the first set 6-2. At 5-3 and match point in the second set, Teltscher hit an approach shot to McEnroe's backhand and came to the net. Mac stretched and hit a backhand cross-court slice that landed on the line. It was one of the most memorable shots in college tennis history. McEnroe went on to win the match 6-3 in the third. In the 1982 video documentary, *The John McEnroe Story: The Rites of Passage*, which captured the match, Bud Collins remarked, "What a backhand! McEnroe has saved the match. This would be another of McEnroe's trademarks, saving match points, tap dancing through a minefield before going on to win. He only spent a year in college, but he comes out with a Ph.D. in saving match points."

McEnroe, however, did lose two matches during the season. As he wrote in his autobiography, "While the team was undefeated, however, Mr. No. 1 was not: I lost two singles matches, one of them an embarrassing rout by Eddie Edwards of Pepperdine who completely outplayed me in front of a home crowd." The other loss was to Larry Gottfried of Trinity.

Said Dick Gould, "More than anyone I know, John expects perfection of himself. It's a tremendous con, but maybe that's one of the reasons he's as good as he is."

At the NCAA Championships at the University of Georgia, McEnroe, the No. 1 seed, had two tough three-set matches, first with Trinity's Erick Iskersky in the quarterfinals, and then against teammate Bill Maze (who had beaten Robert Van't Hof in the third round) in the semifinals. On the other side of the draw, North Carolina State's John Sadri upset the No. 2 and 3 seeds; UCLA's Teltscher and South African Edwards of Pepperdine, to advance to the final. Sadri's trademark at the tournament was a large cowboy hat and a red Wolfpack blazer that he wore throughout the tournament. Said Sadri years later, "I looked like an absolute moron but it was cool." In the final against McEnroe, Sadri launched a cannonade of 24 aces with his 135 mph serve, the second time in NCAA tennis history when 24 aces were served in a match. The first occurred when

Chris Lewis won the 1977 NCAA doubles title with Bruce Manson

Roscoe Tanner faced Dick Stockton in 1972. Unfortunately, like Sadri, Tanner lost to Stockton. In *The Rites of Passage*, Collins called Sadri's serve "the most destructive shot in tennis." McEnroe never broke his serve, but was able to chip away in the tiebreakers to emerge the victor. The final score was 7-6, 7-6, 5-7, 7-6 with McEnroe winning 144 points to Sadri's 143. Dick Gould called this match the greatest match he has ever seen.

"John's style was so different than anyone else I had ever coached, and he was so successful at it that I was smart enough not to try to make any basic changes, and I think he respected that," said Gould. "That being said, I did want more firmness on his volleys and to be sure that he was incessantly on the attack—moving to the net. Other than that, he was incredibly fun to be around—one of the best team members I have ever had! I really enjoyed him."

While Stanford took the team title and McEnroe the singles title, John Austin and Bruce Nichols of UCLA won the doubles title.

The 1979 the USC team was led by Van't Hof, a junior who started the season as the No. 2 ranked player in the country. Other returning veterans were Doug Adler, Sean Brawley, Roger Knapp, Jack Kruger, Billy Nealon and Fernando van Oertzen. Jim Agate, a freshman from Beverly Hills, also joined the team.

The team had talent—and also some unique equipment. Adler remembers, "Robert Van't Hof used to grip his racket very loosely on the serve to be able to get a wrist snap. As a result, the racket would often fly out of his hand and sometimes break. He told me that his father came up with the idea to drill a hole through the bottom of the handle and thread a strap through it. The strap would then be looped around his wrist. Billy Nealon gripped the racket loosely as well, and also sweated profusely, so Robert's dad did the same thing for Billy."

Adler remembered playing with Nealon against UCLA at home in 1979 in the decisive match, after UCLA held a 4-1 lead. After he and Nealon won the match, capping a doubles sweep for the incredible 5-4 comeback win, Nealon was so happy that he pulled the strap off his wrist and hurled his racket from Marks Stadium over the fence and onto Dedeaux baseball field.

Said Van't Hof, in another match that he won, "Billy was so happy he wanted to throw his racket in the air. But there was one problem—his racket was still tied to the strap around his wrist. Billy, who had a bit of a temper, got so frustrated when he couldn't get the strap off his wrist that he proceeded to smash his racket on the court into a million pieces. Classic Billy story!"

The Trojans ended up third in the Pac-10 and lost in the quarterfinals of the NCAAs to Southern Methodist 7-2. UCLA won the national title beating Trinity 5-3 in the final. Kevin Curren, a South African playing for the University of Texas, won the singles title over Trinity's Erick Iskersky in straight sets, and Iskersky and Ben McKown garnered the doubles title, beating Tennessee's Andy Kohlberg and Michael Fancutt in straight sets.

In February of 1980, George Toley called the team together to tell them that he would be leaving USC early in 1980 to become Raul Ramirez's full-time coach. In March 1980, Toley left USC after 26 years at the helm. He would be on the road with Ramirez for two years until injuries forced Ramirez to retire from the tour. Over his many years of coaching, Toley's teams at USC won 82% of their dual matches, with Toley notching 430 wins, 92 losses and four ties. Before he left, George tapped former player Dick Leach to take over as head coach.

There are many stories about George Toley's effectiveness as a coach. After decades of observing and coaching the very best players in the world at the Los Angeles Tennis Club and at USC, Toley had soaked up as much knowledge as anyone in the game.

Even though Toley was a master of technique, perhaps his greater gift was a deep understanding of the psychology of the game. He was often able to get inside his own players' heads to improve a stroke and could show them how to determine and then exploit an opponent's weakness. Toley recalled how he got Ramsey Earnhart, who played on the 1963 team, to improve his forehand, "I advised him to go out with the idea that you're going to miss forehands that you know you are going to choke on. So don't try to make them all. Just hit it. If you miss it, think, 'Well, I'm supposed to miss it.' Just bunch a couple together, or maybe make one and break serve and that's all you need anyway.'" Earnhart improved his rank to 11th in the country. He came back and said, "God, what a difference. I'd miss a ball and I didn't give a darn. So when the next ball came, I had a chance of making it."

Katie Dempster, George's daughter, remembered being on the court with him when she was nine and how hard her father worked. "Dad was on the courts at LATC 12 hours a day," she said. "He loved coaching and worked with the USC team, the Marlborough High School girl's team and taught many lessons at the LATC. He always said that tennis was one of the hardest sports to play since there was so much to master. He had great insight into the physiology of the game, too. He said it was really hard to teach someone how to move -- a player had the ability or he didn't -- but just about everything else was coachable. The other key thing that he did was to watch the competition carefully. He would always tell his players to find an opponent's weaknesses and exploit them relentlessly. I remember him telling players, 'Demoralize your opponent beginning with the first point!' He knew a lot about strategy and the mental game."

Chris Lewis testified to Toley's natural ability to figure out how to play an opponent and turn the tide of a match. "The 1976 team championship was truly memorable," said Lewis. "My best story about George's strategic insight is from the NCAA tournament in Corpus Christi. I was seeded tenth and playing my first-round match against a guy who I didn't know and who attended a school in the Midwest that I had never heard of. Anyway, Coach thought I would have no problem winning and instead went off to watch the other matches. At one point he wandered over and asked me what the score was. When I told him 6-2, 3-1, he thought I was winning, but when I explained that I was getting crushed, he completely changed his demeanor. Immediately, he started asking me questions. After 60 seconds, he gave me a completely new strategy. Remember, he had not seen one point of the match. This is what he said, 'Make every rally go as long as possible to increase the chance that your opponent will play back to his normal level. Any of us can make a great shot here and there but only the best can do it time and time again over a long period of time. 'After using his new approach, I won 11 games in a row and the match. Later, I asked him how he came up with the strategy. He told me, 'Neither you nor I had ever heard of this guy. If he was that good all the time he would be the top seed in the tournament.' It was advice that I would use on many occasions. Overall, Coach was a great guy who taught you to be fair and to do the right thing at all times. He was much more than a tennis coach; he really was a life coach. I am forever grateful to him and actually appreciate him more for how he helped me as a person as compared to how he helped me as tennis player."

Said Dick Bohrnstedt, "In my opinion George Toley and Pancho Segura were the greatest tennis analysts of all time. Their knowledge was so deep and they knew how to apply it."

All of Toley's players agree that, as competitive as he was, he never cut corners and held very high standards for himself and his players.

"George was always a gentleman and acted professionally," said Sashi Menon.

"He was very easygoing and never lost his cool. He made us all dress well," quipped Bohrnstedt.

"Coach Toley had very high standards for himself in all aspects," said Dick Leach. "He always looked sharp and expected the same of his players. Once I came onto the court with sneakers that had scuff marks on them. He took me back to the pro shop and gave me new ones. We all had to be well groomed. We were representing USC!"

"If you made any bad line calls or did anything that was considered bad behavior, you heard about it," said Menon.

Bohrnstedt characterized Toley as, "A competitor who didn't like to lose because his teams had won so often. He liked players who were tough competitors. When his teams did lose, he always lost with class and congratulated an opponent and always displayed good sportsmanship. He respected you if you gave it your best effort and would call you out if he thought you hadn't. If he thought you shouldn't be playing the way he wanted you to do, that would make him upset. And if you defied his instructions, he would threaten to default you even if you were winning."

Said George Taylor, "He defaulted me once in a dual match against Larry Parker of California because I dropped my racket on the court. I was ahead 6-4, 5-4! Even though we got along, I think I just got under his skin."

Said UCLA's Billy Martin, "I grew up in So Cal. I practiced with both UCLA and USC, which you can't do now because of NCAA rules. Both George Toley and Glenn Bassett were great coaches and class acts. It didn't matter whether they won or lost, they were classy. George was very soft spoken and all of his players spoke so highly of him and appreciated him as a father figure. Many coaches put too much pressure on their kids. They want to scare them, but that is not how Toley coached."

Said Dick Gould, "George Toley and I competed against each other for many years, and often it was very intense. And yet we never had an unpleasant moment on the court or off. As far as I was concerned, he was still the 'Master' and I learned all I could by watching the way he handled his players. He could just as easily have been aloof, standoffish and non-communicative as his team's place in college tennis was being challenged but this was never the case. George was classy and a true gentleman."

Toley left an astonishing legacy at USC, coaching the Trojans for a 26-year period beginning in 1954 and ending in 1980. His teams won ten NCAA team championships (1955, 1958, 1962-64, 1966-69 and 1976), including the first four-peat in college tennis history, nine individual singles titles and 12 doubles titles. He coached many of the greatest players of all time including, but not limited to, Alex Olmedo, Rafael Osuna, Dennis Ralston, Bill Bond, Tom Edlefsen, Joaquin Loyo-Mayo, Raul Ramirez, Stan Smith, Bob Lutz and Robert Van't Hof.

Toley produced ten Davis Cup players, five of whom played for the United States (Alex Olmedo, Dennis Ralston, Stan Smith, Bob Lutz and Erik Van Dillen) with the remaining five playing for the Mexican Davis Cup Team (Rafael Osuna, Francisco Contreras, Marcelo Lara and Joaquin Loyo-Mayo and Raul Ramirez). Five of Toley's players were also Mexican Davis Cup captains: Francisco Contreras, Eduardo Guzman, Yves Lemaitre, Eduardo Martinez Lanz and Raul Ramirez. Toley was a pioneer who created great opportunities for Mexican and South American players to come to the U.S. to play tennis in an era when other universities weren't doing so. He even conducted a summer camp for young Mexican players in the summer in Ensenada. It is clear why he was called "The Father of Mexican Tennis." In 2003, both George and Dick Leach were inducted into the USC Athletic Hall of Fame.

In the 1990's, George woke up one morning, bent over to pick something up and heard a cracking sound in his back. From that day on, he was unable to stand up straight. His condition, known as spondylodesis, involved a stress fracture of a vertebrae. Athletes involved in sports in which there is repetitive or forceful hyperextension of the spine such as tennis, volleyball, basketball and football are often susceptible to these types of injuries.

On June 16, 2007, over 200 former players, friends and relatives gathered at the Galen Center at USC to pay tribute to Coach Toley. Bruce Manson, Bob Lutz and Chris Lewis organized the event. Some of the players who attended stood

Dick Leach, George Toley and Peter Smith taken in 2007 at Coach Toley's tribute dinner

up to pay tribute to Toley, who was sitting in a chair near the podium. Former player Doug Adler recalled that it was a highly emotional event. Adler waited towards the end of the event to say a few words and, as he approached Coach Toley, he leaned over and said, "Coach, it's Doug Adler." George looked at him for a minute and in a loud voice said, "Adler, Adler... oh yes, not so good at singles, better in doubles." The room erupted.

At the end of the event, George got up to speak. Clearly moved, but not one who liked to be feted, Toley simply said, "Thank you" and sat down. Nine months later, on March 1, 2008, Coach Toley died at Huntington Memorial Hospital in Pasadena. He had suffered a heart attack just two months shy of his 92nd birthday.

6

Dick Leach - Returning to Troy

"I remember that call like it was yesterday," said Dick Leach of the phone call he received on the evening of March 1, 1980. "I was not expecting to be contacted by Coach Toley and had not really thought about coaching at USC."

Leach had already turned down an offer to coach at the University of California at Irvine the previous year, knowing the time commitment it would take to coach a DI tennis team. But, this was his alma mater.

"George and I met at the Pacific Coast Doubles Tournament at the La Jolla Beach and Tennis Club where he said we could discuss the USC coaching job," Leach said. "All of the major universities like Stanford and California played this event." Toley explained that Raul Ramirez wanted him as his coach on the pro tour and he had to leave as soon as possible.

"My partner and I were playing in the tournament and defeated Stanford's No. 2 doubles team in straight sets," Leach said. "After the match, Dick Gould, the Stanford coach, told me that I should take over for Coach Toley. I was thinking to myself, it might be sooner than you think.

"George invited me to Marks Stadium the following Monday to watch the USC-Miami match. Afterwards, we went out to dinner with Athletic Director Richard Perry and they offered me the job. Right after dessert they mentioned my salary and I just couldn't refuse. I met with George for the next two days so that he could explain the details of the coaching job.

"That weekend, George caught a flight to Italy to be with Raul and I traveled to Tucson with the USC team to coach my first dual match against the University of Arizona. Fortunately for me, the team was made up of a great group of guys - Robert Van't Hof, Billy Nealon, Roger Knapp, Sean Brawley, Jack Kruger, Doug Adler, Fernando Von Ortzen, Jim Agate and Marco Novelo. Every day they came to my office in Heritage Hall to help me figure out which players to recruit for the next year and who to avoid due to the lack of fit with the SC culture."

Dick Leach started playing tennis when he was ten years old at Arcadia County Park in Arcadia, California. Wynn Rogers, Leach's physical education teacher, and a member of the U.S. International Badminton team—and a very good tennis player—enrolled him in his first tennis class. Every weekend, all the local high school players from cities like Whittier, San Gabriel, Pasadena, Monrovia, Glendora, and Temple City played at Arcadia Park. Darlene Hard and Billie Jean King also played at the park regularly, as did Pasadenan Stan Smith. The park was a breeding ground for great players as evidenced by Hard, King and Smith all achieving No. 1 rankings worldwide and, collectively, amassing 64 major singles, doubles and mixed doubles titles.

Fascinated with the game, Leach would ride his bike to the park and spend every weekend playing tennis. He was fanatical, playing a minimum of ten sets a day. By his mid-teens, he was ranked No. 3 in the National USTA 15-and-under singles. Leach was also very good at basketball and made first-team All-Pacific League when he was 17. From 1954 to 1957, Leach coached tennis at Arcadia (Calif.) High, amassing a 93-19 record. In 1958, he enrolled at USC and received a partial scholarship for tennis and also got a job on campus during the summers. Leach lived with his grandmother at 1020 West 36th Street. Later, George Lucas, the future famous *Star Wars* movie producer, and Leach's cousin, John Plummer, lived in the same home after the pair transferred to USC from Modesto Junior College. The home was torn down years ago and it is now the site of USC's Life Sciences Building, which coincidentally is located just across the street from David Marks Tennis Stadium. Leach played tennis under George Toley at USC from 1959 to 1961, was captain of the team his senior year and achieved All-American third team honors in 1961.

From 1966-1968, Leach coached the USTA Junior Davis Cup team for boys 21-and-under and also played on the U.S. men's circuit, achieving a high ranking of No. 16 in singles, and No. 5 in doubles. In 1967, he scored an impressive win at the Newport, Rhode Island tournament over Britain's No. 1 ranked player Mark Cox. Later, he teamed with Robert Potthast from the University of Iowa for a dramatic win over Stan Smith and Bob Lutz at the Southern California Men's Sectionals at the LATC in 1964. Leach won an astonishing 15 United States Tennis Association National Father and Son doubles titles—ten with his eldest son Rick and five with son Jon. From 1969 to

1976, he was the head pro at the San Marino Tennis Club and has been the general partner and owner of four tennis clubs: Big Bear Tennis Ranch, Westlake Tennis and Swim Club, Ojai Valley Racquet Club and the Racquet Club of Irvine.

"Right from the start, my goal, which later became somewhat of an obsession, was to win an NCAA team championship for USC, so I wanted to improve the way that everyone played," said Leach. "The first thing I did was to conduct an interview with each of the players on scholarship. I would ask them to discuss their weaknesses and the conditions under which their strokes broke down. I would then prescribe a course of action with a timetable to overcome these shortcomings. Most of the players were coachable, but over the years, there were a few who resisted my coaching."

One of Coach Leach's true strengths was his knowledge of doubles.

"The next significant thing I did was to work on the doubles lineup," he said. "As I watched the teams play in La Jolla, I knew they could do better if I changed all three partnerships. After everyone switched, we had a good first season going 27-7, and even defeated UCLA in both dual matches. We tied with Stanford for first place in the Pac-10."

Leach had very specific rules for his players, especially his doubles teams, and laid them out for each partnership:
For the team returning serve:
- If the service return is hit well and at the server's feet, the person at the net should poach every time. Breaking serve is critical to winning a match and this is one way to steal a point.
- If you are the receiver's partner, go straight towards the net and then try and cut off the half volley. Most players just cut across the service line and this leaves

the alley wide open allowing the server to get a cheap point by pushing the ball up the line. Remember, it's hard to make a put away volley from your own service line. Also by going straightforward you will get a ball that is above the net rather than a low volley that you can't put away.

- Play the angles, but remember if you hit an angle you set up a bigger angle coming back at you and you could also be putting your partner in a vulnerable or difficult position.
- For a right-handed player in the deuce court, if the serve is up the middle and jams your backhand, hit your return hard up the alley rather than try to hit an inside out backhand. A chip lob is also very effective when you get jammed on your backhand.
- There is nothing wrong with setting up a point. Hit a heavy cross-court shot at the feet of the opponent and charge the net anticipating a high volley.
- When in doubt, hit the second and third shots up the middle of the court forcing the other team to choose who takes the volley.
- A cross-court lob in doubles can be very effective because of the alleys and increased size of the playing area.
- Use a safe slice return at the server's feet and then rush the net to put away a half volley from the opponent.
- Communication is critical with your teammate. Use signals or verbal communication between points.
- Err on the side of a high percentage of first serves. At the highest levels of tennis your opponent loves to have a second serve to crush.
- As a doubles team, move laterally together. If one person is forced out wide the teammate must cover the middle.

For the team serving:

- The player at the net has to keep moving. That person has to distract the player who is returning serve and have him think about what the net person is doing.
- If you are the net player, give the alley away and play more to the middle of the service box. In other words if you take one step and use the length of the racket you can still get to any ball that is hit up the alley. This also makes it difficult for the receiver to hit cross-court without his shot being cut off.
- The role of the net person is critical. If the team serving loses serve it is most likely the fault of the net player because he is not aggressive enough.
- Volleying is highly underrated. It is not that difficult to be a good volleyer but most players neglect the importance of the volley and do not practice it enough.
- Err on the side of serving up the middle. The wide serve creates too many angles for the player who is returning serve.

With these rules, and some very talented players, Leach was ready to achieve his goal of a championship for USC.

"The 1980 team was very talented," said Adler. "I think it helped that we had we had four left-handers in the starting lineup which gave us a lot of versatility, especially in doubles."

UCLA's Billy Martin, one of the most respected coaches in the game, noted, "Dick Leach was a real doubles specialist. He was able to match his team members up very well. He was better than me at that."

Frustratingly, at the 1980 NCAA Championships at the University of Georgia, USC lost to Cal-Berkeley 5-2 in the semifinals, with only Robert Van't Hof (at No. 1) and Sean

Brawley (at No. 4) winning their matches. The Trojans placed third, overcoming Pepperdine 5-4 in a third-place playoff, with Van't Hof and Adler clinching the match by beating Eddie Edwards and Garth Haynes in three sets.

Stanford beat Cal-Berkeley for the national title 5-3, claiming their third title in four years. The loss was difficult for the Bears since they had beaten Stanford in two out of three meetings during the regular season and were up 3-1 during the final match. The clincher for the Cardinal occurred when Peter Rennert and Lloyd Bourne beat Cal's Chris Dunk and Marty Davis 6-2, 1-6, 6-1. It was a tough day for the duo as they had beaten Rennert and Bourne in three previous dual meets.

In the singles championship, Van't Hof, the No. 5 seed, battled top-seeded Peter Rennert of Stanford in front of a crowd of 3,000. Van't Hof and Rennert were close friends, but on the court that mattered little. Van't Hof, sporting a huge mop of curly blond hair, upset Rennert in straight sets 6-3, 7-5.

"I was playing very loose in the match," said Van't Hof after the match. "Everyone had been gunning for me all week and I finally got to gun for somebody else. I was a little tired, but the adrenalin kept me going." He received his winner's trophy from former Secretary of State Dean Rusk, a native Georgian on the faculty at the University of Georgia. Van't Hof turned pro and later achieved career-high singles and doubles rankings of No. 20 and No. 25, respectively. His doubles partner Adler, with whom he got to the semifinals of the doubles tournament, graduated and stayed on as Dick Leach's assistant coach for 1981. In the 1980 doubles final, the University of Tennessee Volunteers won their first national title when Mel Purcell and Rodney Harmon beat Trinity's Tony Giammalva and Jon Benson 7-6, 7-6.

Robert Van't Hof won the NCAA singles title in 1980

In 1981, Billy Nealon assumed the top singles position for the Trojans. New to the team were Hugo Scott, Brad Cherry and Sean Rodriguez. In the semifinals of the NCAAs, USC lost to UCLA 5-4. Hugo Scott and Jack Kruger won their matches at No.'s 4 and 5, and Scott-Brawley and Kruger-Agate won at second and third doubles. The Trojans played the University of Georgia for third place, but lost 6-3, with their only wins coming from Sean Brawley and Jack Kruger and Nealon and Knapp in doubles. Historically, while the intense competition with UCLA, Stanford—and Trinity to some extent— continually occupied the minds of Trojan coaches, players and fans, this match between the Trojans and the Bulldogs would be the start of a cross-country rivalry that would come to a head in 1987.

In the NCAA team final, Stanford edged out No. 1 seed UCLA 5-4. Stanford won five of the six singles matches, with the only Bruin victory coming from Robbie Venter (father of future USC player Kristen Venter) who beat Scott Davis in straight sets. The NCAA singles final was an all-Stanford affair with Tim Mayotte (who would later win 12 singles titles as a pro) defeating teammate Jimmy Gurfein 6-7, 6-3, 6-3. David Pate and Karl Richter of Texas Christian bested Pat Serret and Peter Doohan of Arkansas in three sets to win the doubles title. The Trojans finished the season with a 28-10 record and came in third in the Pac-10 and fourth nationally.

Dick Leach recruited four top freshman in 1982, including Wimbledon junior champion and world No. 2 junior Matt Anger, Roy Emerson's son Antony Emerson, No. 4 U.S. junior Todd Witsken and No. 2 Canadian junior Ric Bengtson, a superior athlete who had spent his junior and senior years at Corona Del Mar High School with Emerson. No. 1 player Billy Nealon would miss most of his final season due to injuries. Danny Moore, a former top high school player from Illinois and experienced coach, joined the team as Leach's new assistant coach.

Witsken played at Carmel High School in Indiana. Not only was he one of the top juniors in the country but was also a member of the Junior Davis Cup team. Dick Leach said he was "the most natural athlete of anyone on the team."

"With the proper dedication and hard work, he'll become a top pro in the future," Leach said.

Born in Brisbane but growing up in Newport Beach, Emerson was the No. 8-ranked junior in the United States. He won three CIF titles at Corona Del Mar High School as well as the Ojai Interscholastic 18-and-under singles event. To boot, he had the genes of his father, who won a then men's record 12 major singles titles.

Matt Anger was a very highly-decorated junior champion winning the 1981 Wimbledon junior title and the U.S. National 16-and-under singles title. He was also a member of the Junior Davis Cup team and was All-American at Amador Valley High in Pleasanton, California.

"There were many factors that led to my choice of USC," said Anger. "I really liked my recruiting class of Ric Bengtson, Todd Witsken and Antony Emerson, and the other great guys on the team, but my main reason for going to USC was that Coach Leach had a specific plan for my tennis development. My goal after college was to play on the ATP Tour and he very directly spelled out my strengths and weaknesses."

Anger said his first road match against Trinity as a freshman in 1982 was one of his strongest USC tennis memories.

"I had heard about their rabid fans from Ken Walts, who coached me in the juniors," said Anger of the Trinity fans. "Ken's son, Butch Walts, had played at USC before me and told me stories about having things thrown at them while at Trinity. Sure enough, they had fans hanging all over the courts, but

Matt Anger was a standout singles player and three-time All-American for the Trojans

despite that I saved three match points in singles to keep us alive. Later, Todd Witsken and I won the deciding doubles in three sets to clinch the match 5-4.

"Our team had a lot of talented players," continued Anger. "I spent most of my time trying to learn to develop as solid a game as I could, but there were other guys—like Witsken—who had shots that I didn't have. He was able to hit an 'over and back drop shot' which is when the ball goes over the net but has so much backspin that, after it lands, it reverses direction and comes back over the net. He could also hit drop shot service returns and angles and shots from all different places on the court."

Under Leach's coaching, the team had a very good year, finishing the season with a 30-5 record, placing second in the Pac-10, and fifth nationally. In the NCAA Championships, UCLA beat Pepperdine 5-1 in the final in Pepperdine's first appearance in the team final, led by coach Allen Fox. Glenn Michibata, playing No. 1 singles, notched the only victory for the Waves beating UCLA's Marcel Freeman in straight sets. In the singles final, unseeded Mike Leach of the University of Michigan upset No. 12 seed Brad Gilbert 7-5, 6-3. Gilbert left Pepperdine in 1982 to join the pro tour and went on to win 20 career titles and ranked as high as No. 4 in the world.

Several new players joined the team in 1983, including Tim Pawsat, who had dreamed of playing for Leach since he was a ten-year-old at Leach's Big Bear Tennis Ranch. Pawsat was a champion from Foothill High School in Tustin, California, and a member of the 1982 Junior Davis Cup team who had played doubles with Leach's older son Ricky. Others included Jorge Lozano, who played on the Mexican Davis Cup team from 1980-1982, and Rafael Belmar Osuna, nephew of USC legend Rafael Osuna and a top player at Miraleste High in Rancho Palos Verdes. Belmar Osuna, a passionate proponent of the history of Mexican tennis, had dreamed of following in his uncle's footsteps and playing at USC. The Miraleste team that Osuna played for was considered one of the best high school prep teams in the country, and in addition to Osuna, consisted of Lozano, John Letts—who went on to Stanford—and Eric Amend.

1982 Men's Tennis Team. Front Row: Jim Agate, Bill Nealon, Sean Brawley, Brad Cherry, Todd Witsken. Back Row: Coach Dick Leach, Matt Anger, Ric Bengtson, Roger Knapp, Antony Emerson, Gary Lemon, Assistant Coach Danny Moore

The 1983 season saw the team win 29 matches and lose five, finishing second in the Pac-10. At the NCAA Championships, USC faced Stanford in the semifinals. Stanford won four of the six singles matches and USC won the first two doubles matches to tie the score at 4-4. One of the highlights of the singles matches occurred when Ric Bengtson, playing perhaps the best match of his college career, beat Jim Grabb 6-3, 4-6, 6-4. Bengtson known for his big serve and ferocious one-handed background, snapped Grabb's 22-match winning streak. In the deciding match, Trojans Anger and Emerson played Stanford's Grabb and Mark McKeen. In true nail-biting fashion, Stanford won the contest, surviving three tiebreakers 6-7, 7-6, 7-6. Stanford went on to win the national title defeating No. 1 seed Southern Methodist University 5-4. In the singles final, Greg Holmes, the top seed from the University of Utah, beat Minnesota's Fredrik Pahlett in straight sets. In the doubles,

Georgia's Allen Miller and Ola Malmqvist upset the top seeds Roberto Saad and Paul Smith of Wichita State en route to the final where they beat Ken Flach and Robert Seguso from Southern Illinois-Edwardsville 7-5, 6-3. Both Flach and Seguso were promising young tennis players who had dropped out of high school and met when they enrolled at Southern Illinois—Edwardsville (SIU), a Division II University. Each decided to go to Edwardsville where they could start playing tennis right away with a high school equivalency diploma rather than attending a Division I school were they would have had to sit out a year in residence. While SIU-Edwardsville was a DII university at the time, (it is now DI), the NCAA allocated spots for the winners of the DII singles and doubles championships (Flach and Seguso that year) to play in the DI tournament. Flach and Seguso, who would later become one of the leading doubles teams in the world, were victorious over Trojans Lozano and Pawset in the quarterfinals and Arkansas Razorbacks Doohan and Serrat in the semifinals.

USC took third place in the team tournament, beating Pepperdine 5-4, with wins coming from Matt Anger (No. 1), Lozano (No. 4), Lemon (No. 5) and Bengtson (No. 6) in singles, and Bengtson and Lemon at third doubles. Lemon, who played a great tournament, joined the Trojan team after sitting out a year as a transfer from Tennessee.

In 1984, four All-Americans, Matt Anger, Todd Witsken, Tim Pawsat and Jorge Lozano led the team. Antony Emerson, Ric Bengtson, Brad Cherry and Rafael Belmar Osuna, together with Rick Leach of Laguna Beach, joined them. Leach was the No. 2 U.S. junior and Coach Dick Leach's eldest son. While the team was young, they earned a first-place finish in the Pac-10 with a 32-4 record.

"I had total confidence in our team that year," said Anger. "Personally I think we were the best team in the country. We lost only one match to UCLA in February, 1984—one that I think is still controversial."

Rick Leach said of the match, "I remember Todd Witsken was playing against Michael Kures of UCLA at the Intercollegiate Tennis Coaches Association Team Championship. Witsken was up 6-7, 6-0, 5-4 (40-0 and serving). In those days, we used no ad scoring at deuce, so Todd had quadruple match point. Todd hit a serve out wide and thought he had aced Kures to win the match, but Kures called the ball out."

Anger continued, "Todd turned to me as I was right on the service line. In retrospect, I should have told him not to worry about it (he had four match points!), but instead indicated that I thought the ball hit the line. Todd asked Michael where he thought the ball landed and Kures pointed to a spot in the alley."

A heated argument ensued. Witsken, known as sometimes having a short fuse, threw down his racket, went around the net and pushed Kures. After the scuffle was broken up, the officials conferred and then defaulted Witsken. A rule was subsequently created that prohibits a player from going around the net to engage an opponent. If caught doing so, the player is immediately defaulted.

"After the singles, we played two of the doubles matches and the score was tied 4-4," Anger continued. "Lozano and Witsken won the first set, had two match points in the second, but then lost the set. It was getting dark and they called the match until the following morning. UCLA then came out fast and were up 3-0 in a matter of minutes. They kept the momentum going and we lost the third set 6-0, and the match 5-4. We played Clemson for third place and took our frustration out on them winning 6-0."

Two months later, in April of 1984, the Trojans once again faced the Bruins. Coach Leach changed the lineup, with Witsken moving up to No. 1 singles to avoid another confrontation with Kures. Witsken, Anger, Leach and Lozano all won their singles matches to go up 4-0. The lead seemed insurmountable, but UCLA's Jim Pugh and Craig Venter came back to win their singles matches, narrowing the lead to 4-2. Leach and Pawsat and Witsken and Lozano lost both of their doubles matches, tying the score at 4-4. In a long, see-saw battle, Anger and Emerson hung on to beat Pugh and David Livingston in three sets 7-6, 6-7, 6-4, avenging their loss from two months earlier. The crowd had been treated to college tennis at its grittiest. Even George Toley, who had come by to watch the match, commented that in his 27 years of coaching he had never seen anything like it. And UCLA's Glenn Bassett told the *Los Angeles Times*, "I don't remember any UCLA-USC match—or any match, for that matter—that went like this!"

At the 100th anniversary NCAA Championships in 1984, unseeded Georgia upset No. 2 seed USC 5-4 in the quarterfinals, handing the Trojans a fifth-place national finish. "In '84 we had a great team, but in that match we found ourselves down 4-2," said Tim Pawset. "The crowd was definitely a factor. There must have been 5,000 people there. We started to play the doubles and Lozano and Witsken and Emerson and Anger both won very quickly. It started to get dark and my doubles match with Rick against Allen Miller and Mikael Pernfors was moved indoors. We lost 7-6, 4-6, 6-2. There were no bad calls or anything like that, but the crowd really made a difference. Three days later, when we played the individual doubles tournament, we got our revenge

Tim Pawsat, NCAA Doubles Champion, 1986 (with Rick Leach)

against Pernfors and Miller 6-2, 6-2, but then lost in the finals to Jerome Jones and Kelly Jones of Pepperdine. I have to say that, despite the home court advantage, the University of Georgia always put on a great event. Everything was done in a first-class manner."

Led by Coach Dan Magill, a legend at the University of Georgia, the Bulldogs fell to Stanford 5-3. UCLA dominated Pepperdine, also 5-3, in the semifinals. UCLA went on claim the title by beating Stanford 5-4, with UCLA's Michael Kures and Mark Basham winning the decisive doubles match. Clemson freshman Lawson Duncan, a largely self-taught player from Cullowhee, North Carolina, had a very successful freshman year earning him the No. 3 seed in the singles tournament. Duncan beat many top players, including USC's Matt Anger and top seed Paul Annacone of Tennessee, to face Pernfors in

177

the final. Duncan had beaten Pernfors earlier in the season 6-2, 6-1, but the 5'8" 150-pound Pernfors was unstoppable, and in front of 5,000 barking fans, overcame Duncan 6-4, 6-1.

Pernfors had come to the U.S. from Sweden to obtain some needed experience before joining the pro tour, and he also wanted to pursue a degree in economics. A friend at Old Dominion suggested he apply there, but their coach didn't want to use up a scholarship on a foreign player. He did, however, help Pernfors get in to Seminole Junior College in Florida in 1982 when he was 18. At Seminole, he won the national junior college singles and doubles championship and—now on scholarship—promptly switched to Georgia, where Coach Magill was building a powerful team. In an interview with a local paper, Pernfors said, "I don't think Coach figured I'd be a No. 1 player for him—maybe a No. 3 or 4."

"For me Pernfors and Stevie Johnson are two of the best players to emerge from the college ranks," said Rick Leach. "Mikael had amazing skills. I remember seeing him hit a ball around the net post from a crazy position on the court for a winner. It was probably the best shot I have ever seen. The crowd went nuts." Anger remembered the quarterfinal team match that he played against Pernfors in the 1984 NCAA tournament in which he lost 2-6, 6-1, 6-1. "Pernfors was simply darn good, but I wasn't quite good enough yet to attack him consistently. I really didn't have that ability for another year. He was able to pass me well when I did attack and he had an incredible topspin lob. He was just too good for me on that day. We played no-ad scoring and I got to deuce countless times, but I couldn't get over the hump after the first set. One match is usually no big deal and you can brush it off, but this match was different and it hurts to this day. Mikael is a good guy and when we were on tour, he would give me a hard time about that match whenever he could."

Pernfors went on to win back-to-back NCAA singles titles in 1984 and 1985, following in the footsteps of Tulane's Ham Richardson in 1953 and 1954, and SC's Dennis Ralston in 1963 and 1964. During his tenure as a Bulldog, Pernfors won 42 consecutive college matches, a record that stood for over 20 years until Stevie Johnson shattered it in 2012 with an astonishing 72 consecutive wins. Pernfors put Georgia tennis on the map. In the years that followed, Georgia would win the NCAA team title six times and finish as runner-up seven times.

Perhaps unsurprisingly, Coach Leach's son Rick got an early start in tennis. His father said he began playing when he was five years old and took to the game immediately.

"We would go to Lacy Park in San Marino and hit with the ball machine at 6:30 a.m.," said Coach Leach. "I believe kids have to find their passion and that parents shouldn't push them too hard. My way of finding out how much he liked the game was to purposefully quit playing with him each day before he was ready to stop. So after hitting with him for a while, I would tell him that we had to leave. He didn't want to go and sometimes kicked up a fuss. I had a long drive from USC to Laguna Beach, and most days I would come home exhausted, but Rick was yearning to hit. I started telling him that he had to finish his chores before we could go and figured that if he really loved the game, he would get the chores done. On one occasion when I came home, he was waiting at the curb with a bucket of balls. I told him he had to cut the grass first and he smiled and said that he had already done it. I knew then that he had found his passion. I would recommend this approach to any parent trying to encourage their kids to play sports."

When Rick was six-and-a-half years old, he played a tournament at Redlands and won four matches. He was so small that he couldn't see over the tournament desk. At the end of that tournament he told his dad that his left, tennis-playing arm really hurt. Dick had the arm checked out and discovered that Rick had osteoporosis. The doctors put a cast on him and told him not to touch a racket. Said Dick, "Rick begged me to teach him to play right-handed. I agreed because he was so motivated. Amazingly, he got so good that he actually won a tournament playing right-handed, but he played so much that he ruined his right arm, too. Several people told me that I should have been arrested for child abuse. Once his left arm healed, I only allowed him to hit once a week and then gradually increased this to twice a week. To keep his body balanced he started to lift very light weights with both arms."

Rick, known as one of the game's truly great doubles players, started to develop his doubles skills at a young age. When he was 12, he started playing with his father and former Trojans Sashi Menon and Dick Bohrnstedt.

"By the time Rick was in junior high he was in my advanced junior workout clinics," said Bohrnstedt. "Rick was not only a good player at a young age, but also a great example to the other kids. He was physically strong with quick hands and he had his father's brain for making the right play."

The doubles experience paid off as father and son won ten national father-son doubles tournaments. With his junior doubles partner Pawsat, Rick was half of the top-ranked U.S. junior doubles team in 1982 and the two won the Grand Slam of American junior doubles: Indoors, Hard Courts, Clay Courts and Nationals. En route, the pair never lost a set, a feat that has not been accomplished since. Leach also played on six U.S. Junior Davis Cup teams, ultimately becoming one of the top doubles players in the world. "I was always better at doubles than singles," said Rick. "I had good hands and was quick at the net."

Said Pawset, "My coach, Chuck Pate from Tustin, and Dick Leach used to play against Rick and me when we were young. They would always beat us, but never gave us any real doubles tips. What they wanted us to do was to figure out how to be better. By the time we were 14, Rick and I were way ahead of our peers in doubles."

For Coach Leach, the challenge to building his team often came down to too many good choices. He explains, "One of the toughest things about coaching tennis is that you only have four-and-a-half scholarships," said Leach. "You have to be very creative in figuring out how to divvy these up. In some instances, you give some players a full ride—but that takes one full scholarship away. You offer some other players a half scholarship. It is not a pleasant task. You can imagine how happy I was when I knew Rick was committing to USC. Because of my position as a USC employee, I got

Rick Leach won the 1986 NCAA doubles title with Tim Pawat and the 1987 title with Scott Melville

tuition remission when Rick joined the team, allowing me to allocate my scholarships to other players.

"I remember when we went up to the national hard courts at Stanford, just before Rick enrolled at USC. We stayed with our good friend Dick Gould. Dick was the best recruiter in the country. When we came down to breakfast that first morning, Dick had Rick's favorite cereal and juice waiting for him. He was actually trying to recruit him! Rick won the tournament. Later, Dick said to me with a straight face, 'I want your son; he's too good a kid and it would be better if he came to Stanford. And, if you don't let me have him, I am going to report you to the NCAA.' 'Why,' I asked? Dick replied, 'First of all you gave him a car and that is illegal (I had given Rick a vintage 1969 Porsche for his birthday). Second, according to NCAA rules, a player can only make three visits to campus and your son has had hundreds (he came to work with me or visited the campus many times all the time). Third, and this is the worst violation, you're not allowed to sleep with a recruit's mother.... I've got to turn you in!' That was Dick Gould for you!"

Rick Leach made history when he became the NCAA's first four-time Division I All-American singles and doubles player while at USC. He finished his collegiate career ranked No. 1 in doubles and No. 4 in singles, after claiming his second-straight NCAA doubles championship in 1987. The first title was with Tim Pawsat and the second with Scott Melville who had transferred to USC from Rice.

In 1985, Coach Dick Leach was looking forward to a banner year. Amazingly, he had five returning All-Americans, (Leach, Lozano, Emerson, Pawsat and Witsken), five of the top six singles players and two out of three doubles teams from the previous year's Pac-10 championship team. Incredibly, Leach, Lozano, Pawsat and Witsken had earned All-American honors in both singles and doubles. In 1984, the Intercollegiate Tennis Association changed its criteria for selecting men's and women's DI players its for All-America designation. In singles, a player has to 1) be a top 16 seed in singles at the NCAA Championships; or 2) reach the round of 16 in singles at the NCAA Championships; or 3) finish in the Top 20 of the final ITA Rankings. In doubles, a team must 1) be a top eight seed at the NCAA Championships; or 2) reach the doubles quarterfinals of the NCAA Championships; or 3) finish in the Top 10 in doubles of the final ITA Rankings. It is the dream of many college tennis players to achieve this designation, a testament to how incredible it was that USC had five All-Americans on the same team.

The biggest loss to the team occurred when Anger turned pro, however Eric Amend, another top player from Miraleste High in Rancho Palos Verdes stepped in. Amend was the No. 2 ranked junior in the U.S. and a member of the four-man 1984 U.S. Olympic tennis team, comprised of players age 20 and under. Amend first met Rick Leach when he was 10 years old at a national tournament in North Carolina before he moved to California. When his family moved to Rolling Hills Estates he played at the Jack Kramer Club where he became friends with many future USC players such as sisters Anna Maria, Anna Lucia and Cecilia Fernandez and Trey Lewis.

"I saw Rick Leach at every SoCal junior tournament and I played him many times," said Amend. "In fact, I played one of my best matches in front of his father and the SC team, against him in the finals of the boy's 16-and-under at Ojai—where I won in three sets. Rick and I also played some national junior doubles tournaments together and we won a national championship at the 1983 USTA National Junior Clay Court

Eric Amend won the NCAA doubles title in 1989 with Byron Black

Championships in Louisville, Kentucky. Dick also coached the SoCal Junior Sectional Team, which consisted of future Trojans Rick, Tim Pawsat, and me."

Amend and his father traveled to Marks Stadium in 1978 to watch Robert Van't Hof play John McEnroe, Amend calling the excitement "incredible." His choice to attend USC was driven by a bigger goal, "My dreams were to be a Trojan *and* an Olympian and I was thrilled to have achieved both of these goals in my life," he said.

In 1984, Amend beat his good friend and Miraleste High School teammate John Letts for the last spot on the U.S. Olympic Team, joining professional player Jimmy Arias, Pepperdine's Kelly Jones and Stanford's Derrick Rostagno.

The Trojans had a good year with 34-4 record and were seeded No. 2 behind UCLA. USC advanced to the NCAA semifinals where they were upset by No. 6 seed Georgia 5-3. Leach and Lozano won at second and third singles and Leach and Amend won easily at second doubles; but Georgia was too strong. In the final, Georgia beat UCLA 5-1, winning five of the six singles matches to clinch the victory. This was the first time that Georgia had ever won the NCAA team title, and the first time since Trinity in 1972 that a non-California university had won the title. In the individual singles, Mikael Pernfors overcame teammate George Beznecy 6-2, 6-3 in the singles final and Pepperdine's Kelly Jones and Carlos Di Laura defeated Charles Beckman and Royce Deppe of Texas 7-5, 7-6 in the doubles final.

In 1986, the Trojans lost four of their top seven players: No. 1 singles player and three-time All-American Todd Witsken, All-American Antony Emerson, Ric Bengtson and Jeff Ewing. While Eric Amend took time off to improve his grades, Rick Leach, Tim Pawsat, Jorge Lozano, Rafael Belmar Osuna and red-shirted freshman John Carras returned to the team. Other players included freshman Rick Kepler, junior John Simerson and transfers Jonas Wallgard, a junior from Pierce College in Woodland Hills, and John Washer. Wallgard came from Hollviksnas, Sweden, the same town as Mikael Pernfors, and had notched a winning record against him as a junior. The Trojan's top freshman recruit was Luke Jensen, a completely ambidextrous player from Michigan.

Jensen grew up on a Christmas tree farm in the small town of Ludington, in northwest Michigan. Both of his parents were athletes, his mother being a 6'2" basketball center who averaged 50 points in high school games even before there were Title IX opportunities for women in college sports, while his father played pro football briefly for the New York Giants, after playing at Minnesota and Memphis State in college. "Football was my main game and I being was groomed to be a quarterback," said Jensen. "Dr. Richard Slager, who owned a summer cottage in Ludington, had been a quarterback at Ohio State and also played on the varsity tennis team. He told my Dad that tennis would be a great sport to help develop my footwork for football."

Dr. Slager's son Rick was also a versatile athlete and the 1971 and 1972 Ohio state high school champion playing for Upper Arlington High School. Rick went on to become the quarterback at Notre Dame and his career overlapped there with Joe Montana.

Luke Jensen

"I grew up throwing footballs and baseballs with my left hand," Jensen said. "But I started playing tennis with my right hand. So Dad thought that since I had a natural lefty throwing motion, I could serve left-handed as well. Thus, I have the unique ability to serve left and right-handed. I was a thrower, trying to ace my opponents on every serve. For me, Coach Leach was a visionary. He changed me from a thrower into a pitcher and helped me explore the many options in my game. I was battling Stanford's Patrick McEnroe in a pivotal point and Coach told me to put so much lefty spin on the ball that it would go into Patrick's right pocket and stay there. If you're trying to get your mind around what that threat looks like, well that's exactly what Coach did—he helped me think through these types of situations. Coach Leach was a father figure who taught me fundamental core values and the kind of work ethic it would take to maximize my ability and the responsibility of being a Trojan. These lessons have lasted my entire life."

One of the strengths of Jensen's game was his serve, clocked at over 130 mph with both right and left arms. Jensen said that lefties have a big advantage in tennis for two reasons. "First, there aren't that many lefties out there and the ad scoring system puts most of the big points in the ad court," he said. "Lefties have the advantage of swinging their serve out wide on the ad side to pull their opponents off the court at critical moments in a match."

Even though Jensen threw the ball with his left hand, he had learned tennis right-handed, hitting a two-handed backhand because the rackets were so heavy at the time. When he was 14, his father thought it would be best to develop a left-handed serve that would work to his advantage. "I didn't have a developed game at that point," Jensen said. "So I just added these shots as part of my training process. Most tennis coaches

I came across thought this was a bad idea and discouraged me, saying that it was a waste of time and took time away from developing my right-handed serve. I wanted to prove them all wrong and Don Dickinson, my first tennis coach, who had a background in basketball where ball handling and shooting with both hands was the norm, encouraged me. Coach Dickinson had me hit 200 right-handed and 200 left-handed serves every day. He told me that my left-handed serve couldn't be just a part-time shot. He also made me use my left-handed serve every time I had to hit a second serve to develop a pressure-proof stroke. It took about three months for me to become ambidextrous on both the serve and overhead. Another real benefit was that I never had to serve into the sun and I had twice as many service options as my opponents. I used all my options and served with one hand on the first serve and another on the second serve. I'm still surprised that more players don't develop these skills. You can do it if you try."

Said Dick Leach, "Luke Jensen was the No. 1 junior tennis player in the world in singles. In '84, he and his partner Patrick McEnroe won the junior French Open and USTA Boys' 18 National and Clay Court doubles giving Jensen a No. 1 ranking in doubles by the time I recruited him. He was a great team player and an extremely loyal Trojan. Luke was ambidextrous but only on his serve. He did use both hands in every match. His first serve was very good from both sides, but I thought his second serve was better right-handed. He hit groundstrokes and volleys right-handed most of the time."

The Trojans had a 25-7 season, earning second place in the Pac-10. The team lost to UCLA 5-4 both at home and in Westwood. In April, Jorge Lozano decided to leave the team for the professional tour. Pepperdine beat the Trojans in the quarterfinals of the NCAA team tournament 5-2, with Pawsat and Wallgard winning at No. 2 and No. 5. Stanford dominated Pepperdine 5-2 in the final, with Patrick McEnroe and John Letts beating Gilberto Cicero and Robbie Weiss 6-2, 6-3 to clinch the match and the national championship. USC was ranked sixth at the end of the season.

Certainly the high point of the season for USC occurred when Rick Leach and Tim Pawset won the NCAA doubles title coming from behind to defeat Michael Kures and Dan Narhirny of UCLA 6-7, 6-4, 6-2 in the final, earning a No. 1 doubles ranking, and USC's 18th NCAA doubles title. Rick Leach also finished the season ranked No. 1 in singles, despite Dan Goldie of Stanford beating SMU's Richey Reneberg in the NCAA singles final, becoming the first player to accomplish double No. 1 rankings since John McEnroe in 1978.

The Trojans entered the 1987 season ranked as the No. 1 college team in the nation. Senior Rick Leach and sophomore Luke Jensen were the No. 1 and No. 3 ranked pre-season players in the country. At the start of the season, Coach Leach said that Rick and Luke were the strongest one-two combination at USC since Stan Smith and Bob Lutz in the 1960s. The team was supported by freshman Greg Michaels and Paul Brandt, sophomores Eric Amend, John Carras and Rick Kepler and juniors Jonas Wallgard, Scott Brownsberger, Andy Olyphant, Chris Dundas and Scott Melville. Seniors John Washer and John Simerson rounded out the team. Former two-time All-American at USC and pro player Roger Knapp began his first season as assistant coach to Dick Leach.

The squad had an incredible 32-0 record, one of the longest pre-tournament streaks in DI college tennis history, and finished first in the Pac-10. Only two other teams had achieved an undefeated record until then, Trinity's 1972 team led by Dick Stockton at 27-0 and John McEnroe's 1978 Stanford team at 24-

0. Heading into the NCAA tournament, the Trojans felt very confident in their quest to win the national title.

Also gunning for a title was the University of Georgia, ready to capitalize on their long tennis history that began in 1898. Coach Dan Magill, who played for the Bulldogs from 1940-1941, had been head coach since 1955. Magill had coached a number of successful teams at Georgia, but none had ever been contenders in the NCAA tournament. In 1977, when the national tournament changed to a full team tournament format, a location for the 16-team draw tournament had to be found. The University of Georgia, under Magill's urging, had stepped up and created a truly top-notch facility. The new facilities gave Georgia's program a huge boost, not to mention bragging rights about having the best tennis complex in the nation. In an interview on May 20, just before the 1977 tournament began, Magill told the *Orlando Sentinel*, "My school is honored to host this year's tournament. We anticipate record crowds and recently finished building a $100,000 grandstand to accommodate them. We expect to hit a record gate of $50,000. This year's championship will have a new format, and the Men's Intercollegiates will truly determine the national team and individual champions. Did you know that 12 of the top 20 money winners in recent ATP listings are former participants? The list includes Connors, Ashe, Stockton, Smith, Lutz, Eddie Dibbs, Harold Solomon, Raul Ramirez, Roscoe Tanner, Vitas Gerulaitis, Sherwood Stewart and Brian Gottfried." He further opined, "That's why my colleagues and I consider the Men's Intercollegiates as a springboard to fame and fortune. I'm convinced that the greatest tennis tournament in the world isn't Wimbledon or Forest Hills, it's the Men's Intercollegiates at Georgia."

1987 men's tennis team. Front Row: Eric Amend, Rick Kepler. Middle Row: Andy Olyphant, Jonas Wallgard, Luke Jensen, Rick Leach, Paul Brandt, Scott Melville. Back Row: Roger Knapp, Assistant Coach Scott Brownsberger, John Simerson, John Washer, John Carras, Greg Michaels, Head Coach Dick Leach

The Trojans had not had much experience playing Georgia until 1981, when USC lost to the Bulldogs for third place, and again in the quarterfinals in 1984. In 1985, USC fell to the Bulldogs in the semifinals as Georgia went on to win their first NCAA team title. While Georgia created an unparalleled collegiate championship experience hosting the NCAAs, Leach felt it was not the most fair environment. "We all appreciated the huge effort that went into creating the tournament, but at the same time, many of us believed that this gave the Bulldogs a huge advantage given the enormous hometown crowds they could draw," he said.

As fate would have it, the then 34-0 Trojans faced the hometown Georgia Bulldogs in the semifinals of the team tournament in Athens.

"We were playing Georgia in the semifinals with the best team I had ever coached," Leach said. "The Georgia fans were very boisterous and even antagonistic that year. It was a particularly difficult environment in which to play. Earlier, in the season we had beaten Georgia 5-1 in the Blue Gray National Tennis Classic in Montgomery, Alabama—a prestigious tournament with history that began in 1949."

In the semifinal match, Leach, Melville and Amend— playing one, four and six, respectively—won their singles matches, and Leach and Melville won at No. 1 doubles. With the score tied at 4-4, Amend and Jensen at No. 2 doubles lost their match in straight sets 7-5, 6-3 to Trey Carter and T.J. Middleton.

Said Leach, "I was upset at how much influence the crowd had not only on our players but on just about every other team that played them and exchanged some angry words with several of the spectators who taunted us."

The upset loss greatly affected Amend. "The 1987 team was really tight and felt like a family," he said. "We would all sacrifice for each other with title hopes on our minds. Rick Leach took the fall semester off to play pro tennis, but he wanted to come back for his senior year to win the title for his Dad. The guys who were there felt a duty to be prepared to win, since Rick was coming back for the sole purpose of winning that team title. I think his decision to come back added to the pressure and, going into the NCAA Tournament undefeated created extremely high expectations. We didn't play our best when we needed it the most. Losing that match was the biggest disappointment in my entire life. We only get four chances to win a team title as an athlete, so opportunities like the one we had in '87 are precious and extremely difficult to come by. It continued to haunt me for two decades. Even with winning an individual title in 1989, I felt my college career was a failure since team championships are how college careers are measured in my mind. In all of the years afterwards, I never ever dreamed that I'd be able to exorcize that ghost. A second chance at a team title never even crossed my mind until 2009 came along and we won the title when I was the Trojans assistant coach under Peter Smith. It was divine intervention for me."

"There is no other single moment in my life where I felt I let everyone down," said Jensen "I have lost Grand Slam finals and have emotionally healed from them, but not from the 1987 NCAA semifinal match with UGA. I think about this match more than any other that I have ever won or lost, and have lost more sleep because I didn't do my job on a very hot and humid day in May in Athens, Georgia. That year, I had performed very well for USC as did everyone else on the team. We won the national team indoor championship and I won the national individual indoors singles and doubles championships with Rick Leach. Coach Leach had prepared one of the greatest teams in NCAA tennis history for this run and nothing was going to stop us. He knew what the challenges would be in Athens and had brought other elite USC teams in earlier years that had been upset by Georgia under those crazy conditions. Their fans bring incredible energy and passion to watch their beloved Bulldogs. As soon as we pulled into the tennis court parking lot, we saw trucks with gun racks and fishing poles. This was not your country club crowd! This was an SEC football crowd at a tennis match. The fans barked like dogs and during our grueling match and would scream, 'Let the big dog eat!'"

Jensen noted that USC got off to a good start, with Rick Leach at No. 1 winning in straight sets. Melville and Amend survived tough three-set matches at four and six against Carter and Middleton, but Carras and Wallgard were beaten. In Jensen's match at No. 2 against Stephen Enochs, things started out well, but then went south. "Coach Leach stressed all season what we would face in Athens," Jensen said. "Every win during the season was always met with Coach Leach saying, 'I'm pleased but not satisfied.' We knew we were preparing for a great Georgia challenge, as every team in the country was looking to wreck our perfect season. Coach told us to sleep and study, and to stay away from the USC co-eds or bonnies as he called them! He knew about the heat and humidity and once finals were over, he took the entire team to Palm Springs to train before the tournament. Palm Springs was really hot but it didn't have the Athens humidity.

"In my match with Enochs," continued Jensen. "I won the first set 6-3 and was up a break with break points to blow open the match. It was at this point where I made tactical blunders and failed to close out the match with the many opportunities I had to do so."

Coach Leach blamed the heat and humidity for undercutting Jensen's performance. While Jensen was aggressive, coming to the net often, his opponent kept lobbing him and forcing him back. The crowd also had an undeniable impact and Jensen remembered being annoyed by the fraternity guys sitting on top of him. Coach Leach moved to Jensen's court and was calling plays and giving him tactics to change the momentum, but the match got away from him and he lost the next two sets 6-4, 6-2.

The match was tied 3-3 after singles, but USC was going into their real strength, their doubles teams. The 1987 squad had two All-American teams with Rick Leach and Melville at No. 1 and Amend and Jensen playing at No. 2. Carras and Wallgard played the No. 3 doubles line. Amend and Jensen were up against two tough competitors in Middleton and Carter. As the doubles matches were being played out, Leach and Melville won 6-3, 6-1 against John Boytim and Stephen Enochs, but Carras and Wallgard lost to Phillip Johnson and Jim Childs 6-3, 6-3.

The match came down to Amend and Jensen. Said Jensen, "I loved playing with Eric. He is one of the most competitive and passionate people I have ever met. He was a true Trojan—down to his DNA. This opportunity was a once in a lifetime chance to lift our team in hostile territory to an historic final. My role on the doubles team was to set Eric up. I served first in the rotation and I returned from the deuce court. Coach Leach stressed the importance of the player in the deuce court whose job it is to make returns that set up his teammate at the net. Eric Amend is a shot maker whose role was to go for big plays and fly around the court. He and I competed well together and I felt that walking on the court with him was walking into a back alley fistfight. He was an assassin. The atmosphere was always intense when we played doubles.

"That final doubles match was like nothing I have ever been a part of before or since. I remember vividly being in the cool air-conditioned locker room underneath the main stands. The room was shaking from the noise and vibrations coming from the 5,000 fans in the crowd. Middleton and Carter never played better in their lives. They rode a tsunami of support and momentum from the Bulldog faithful. At every move they seemed to play the right shot. When Eric and I would change tactics or formations, they were ready. This was the only time in my career where the team across the net outplayed me. It was a very impressive performance by the Bulldogs.

"Personally it was my job—my responsibility—to win both of those matches for USC. I have always prided myself in being able to win in the biggest moments. Unfortunately, I did not take care of business when I had the singles match under control, and my game did not rise to the level needed to beat Georgia that day. I still remember the crowd, the competition, the historic situation and the outcome. This was a loss that has never left me."

A few days after the match, Dick Leach said he believed he had made a mistake with the doubles lineup. "In retrospect, I think I should have split Rick Leach and Scott Melville up at No. 1 doubles, since they won so easily, and instead moved Carras up to play with Rick," he said. "Then, I should have paired Melville with Wallgard at No. 3 doubles because Georgia had placed their No. 1 player, Philip Johnson at third doubles. Johnson was an excellent player and took over the match. I think that having Scott on that court might have made a difference."

After Georgia's historic 5-4 win in the semifinals, they won their second NCAA team title with a 5-1 win over UCLA in the final.

In the NCAA individual tournament, Leach lost to Furman's Ned Caswell 7-5, 6-7 (4), 7-5 in the third round, having upset Jeff Tarango of Stanford earlier.

"During Rick's singles match with Caswell, there were only about 25 people watching and they were relatively quiet," said Coach Leach. "However after the match was done and we were leaving the complex, one of Georgia's reserve guys started heckling Rick and saying bad things about me." Rick, who is an extremely mild mannered person, reached his breaking point and confronted the Georgia player. A very heated altercation and war of words on both sides ensued. The incident has been sensationalized over the years, but ended peacefully after campus security stepped in and calmed things down.

Andrew Burrow of Miami ended up as being the last man standing in singles, winning the title by beating Dan

Goldberg of Michigan in the final. He was the first Miami player to win the singles championship since Pancho Segura won three in a row from 1943-1945. Later, in the doubles final, Leach and Melville put their disappointment over the team title aside and beat Julian Barham and Darryl Yates from UC Irvine in a very close 4-6, 6-4, 7-5 match, giving USC their 19th NCAA doubles title.

In August 1987, after the altercation in Athens, an NCAA subcommittee reprimanded the Leaches but acknowledged that they had been provoked. The upside, however, was that new crowd control measures would be implemented. Leach, and other coaches such as Pepperdine's Allen Fox, Dennis Ralston at SMU and Chuck Kriese of Clemson, suggested that the NCAA look for another more neutral site to level the playing field. As a result, the 1990 tournament moved out of the Henry Feild Stadium at the University of Georgia to the Hyatt Grand Champions Resort in Indian Wells, California. The NCAA moved the tournament back to Georgia for the 1991 and 1992 championships, citing that 3,000 daily fans who showed up in Georgia compared to the 1,000 at best daily fans at Indian Wells and that 3,000 fans a day were needed to break even financially. The NCAA also announced they were considering a different format for the championship in which early rounds of the tournament would be held in different regions.

With years of introspection on the loss to Georgia, Rick Leach put the loss in perspective. "I did actually get some benefit from that 1987 match," he said. "In 1990, the U.S. was in the semifinals of the Davis Cup in Vienna, Austria. In singles, we had Michael Chang and Andre Agassi playing for us, and Jimmy Pugh and I were the doubles team. We had to play against Thomas Muster and Horst Skoff, the No. 1 doubles team in the world on clay. Muster wasn't about to lose on clay.

The tournament was played in a soccer arena in which they had built a clay court. The crowd was incredibly rowdy and 15,000 fans, many with painted faces, were constantly doing the wave and chanting everything they could think of including 'Zu-ga-be! Zu-ga-be!' (More! More!) It resembled a World Cup soccer match."

Pugh and Leach were up two sets to one when it started to rain. The groundskeepers put down a tarp, and took it away when it stopped. When the rain started again in the fourth set the groundskeepers inexplicably did not put the tarp on. It rained for 20 minutes, turning the clay to a soggy mess. At 5-5 in the fourth set, in front of a boisterous crowd, Pugh and Leach pulled out the win. Despite the noise and distraction, Leach never lost his serve. "I remember thinking that the NCAA match in Georgia in '87 really prepared me for Vienna. In fact, compared to the Davis Cup, the Georgia match was like a 'Pillsbury Bake-Off Contest.'"

Pugh and Leach won 7-6 (4), 3-6, 6-0, 7-5 to give the United States an important 2-1 lead, setting the stage for Chang to win the deciding match in heroic fashion by beating Skoff after being down two sets. The U.S. then went on to beat Australia in the final to win the Davis Cup for the first time in eight years.

In looking back at his son—and top player's—career, Coach Leach said, "For me, Rick had two very memorable professional doubles matches. The first was when he and former Bruin Jim Pugh played against John Fitzgerald and Anders Järryd—one of the best doubles teams in the world—in the 1989 Wimbledon final. Jim and Rick were up a set and a break, but then they stopped playing to win and started playing *not to lose*. Things turned sour and they lost the match, 3-6, 7-6,

6-4, 7-6. I went up to Rick and told him, 'You've got to grab the brass ring, no one is going to give it to you.'"

The next year in 1990, Leach and Pugh played again in the Wimbledon final—this time facing South Africans Pieter Aldrich and Danie Visser. The match was extremely tight, and the score was 7-6 (5), 7-6 (4), 6-6, and 4-4 in the tiebreaker. Leach hit a forehand up the line to go up 5-4 followed by an ace on his next serve. His next serve was a near ace that set Pugh up for a put-away volley to win the title. Rick went up to his father after that match saying, "Did I grab the brass ring, dad?"

Rick Leach had an illustrious career at USC leading the Trojans to the NCAA semifinals in 1985 and 1987 and the quarterfinals in 1984 and 1986. He was the first player to be an eight-time All-American winning both singles and doubles distinctions for four straight years. The only other player to match this feat is J.P. Smith at Tennesee in 2011. Rick played on the pro circuit for 15 years and retired in 2005. He achieved a No. 1 doubles ranking in the world in 1990, winning a total of 46 professional doubles titles including the Australian Open in 1988, 1989, and 2000, Wimbledon in 1990, and the U.S. Open in 1993.

In 1988, two very different but talented players—Byron Black from Zimbabwe and Luke Jensen's brother Murphy from Michigan—joined the team. Rick Leach had graduated and Luke Jensen left school after his second year, both headed for the pro tour. Returning players included four seniors, Scott Melville, Jonas Wallgard, Scott Brownsberger and Chris Dundas and four juniors, Eric Amend, Rick Kepler, John Carras and Andy Olyphant. In addition to Byron Black and Murphy Jensen, Donny Isaak from San Marino, Kent Seton from Beverly Hills and Greg Michaels from Claremont signed on as freshman.

Black started playing tennis with a sawed-off racket when he was three years old. The racket was too big for him so he developed a two-handed forehand and backhand (similar to Hans Gildemeister from the 1976 Championship team). In 1986, he left Zimbabwe to train at John Newcombe's Tennis Academy in New Braunfels, Texas. Dick Leach remembered a call from Clarence Mabry, the former coach at Trinity and the co-founder of Newcombe's Academy, who mentioned an outstanding player from Zimbabwe who was on their Davis Cup team. Trinity had changed its status from a DI to a DII school, thus dropping scholarship athletics. Mabry suggested that Leach visit and watch Black play at an indoor Thanksgiving tournament. Leach was so impressed with Black's play that he immediately recruited him.

"After I met Coach Leach, I went to visit USC," said Black. "On my recruiting trip, I watched USC beat UCLA 6-0 at UCLA. It was an incredible day, with Luke Jensen playing No. 2 and the event broadcast on Prime Ticket cable television. I vividly recall Luke diving for a volley and cutting open his hand and still managing to win the match. The whole court was covered in Luke's blood. It was an amazing spectacle. Next thing I knew he was driven away by a beautiful blonde in a red corvette to get stitches! I was so blown away by the spectacle, but still very wet behind the ears. USC was the only university for me because Coach Leach had built such a tennis powerhouse and they had a strong business school, but at the same time, I felt so physically small compared to that '87 team that I did not think I was worthy of a full scholarship. When I arrived, Roger Knapp took me under his wing and made me feel welcome and showed me the ropes,"

Said Jensen of what he called "the blood match," against UCLA in 1987, "Even if you were friends with a Bruin player off the court, on the court it's the height of the Cold War and UCLA are the Soviets to us. I was playing No. 2 singles against Buff Farrow. At the end of the first set, I dove for the ball and made a gash in my playing hand in a place that could not be taped. The bleeding would not stop. I had to modify my game by serving left-handed only and moving forward to volley every ball I could. Groundstrokes made the cut split open even more, with the blood pouring out as we entered the third and decisive set. I had bled through my SC uniform and all over Bruin court No. 2. The blood covered my gold Prince Boron racquet to make it a true Cardinal and Gold frame. By the end of the match, I had bled out over every part of the court. The windscreens even had to be bleached from the bloodstains. The court was ruined and had to be resurfaced, while my shoes, socks, shirt, shorts and racket would be placed into the team's trophy case with all the other USC historic trophies. It was the clinching match for the dual meet and one of the greatest highlights of my tennis career. To bleed out in a victory against the Bruins in Westwood is a feeling I wish all Trojans could experience.

"And Bryon is right about my ride after the match," Jensen continued. "I was dating a knockout from the Delta Gamma Sorority. After the match, she drove me to the UCLA training room in her dad's red Corvette where I received 12 stitches. There was nothing more the medical staff could do. I had disfigured my finger from the constant pressure of gripping the racket for the final two sets. Along with nerve damage that causes numbness and tingling to this day, I also managed to rip open the stitches the following weekend against Stanford and Cal."

Jensen's younger brother Murphy had already made a name for himself as a top junior. "I won a number of national doubles titles including two Orange Bowl world championships in doubles in the 16s and 18s with Al Parker. We were ranked No. 1 in the world in doubles in the 18s. I was ranked as high as No. 2 in the nation in the 18s in singles." Parker went on to Georgia and Jensen went to USC to follow in his brother's footsteps, believing that, under Coach Leach, USC was "the best school in the nation."

Continued Murphy, "I think my USC tennis experience was different from those of players in previous years, as I entered a situation in which an undefeated team had just experienced great disappointment. It seemed like there was a dark cloud hanging over everyone after that loss. Ricky and Luke had turned pro and the remaining players on that team were still healing from that experience. Coach Leach was still the best coach in the country and he really knew tennis. I learned everything I needed to learn from him to prepare me to be successful and to win on a professional level. It wasn't until years later that I realized what a tough job Coach Leach had in trying to coach me and the other very accomplished players. In the end, I realized that he had the biggest impact on my success as a player because he was so tough on me. He didn't put up with nonsense and taught me what it meant to compete with class as a Trojan."

The Trojans began the season ranked No. 3 in the country and finished with a 25-5 record and second place finish in the Pac-10. Leach had put together three great doubles teams in Melville and Amend, who won four doubles titles (including the Pacific Coast and Pac-10 championships), Brownsberger and Jensen, ranked the best second doubles team in the nation, and Carras and Black who had a 14-4 record. The team got to the semifinals of the NCAAs, beating Southwest Louisiana 5-2 and Irvine 5-2 before facing Stanford. Carras notched a great win over Jeff Tarango 6-0, 5-7, 6-3, Byron Black beat Patrick

McEnroe 6-3, 7-5 and Brownsberger defeated Glenn Solomon 7-5, 6-1, but the Trojans lost 5-3. Stanford defeated LSU 5-2 in the final to claim the team title, the Trojans finished No. 3 nationally. Amend and Melville lost in the semifinals of the doubles tournament 6-3, 6-4 to UCLA's Buff Farrow and Robert Bierens but still finished ranked No. 1 in the nation in the final doubles rankings. Robbie Weiss from Pepperdine beat UCLA's Brian Garrow in three sets to win the singles title, while Garrow returned with Patrick Galbraith to beat their Bruin teammates Farrow and Bierens in an all-UCLA doubles final. Dan Magill, Georgia's legendary coach retired shortly after the national championships with Manuel Diaz, his assistant coach of six years taking over the job.

In 1989, Roger Knapp started his third and final season as Dick Leach's assistant as the team had one of its most difficult years with a 17-13 record and a third-place Pac-10 finish. Leach felt the loss of three of his top players Scott Melville, Jonas Wallgard and Scott Brownsberger. In particular, the departure of Melville, who was Troy's No. 1 player the previous year, and who won the 1987 doubles title, left a very big hole in the team. Veterans Byron Black, Eric Amend, John Carras, Murphy Jensen, Andy Olyphant, Rick Kepler, Paul Brandt and redshirted freshman Donny Isaak were joined by Greg Failla, a two-time All-American at Cal State Long Beach who transferred for his senior year, and incoming freshman Greg Michaels.

Going into the NCAA tournament, the Trojans were missing two key players—Carras who was on academic suspension, and Jensen who was ill—weakening the team significantly. USC once again was drawn to face Georgia in its opening match in Athens. Going into the match, the Trojans were 0-4 in their NCAA matchups against the Bulldogs since 1981. And again they lost by a 5-1 margin with only Isaak at

No. 4 singles beating T.J. Middleton 6-4, 6-0. USC ended their season ranked No. 10 nationally.

Georgia went all the way to the final, only to lose to Stanford 5-3 as the Cardinal claimed their 10th NCAA team title. Donni Leaycraft from Louisiana State defeated Steven Jung of Nebraska in three sets for the individual singles title. Dick Leach proved what a great doubles coach he was once again, when Amend and Black won USC's 20th NCAA

doubles title in a closely contested seesaw match against Mike Briggs and Trevor Kroneman of UC-Irvine 7-5, 6-7 (5), 7-5.

Between 1980 and 1989, Stanford had won the NCAA Team Tournament six times, while UCLA and Georgia had each won it twice. While USC had many outstanding players and outstanding teams, they consistently fell short at the final. All of that would change when the new decade began.

Byron Black won the 1989 NCAA doubles title with Eric Amend

204

7

Championship
Seasons

In the 1980's, Dick Leach had recruited many top players, experienced some great individual wins, but also endured some very difficult team losses. As the 1990 season started, he questioned whether the Trojans had peaked without achieving their ultimate goal.

"In 1990, I still had a lot of energy and really wanted to win a National Championship, but every day as I commuted to USC, I began to doubt that it was going to happen," said Leach. "I kept thinking back to that 1987 season when we had the best team in the country." Members of that '87 squad, many now facing their last year as a team, shared Leach's feelings of uncertainty. New recruit Byron Black said he remembered feeling like the "team was fragmented, with the seasoned players being down and the new recruits, like me, not really understanding how much that previous loss affected everyone."

At the end of the 1989 season, Murphy Jensen left USC for the University of Georgia to join his comrade and long-time doubles partner Al Parker. The entire Jensen family also decided to relocate to Atlanta, not only to be close to Murphy, but because Luke believed that there would be more tennis opportunities in what had become the most active tennis city in the country.

Leach felt the pressure. He knew that Stanford was having a great deal of success recruiting many of the top American juniors. In fact, Leach said he only recalled prying two players, Matt Anger and Tim Pawsat, away from Dick Gould's Stanford recruiting machine during the entire 1980s. An increasing number of top players were also going to college either for a short time before turning pro, a trend started by Jimmy Connors and John McEnroe in the 1970s, and continued by Michael Chang, Pete Sampras, Andre Agassi, and Jim Courier who skipped college completely, going directly onto the tour.

So Leach turned to another talent pool—top international players who wanted to get great training and experience, *and* a first-rate education at an American university. Leach faced opposition however. Favoring even a few foreign over domestic students was not a popular idea with the parents of top U.S. players, since attaining a tennis scholarship was already competitive enough. Even Mike McGee, the USC athletic director at the time, was hesitant; but he eventually came around after being impressed with Byron Black's athletic and academic prowess. Years later, Dick Gould told Leach that, while he wasn't inclined to recruit international players, he supported those schools that did because the caliber of players gave his teams greater competition.

With this new strategy, Leach had a solid recruiting year in 1990, bringing in a good mix of players, including four new freshman: Martin Dionne from Quebec, Perre-Andre Genillard from Geneva, Andras Lanyi from Budapest and local player Chris Swortwood from Del Mar. Returning were Byron Black, the Trojans' No. 1 player, junior Paul Brandt, and sophomores Donny Isaak, Mehdi Benyebka and Kent Seton. In addition to recruiting top players, Leach hired Carl Neufeld as his assistant coach. A former top player for Northern Illinois University from 1976-1979, Neufeld had coached for nine years at NIU, where he had amassed a top record as the winningest head coach in the school's history. The Trojans had a respectable season with a 22-8 overall record, tying with Stanford for the Pac-10 title.

The 1990 NCAA tournament took place at the Hyatt Grand Champions Resort in Indian Wells, California. This was the first time since 1976 that it was held away from the University of Georgia. In the new venue, USC beat South Carolina 5-2 in their opener to set up a quarterfinal match against Georgia, with the opportunity to avenge their 1987 loss to the Bulldogs in a neutral location. Byron Black beat Al Parker 6-4, 7-5 at No. 1 singles, but in an odd twist of fate, Murphy Jensen, now playing for the Bulldogs, faced USC's Martin Dionne and lost 7-6 (6), 6-4. At the end of the match Jensen said, "It was the most unusual match I've ever played. I spent two years trying to win matches for the Trojans and now I come here and am trying to beat them." The Trojans ended up winning the match 5-1. Dick Leach told the *Desert Sun*, "Our team started off slowly this season. It looked for a while like we wouldn't get invited to the tournament at all when we were the host school. It would have been very embarrassing."

In the semifinals, Stanford, who had tied with USC for the Pac-10 title, overcame the Men of Troy 5-3. Black scored a tough victory over Jonathan Stark, the No. 2 player in the country 7-6 (6), 6-7 (4), 7-5 and Andras Lanyi had a straight-set victory over Jeff Cathrall 6-2, 6-2. Lanyi then teamed up with Isaak to beat Cathrall and Alexis Hombrecher in three sets.

The Tennessee Volunteers, coached by Mike DePalmer, entered the NCAA tournament as the No. 1 seed, having amassed a spectacular 34-0 record. The 34-match streak surpassed the 32 consecutive victories set by USC entering the 1987 NCAA tournament. In the final, the Vols faced the No. 2-seeded Stanford with the Cardinal overpowering Tennessee 5-2 to win their third consecutive team title—Dick Gould's 11th title in 24 years. It was a devastating outcome for the Vols and they more than likely endured the same kind of disappointment that the Trojans had in 1987. Any team playing in their first NCAA team final feels pressure that is so intense that even the best teams get stressed but going up against a highly experienced powerhouse like Stanford, who had won many finals before, was certainly unnerving.

One player who stood out for the Volunteers was Doug Flach (Ken Flach's brother) who played No. 1 singles. Despite not being a highly-ranked player, Flach gave it his best shot, coming up short as he played four grueling three-set matches in a row facing off against top players including UC Irvine's Trevor Kroneman, Miami's Conny Falk and UCLA's Jason Netter. In the final, Flach lost 6-1, 2-6, 7-5 to Stark and said, "I played four, three-set matches here and lost them all. Physically I just broke down." Steve Bryan from the University of Texas beat Jason Netter from UCLA in straight sets to clinch the singles title and Doug Eisenman and Matt Lucena from Berkeley won the doubles title defeating Mitch Michulka and Michael Penman from Texas in the final.

At the end of the 1990 season, USC's Byron Black was awarded the ITA/Rafael Osuna Sportsmanship Award bestowed to the "Division I men's player who displays sportsmanship, character, excellent academics and has had outstanding tennis playing accomplishments." He was the fourth Trojan to win the award since it was established in 1969 to honor Rafael Osuna, following in the footsteps of Joaquin Loyo-Mayo in 1969, John Andrews in 1974 and Roger Knapp in 1982.

As the 1991 season began, Dick Leach was optimistic about his team's chances, predicting, "This will be the strongest team that we've had in many years. We've improved talent-wise at all three doubles positions and at three of the six singles spots. And this could be the most balanced singles lineup I've ever had." Leach's optimism was rewarded as the team placed first in the Pac-10 and went 30-2 overall.

Mehdi Benyebka and Martin Dionne had transferred to other schools and Paul Brandt had graduated. But Byron Black was returning for his senior year and was joined by junior Donny Isaak, sophomore Andras Lanyi from Hungary, Auburn transfer David Ekerot of Sweden, Kentucky transfer Phil Whitesell, Foothill Community College transfer Chad Rosser, Kent Seton from Beverly Hills, and Chris Swortwood from Torrey Pines High School in Del Mar. Two very talented freshman, Brian MacPhie from Gunderson High—who Leach characterized as having "God-given talent," and Rick's younger brother Jonathan Leach from Laguna Beach High, also joined the team.

Dick Leach would likely have wanted to recruit Jon—even if he hadn't been family. "My second son, Jon, started playing when he was six-and-a-half, and got very good very quickly," he said. "He saw Rick succeed and emulated him."

Jon came up through the juniors and was ranked No. 3 in the nation in the boys' 14-and-under division. He also won four national doubles titles in the 14s and the Ojai 16-and-unders and was the first player ever to win the CIF-5A singles title as a freshman. "Jon was a very aggressive player and had a different temperament to Rick's," said Coach Leach. "Rick was mild mannered but when Jon was young he had a fiery temper and wouldn't back down from anyone. Sometimes it got him in to trouble, but over time he channeled his aggression into becoming an excellent tennis player."

The other newcomer to the team, Brian MacPhie, came in from Gunderson High School in San Jose, where he had amassed an incredible 75-0 prep singles record and was the No. 1 ranked player in Northern California. Both

Leach and MacPhie were top students and had played together before entering USC, having reached the semifinals of the Wimbledon junior championships and as members of the U.S. Junior Davis Cup Team.

At the first meeting of the year, Coach Leach addressed the players sitting on the Trojan bench at court three where the team met everyday at 1pm before beginning practice. Freshmen sat in the back row, with the upper classmen up front. From the front of the bench, Coach noticed that two

Jon Leach clinched the 1994 NCAA title for the Trojans

of his players, Lanyi and MacPhie, were sporting earrings. "I mentioned to the team that the USC alumni probably wouldn't like to see them wearing earrings during their matches," said Leach. "I was so old school that I would prefer they remove them during tennis matches and events. Everyone agreed, under one condition: if we won the NCAA Championships in Georgia—the tournament had moved back there—I would have to get an earring. It seemed like a safe bet, as we couldn't seem to pull off an NCAA Championship there, so I agreed.

"We went down to Athens a week early to get used to the humidity and trained very hard. In the first round we played a very good Notre Dame team and won 6-0. After the match I got my team together to debrief. They told me there was nothing to talk about because in three more matches we were all going to the local mall and I was getting my ear pierced!"

In the next match USC played a very good Florida team in sweltering conditions and wore them out, winning 6-0. The team didn't want to talk about the match, they were focused on the fact that, in two more matches they would be taking Coach to the mall.

"They were having fun and so intent on having *the old guy* get an earring, that their attention was diverted from the pressure of the NCAA title," he said.

In the semifinals, USC faced Stanford in the rubber-match for the year between the two Pac-10 powerhouses, winning a 5-4 decision and losing 1-5 in another. Stanford had three future U.S. Davis Cup team members on their team – Stark, Alex O'Brien and Jared Palmer, but the Trojans still triumphed 5-2. "I couldn't wait to have a team meeting, since I was proud of them," said Coach Leach after the win over Stanford. "But the team only wanted to have the same conversation as before— after the finals, we were going to be going to the mall. I wasn't so sure. Georgia was playing Cal after our match, and if Georgia won, we would be facing them once again on their home turf. I envisioned the rabid Bulldog fans making things very difficult, as they had in the past. And, as luck would have it, Georgia beat Cal 5-4. I had a bad feeling that once again I would be denied my first NCAA Championship either as a player at USC or as a coach.

"The night before the championship match, I cramped up in bed," said Leach. "This was so odd as it had never happened to me before. At midnight I was in so much pain I couldn't sleep. The next morning at breakfast I knew I had to be cool and act like this was just another match. I asked assistant coach Carl Neufeld to take over the team's morning practice before the match. I kept my distance, afraid they would get bad vibes from me."

As the match commenced, USC went up 4-2 with Black, Isaak, Ekerot and Lanyi winning in singles and MacPhie and Jon Leach losing in very close matches. The team only needed one doubles win for Leach's first NCAA championship. The No. 1 doubles team of Black and MacPhie was the first to play, facing Georgia's top two players Al Parker and Patricio Arnold from Argentina. It was Parker's last chance to lead Georgia to an NCAA team title, coming to Georgia after the 1987 NCAA Championship team as the greatest junior tennis player in USTA history with 25 national titles.

"We were up 6-2, 2-1 with a break, when the other two doubles matches started," said Coach Leach. "I knew we could win any of these matches; however, all eyes were on court one. We had championship point at 5-3, with Parker lining up for his second serve. Al hit a great serve that landed on the line and went on to hold at 4-5, still in USC's favor. I ran over to talk to my team as they switched sides and noticed Byron was very nervous. Brian was only a freshman but he had the best left-handed serve in college tennis and he was highly self-confident. I instructed him to serve to Parker's forehand and wide to Arnold's backhand. I asked Bryon, who was at the net, to look over at me before each serve and if I placed one finger down my leg, poach on the first serve; two fingers down meant poach on Brian's second serve. If I put three fingers down my leg, poach on both serves. I said to Byron, 'If they pass you down the line it will be my fault, not yours.'"

On the first point Byron, looked over and Leach placed three fingers down. Byron crossed and hit a volley for a winner. On the second point Byron saw three fingers down. Brian hit a great serve and Byron knocked off the volley. Both players were now very confident. At 30-love when Bryon looked at Coach, he saw three fingers down again, crossed, and bounced the volley over the fence. Brian stopped before serving for the match and looked over to his teammates on courts two and three and held up one finger indicating, *one more point*. Said Leach, "Brian hit the biggest left-handed, un-returnable serve I have ever seen and we won the NCAA Championship." The 15-year drought had ended for Coach Leach.

Said Black, "The match against Parker and Arnold was one of my two best matches in college. It was extra special for Coach Leach as it was his first team win. It was also my last year as a Trojan, and it was a way for me to thank Coach for the opportunity to play under him and for my scholarship. Most importantly at this tournament, any discord that we might have felt as a team went away and we really pulled together. I believe that team unity is why we won the national championship."

Black would go on to win 22 professional doubles, gaining a No. 1 world doubles ranking in 1994 when he and

Jonathan Stark from Stanford won the French Open doubles championship.

Right after the award ceremony, Coach Leach knew what was going to happen next. "As soon as the match was over, the team dragged me to the mall for their real payoff," he said. "You have never seen a happier bunch of young men. The guys picked out a gold stud and I got a hole poked in my ear. I had to wear this thing during the individual singles and doubles parts of the tournament." In the singles tournament, Donny Isaak

Brian MacPhie clinches the 1991 NCAA title for USC

played very well and got to the semifinals, but was beaten by Stanford's Palmer. Palmer went on to win the tournament beating Georgia's Arnold 6-2, 6-0 in the final. The California Bear's duo of Matt Lucena and Bent-Ove Pedersen beat Palmer and Stark in straight sets to claim the doubles title.

At the airport flying back to California, Coach Leach felt that everyone was looking at him and wondering why an old guy was wearing an earring. "When I got home, my next door neighbor saw me and said he was going to sell his house as the neighborhood was deteriorating, and on campus, Athletic Director Mike Garrett thought I had lost my mind," he said. "For me this was a tiny price to pay for winning the title, but most importantly, having the team focus on the earring kept them loose. That's one of the secrets of doing well at the NCAAs—relax and keep it light."

In addition to keeping things light, Coach Leach had three other goals for the team to keep in mind as they entered the 1992 season. In the USC Media Guide, he shared these goals that were now posted on the main scoreboard: 1) Have the highest USC athletic team GPA; 2) Win the Pacific-10 championship and 3) Win the national championship. Having achieved each of these goals in 1991, Leach had his focus on repeat seasons.

In the pre-season poll, the Trojans were ranked No. 2, but Leach was anxious. Black, the seven-time All-American in singles and doubles had graduated and was on the pro tour. Isaak, USC's No. 3 player, left to play for Roger Knapp, now head coach at Drake University. Returning to the team were David Ekerot, Andras Lanyi, Jon Leach and Brian MacPhie, who had won All-American honors in both singles and doubles as a freshman, a feat that had only been accomplished before by Jimmy Connors, John McEnroe and Rick Leach. Other team members were junior Kent Seton, who was redshirted the previous year, Phil Whitesell and freshman newcomers Wayne Black—Bryon's younger brother from Zimbabwe—and Leonard Lee, an accomplished player from San Marino High School. The team had another strong season at 21-3, winning the Pac-10 conference title.

Much like Byron, Wayne Black began tennis early. "When I was around four-years-old, my dad sawed off the handle of an ancient wooden racket, shaved down the throat for my grip, and strung it with regular house string so it was small and light enough for me to maneuver," he said. "We actually had two grass and one hard court at our home, so you can imagine that my dad had a slight passion for the game. Dad had me playing three hours every day—birthdays, Christmas, it didn't matter, and I had no choice. I did feeding drills all day and either my dad would hit the ball to me, or our gardener would throw balls to me for an hour at a time as another gardener would be picking them up. So I hit non-stop at assorted targets in the corners of the court. My schedule was to hit for an hour before school, an hour from 2 to 3 p.m. and then play a match against someone at 5 p.m. I also played club matches and tournaments on the weekends and holidays. The International Tennis Federation had set up a development fund for the poorer nations and that is why Bryon and I, and others from Africa, got scholarships to John Newcombe's Tennis Ranch."

Byron had told his younger brother many stories about life at USC—about winning the NCAAs in his final year and the long history and tradition of tennis there—so it seemed destined that Wayne, too, would become a Trojan. The big question was whether USC would have space for him. There were a few factors working against him. "Our parents didn't have the funds so I had to get a full scholarship," said Wayne. "I did not have a junior career like Byron's and my ranking was average to say the least, so I was contemplating going to another school for a year and then hopefully transferring to USC from there. Roger Knapp offered me a spot at Drake. I went there for a recruiting trip and it was the first time I had seen snow. Although I liked the campus, the cold weather was not for me. But Drake was the only college that offered me anything. Fortunately, Coach Leach had one open scholarship and offered it to me. I met Carl Neufeld on a trip to USC and he definitely had something to do with Coach's decision. Carl seemed confident I would be a hard and dedicated worker."

Neufeld concurred in a later interview with the *Los Angeles Times*, "Quite frankly, the only reason Wayne got a scholarship was that he was Byron Black's brother. In fact, we were the only school to offer Wayne a full scholarship and we didn't even do that until May, just three or four months before he had to come to school. The truth is he just didn't have the results that would warrant a scholarship offer. We were going to work on Wayne's game his freshman year and probably have him sit out the season as a redshirt, but he started playing so well that we scrapped that idea."

Neufeld and Black developed a strong friendship. The pair met at the courts to hit every morning at 8 a.m. When Neufeld was busy, Black found other people to hit with, including a graduate student from Germany. "I remember he wasn't a tournament player, but he was rock solid from the baseline," Black said. "He and I would hit cross-courts for two hours, every weekday. Carl would come over and offer tips from time to time. I ended up arranging my classes from 10am to 1pm with a few night classes as needed. I didn't spend that much time on schoolwork, as I knew I was not going to achieve much there. Team practice was from 1 to 3 p.m. and I would stay and hit with my doubles partner Kent Seton, who was an excellent doubles player, until 5 p.m. If I wasn't hitting I would be in the gym or on the track. So while I did start a little slow, I was highly motivated, not only to keep my scholarship, but also because I loved what I was doing with Carl and improved very quickly with such good players surrounding me. I started at No.

6, and once I got the taste of a team victory, it consumed me. I didn't lose a match the entire season, except that last match in the NCAAs—which broke my heart. But, in a nutshell, I owe the improvement in my game to Carl Neufeld who believed in me from the start."

At the 1992 NCAA Championships at Georgia, the Trojans were seeded No. 1. Brian MacPhie was playing the No. 1 position, followed by David Ekerot, Jon Leach, Andras Lanyi, Wayne Black and Kent Seton. USC opened with a win against Texas 6-0 and then beat Kentucky 5-3. In the semifinals they faced No. 10 seed Notre Dame. Said Coach Leach, "Andras Lanyi had a very sore back so I took him out of the lineup in the matches against Kentucky and Notre Dame. I wanted to save him for the finals if we got there. "But the Fighting Irish stunned the Trojans, winning five out of the six singles matches. The Irish's David DiLucia won a very close match over the No. 5 ranked Brian MacPhie 7-5, 4-6, 6-3, with only Kent Seton winning at No. 5 singles. "Notre Dame played so well," Leach said. "It was their day." In the final, No. 2 seed Stanford blew out Notre Dame 5-0, the first shutout recorded since the start of the team championship format in 1977. Stanford players also won the singles and doubles titles giving Stanford the first sweep across all three titles since the team tournament era began in 1977. In the singles final, Alex O'Brien beat Wade McGuire from Georgia in straight sets and then teamed with Chris Cocotos to win the doubles championship, vanquishing their own teammates Vimal Patel and Jason Yee in two close sets. O'Brien's sweep of both singles and doubles titles was the first since the Cardinal's John Whitlinger had done so in 1974.

The Trojans began 1993 as the No. 1 ranked team in the nation once again. Leach confidently compared the level of talent on this team as equal to that of the 1987 squad. MacPhie, USC's No. 1 player, along with David Ekrot, Jon Leach, Wayne Black, Andras Lanyi, Kent Seton, Phil Whitesell, Pierre-Andre Genillard and Chris Swortwood were returning. Two freshman, Lukas Hovorka from Brno, Czechoslovakia, and Adam Peterson from Orange, California also joined the team along with junior walk-on Chad Rosser. The team achieved a 22-2 record, losing to UCLA twice, once at home and once at Westwood. The team did win their fourth Pac-10 title in a row with a 9-1 record, and Dick Leach was named the Pac-10 Coach of the Year for the third time in four years.

During this time both Jon Leach and Chris Swortwood received extra training and tutoring with Professor George Schick, a statistics professor in the business school (now the Marshall School of Business). Said Swortwood, "Dr. Schick loved tennis. He liked to hit with one of us in the mornings and then tutor us in the afternoon. He would devise rules to try to make things fun and challenging. For instance, we would have to play in the singles court, but he could use the entire court. We got one serve on each point, but he got two, and he would start up 30-0 in every game." Said Jon Leach, "Professor Schick had another type of game in which the first person to 100 points won the match, but the catch was that we had to start at our ages and go up to 100. At the time I think he was in his 60's and of course we were in very early 20's. Even though we were top college players, these games proved to very challenging and fun."

The Trojans were again the No. 1 seed in the NCAA tournament and in their opening round beat North Carolina 5-2, with MacPhie and Ekerot losing at No. 1 and No. 2 singles to UNC's Roland Thorqvist and David Caldwell, respectively,

Wayne Black was inducted in the USC Athletic Hall of Fame in 2018, joining Gene Mako, Bob Falkenburg, Alex Olmedo, Dennis Ralston, Rafael Osuna, Stan Smith, Bob Lutz, George Toley, Dick Leach, Byron Black and Rick Leach both in close three-set matches. Later, Leach and MacPhie clinched the match, beating Thorqvist and Daryl Wyatt in straight sets. The Trojans won their next two matches in 5-0 shut-outs, avenging their loss the previous year to Notre Dame in the quarterfinals and beating Texas in the semifinals. On the other side of the draw, Georgia upset No. 2 seed UCLA 5-4 in the semifinals, setting the stage for another skirmish between the Trojans and the Bulldogs.

The championship match was very close as Black and Peterson won their matches at No.'s 3 and 6 while Georgia won at No. 1, No. 2 and No. 5 singles. Jon Leach, playing at No. 4 singles, trailed Georgia's Craig Baskin 4-5 in the final-set and faced a match point. Leach, however, stayed alive, forced a final-set tiebreaker and won the match 6-3, 3-6, 7-6 (5) to even the team match score 3-3. The Trojan teams of Ekerot and Lanyi and Black and Seton won their matches in straight sets clinching the 5-3 win and the 14th national title for USC. Dick Leach later told the *Los Angeles Times*, "It was an unbelievable match. There were barking, screaming Georgia fans, cheering like mad on every point. They sounded like a USC-Notre Dame football crowd. For my kids to be able to deal with that is a real tribute. It's the most amazing show I've ever seen in tennis."

Chris Woodruff from Tennessee, the No. 1 ranked player in the nation, won the singles title beating Wade McGuire of Georgia in straight sets. Florida Gators David Blair and Mark Merklein won the doubles title by beating Stanford's Chris Cocotos and Michael Flanagan in three sets.

In June 1993, former Trojans Luke and Murphy Jensen, who were becoming as well known for their hard-driving, rock and roll lifestyle as their tennis—which Vitas Gerulaitis had coined "grunge tennis"—won the French Open doubles title by beating Germans Mark Goellner and David Prinosil in the final.

An ebullient Murphy declared, "Winning the French Open with Luke was the highlight of my tennis life. A few months later, we were honored at midfield in the Coliseum as a USC Grand Slam Champion, which is something I will never forget. Winning the French was validation of what I have learned from Coach Leach, and I believe that a win like that is as much for the Trojan family as it is for us."

In October of 1993, an enormous fire swept through Laguna Beach, destroying thousands of homes. That morning, Dick Leach noticed that the hot Santa Ana winds that came from the desert were kicking up. He was on campus when he got a frantic call from his wife, Sandy, saying there was a big fire in the Laguna Canyon. He left campus immediately to make sure Sandy was all right.

"I remember it so vividly," said Leach. "As I got close to Laguna Beach I could see large black clouds, but the police stopped me in Corona Del Mar. I went down to the ocean and walked along the beach for five miles to where I lived. The flames were 40 feet high and I stopped and watched from inside the ocean where I felt safe. I knew my home was probably toast. I slept at Jon's apartment off-campus that night. The home phone was dead, which was a very bad sign. Remember, there were no cell phones then. I had no idea where Sandy was, and couldn't get anywhere near our home. I went to my office the next morning and Sandy had left a message to tell me she was fine. She had gone to the gym at Corona Del Mar High School where people from the area were being sheltered."

Incredibly, Rick Leach, who was playing tennis in Europe, saw his family home burning on CNN that night. He and his father talked on the phone that day. Two days later, Dick Leach was able to get back to his home, only to see that it had burned completely to the ground. "All of our friends were so worried and asked how I felt. I told them that the most important thing was that we were all safe," he said. "Immediately, I began to draw up plans for our new home. I wanted the kids to think they were coming back to their old home so we placed the bedrooms in the same locations. We ended up with a larger, better version of our old place."

The Laguna Beach fire was one of the 20 largest fire losses in U.S. history. Over 16,000 acres were burned as well as 400 homes.

In 1994, three-time All-American and former Trojan standout Matt Anger rejoined the Trojans as Dick Leach's assistant coach. The team lost many top players, including All-Americans David Ekerot, Andras Lanyi, Kent Seton and Brian MacPhie. MacPhie had left USC early to pursue a professional career.

"On the pro tour everyone called Brian MacPhie, 'Magic' because of his amazing 130 mph lefty serve that could dance," said Rick Leach. "He and I played together and did very well."

Dana Bozeman, who played with MacPhie after college said, "When Brian hit that big left-handed twist serve at the midpoint of the sideline in the deuce court, the ball would kick up high and swerve with so much spin that it would often hit the fence before you could get a racket on it."

Rick Leach laughingly agreed, "Yeah, no one wanted to play Brian because they didn't want to face that serve."

Two All-Americans, Wayne Black and Jon Leach, returned as did Lukas Hovorka and Adam Peterson. Other players included Chad Rosser, Josh Bridwell, Kent Carl, Chris Swortwood, Phil Whitesell and Leonard Lee. Joining the squad was junior Brett Hansen, a former No. 1 player from UC-Irvine, and freshmen Jason Wilson and Ryan Sellchop.

USC was ranked No. 3 in the pre-season rankings, and Black was ranked as the top singles player in the country with Leach at No. 15. Black and Leach were also ranked No. 19 in doubles. USC won its fourth straight Pac-10 title with a 9-1 record, going 22-3 overall. During the season, two losses occurred because of defaults.

"Someone at another university complained that several universities were using pro players on their teams and there were some coaches who were against bringing foreign players onto college teams in general," said Dick Leach. "At the last minute, the NCAA said that we had to demonstrate that our international players were not professionals."

To prove this, Leach and Anger had to get letters from each player's home federation and copies of all expense forms for the tennis tournaments. Leach and Anger worked for several days to get the necessary information to prove that Black and Hovorka were amateurs. But the delay hurt the team's overall record. "Our compliance office looked at all of the documentation and concluded that our players had not taken any money," said Leach. "But while we were going through the process, two of my players had to sit out of matches against UCLA and the University of San Diego. Because 1994 was a very lean year recruiting-wise for us we didn't have enough players to fill their vacated slots and had to default those matches."

Notre Dame hosted the NCAA tournament at the Courtney Tennis Center in South Bend, Indiana and USC was seeded No. 1 followed by Stanford at No. 2. In the semifinals, USC beat Mississippi 4-0 and Stanford defeated UCLA 4-0. USC had played Stanford twice during the season and had beaten them 4-3 both times.

The NCAA decided to use a new format to decide the tournament winner. For the first time in 17 years, instead of using a nine-point system as they had since 1977, the total number of points was reduced to seven. Each singles match was worth one point and the team who won two out of the three doubles matches won the other point. Teams had to win four out of seven points to win the match. Another change was that doubles matches were played first and consisted of just one eight-game pro set. Said Dick Leach, "I and many of our fans were dead set against this change as it devalued doubles play and was bad for the sport."

Stanford had three match points at No. 2 doubles, but the Trojans fought back and won the match. USC also won at No. 1 doubles to take the doubles point and go up 1-0. After two more hours of play, Stanford won three out of five singles matches to even the score at 3-3.

The remaining match was at No. 2 singles where Jon Leach played Stanford's Jeff Salzenstein. During the regular season, Salzenstein had beaten Leach twice—once at the Farm and once at home. Coach Leach decided to let Matt Anger coach Jon through the match. Jon and Matt were close friends and Leach felt that he didn't need to put more pressure on his son.

"Jon and Jeff split sets and it was 3-3 in the third," said Anger. "It was 30-all on Jeff's serve, when Jon hit a lob over Jeff. Jeff jumped for the ball and couldn't reach. On the way down, he stepped on himself and somehow broke his shoelace. While he was looking for a new shoelace, I remember two things. First, Jon's lob hit the line but he didn't see where the ball landed as he was trying to regain his balance. Some Stanford players were telling with him to call the ball out which, to his credit, he felt he couldn't do since he hadn't seen where the ball landed. I went over to the ref to make sure that the ball was good, and he concurred."

Said Dick Leach, "While Jeff was trading shoelaces with his coach I moved behind the back fence where no one could see me. I told Jon to take away the backhand serve by stepping to the left, because Jeff was a lefty and I thought he would serve wide to Jon's backhand."

Continued Anger, "Jon now had break point, and he and I were talking about what to do next. I thought that Jeff would serve to Jon's forehand or into his body. After a lengthy delay, Jeff served and hit a ball into Jon's body. Jon moved to the left and hit his return down the line for a winner and the break. Jon's hands were so good, he was able to adjust. On the changeover, Jon was pretty excited, but he knew he wasn't done yet. He leaned over to me and said that he was nervous for the first time. While keeping him calm, I said that it would be good to play some power tennis and not worry about any feel or finesse shots, since those are tough if you are feeling tight. Jon played a perfect game to hold easily and go up 5-3. Jon won the first point on Jeff's serve and I remember telling him to keep hitting out. On the next point, Jon feathered a backhand chip lob up-the-line—just the opposite of the kind of shots that we discussed. Somehow Jon got that ball over and around Jeff with perfect placement. It was one of those coaching moments where I was thinking, 'No, no—and then, when it was a winner—yes, yes!' Jon broke serve a couple of moments later to win the title. I was very happy for Jon but also for the team as they were such a good group. Coach Leach had also gone through a lot earlier with his home burning down so Jon clinching the match was a storybook ending for everyone."

Said Dick Leach, "It's one of my best memories of seeing Jon play. He had been in the zone and it was the best set of tennis I have ever seen him play. Just thrilling."

Said UCLA coach Billy Martin of the Jon Leach vs. Jeff Salzenstein NCAA team title decider, "The match between Jon and Jeff was amazing. I remember watching Matt Anger on the court with Dick Leach looking from behind the screen. It's tough enough when you are watching your player in this tense situation, but when it's your son, well, you have to be a nervous wreck!"

The Trojans also had an opportunity to make a clean sweep of the championships since Wayne Black was in the singles final as well as in the doubles final with Jon Leach. Unfortunately for SC, Mark Merklein from Florida, who had won the national doubles title the previous year with David Blair, took the singles title beating Black 6-2, 6-7(8), 6-4. In doubles, Laurent Miquelard and Joc Simmons from Mississippi State edged out Black and Leach 7-6 (5), 2-6, 6-3 to take the title.

At the beginning of the 1995 season, Coach Leach knew that attempting a three-peat as national champions would be an enormous challenge. Even though the team was ranked No. 2 in the nation in the pre-season poll, his two top players, Wayne Black and Jon Leach, were no longer on the team. Black decided to leave in his junior year, just before the season began, for the pro tour. He was very successful and ended up winning two major mixed doubles titles — the French Open in 2002 and Wimbledon in 2004 with his sister Cara. Returning were Brett Hansen, a senior who had a spectacular 23-1 season winning every singles matches at No. 4 in the 1994 NCAA tournament, Adam Peterson, ranked No. 48 going into the season, and Lukas Hovorka, an honors student who had amassed a 24-9 record. Two new recruits, junior Manny Ramirez, a transfer from College of the Desert, and standout freshman Fernando Samayoa from Guatemala, joined senior Leonard Lee, Phil Whitesell and Chad Rosser, redshirted freshman Kyle Spencer,

Jason Wilson from San Francisco and Andrew Hughes from Decatur, Georgia. Ryan McKee, a former All-American in singles and doubles at Claremont-McKenna, became Dick Leach's assistant coach.

Samayoa was born in Guatemala, but from age 12 grew up playing at Spanish River High School in Boca Raton, Florida. There he was a top-five ranked junior in the 18-and-unders. He was also the first Guatemalan born player to be ranked by the ATP (No. 394 in 1992). Samayoa came to USC through a referral from Guy Fritz (the father for future ATP pro Taylor Fritz's father and Dick Leach's close friend), who at the time was the head coach of College of The Desert in Palm Springs. Samayoa met Fritz at the Bahamas Open in late 1993. After Wayne Black turned pro, there was an open scholarship at USC.

"I remember getting a call from the Guatemalan Consulate in Los Angeles asking if they could speak with me about an opportunity to play tennis at USC," Samayoa said. "Of course, I thought it was a joke, so I hung up the phone, probably about three times, until I felt bad for the person on the other end. I was so excited, and within a few months, my papers and transcripts arrived at USC. This was the best decision I had ever made and the opportunity of a lifetime."

However, the team did not fare very well in 1995, going 14-8 overall and 5-5 in the Pac-10 placing third. At the NCAA tournament, the two-time defending champion Trojans were upset by Mississippi in the opening round 4-3. USC lost the doubles point, and Peterson lost at No. 2 singles. However, Hansen, Hovorka and Samayoa won at No.'s 1, 4 and 6 to go ahead 3-2. The Rebels then won two very close three-set matches where Ali Hamadeh defeated Manny Ramirez and Van Vanlingen beat Kyle Spencer. It was the first time in five years that the Trojans did not advance to the final four at the NCAAs. The Trojans finished with a final ranking of No. 11, falling out of the top 10 for the first time since the team championship began in 1977. Mississippi ended up reaching the team final where they were defeated by Stanford 4-0 to clinch their 13th NCAA team title and finish a perfect 27-0 season. It was Stanford's first perfect season since 1978 when John McEnroe led the team.

Brett Hansen was the bright spot for the Trojans during the tournament, defeating Salzenstein in the semifinals of the singles tournament 6-7(6), 6-0, 6-3. Hansen played well in the singles final against the top-seeded Sargis Sargsian of Arizona State winning the first set 6-3 but lost the next two sets 6-3, 6-4. Mahesh Bhupahti and Ali Hamadeh of Mississippi won the doubles titles defeating Chad Clark and Trey Phillips of Texas in straight sets.

In 1996, Dick Leach was still reeling from the previous season's results, but was, nevertheless, excited about the potential of his new team. The major loss for the Trojans was two-time All-American Brett Hansen, the previous year's NCAA singles finalist, who graduated. Coming back to the squad were All-American Adam Peterson, ranked No. 7 in the pre-season poll, seniors Manny Ramirez, the team's No. 4 player, Lukas Hovorka, junior Fernando Samayoa, sophomore Kyle Spencer and senior Reid Slattery, a transfer from Kansas. The top recruit for the team was freshman Cecil Mamiit, a graduate of Nick Bollettieri's Tennis Academy in Sarasota, Florida, who had acted as Boris Becker's practice partner.

Cecil Mamiit grew up in Eagle Rock, California, a city wedged between Glendale and Pasadena and started playing tennis at about eight years old. "My cousin showed me how to play the game initially and then, when I was around nine,

I started taking lessons from former USC great Tom Leonard at the Racket Center in South Pasadena as well as known teaching pro Rusty Miller," said Mamiit. Leonard used what Mamiit called "a cerebral approach" to the game. "He stressed being aware on the court, how to be disciplined, consistent and competitive," he said. Mamiit became a top junior and went to USC on a full scholarship. He worked closely with Coach Leach who had a profound effect on him. "I learned a great deal from Coach Leach," he said. "I believed that his overall goal was to make the boys on the team into men. I think many players will agree with this."

During the NCAA team tournament held at the University of Georgia's Dan Magill Tennis Complex, Stanford beat USC in the quarterfinals 4-1. The final pitted Stanford against UCLA, the No. 1 seed, who entered the tournament with a perfect 26-0 record. The Bruins had not won a team title since 1984, and they hoped that this would be their year to break the drought. Despite winning the doubles point, UCLA's No. 2 through No. 6 singles players were all defeated and Stanford won its 14th overall title by a 4-1 scoreline.

In the individual singles tournament, both Mamiit and Peterson made it to the semifinals, but were unable to make an all-Trojan NCAA singles final happen. Peterson lost 6-4, 6-3 to Fresno State's Fredrik Bergh, a protégé of future Trojan coach Peter Smith. Mamiit beat Stanford's Paul Goldstein in three sets in the second round and UCLA's Srdjan Muskatirovic 6-3, 6-3 in the third round. In the quarterfinals, he crushed Jan Hermansson of South Alabama 6-1, 6-1. Mamiit had lost only 18 games en route to the semifinals and beat Johan Hede of Mississippi 6-4, 6-1 to face Bergh in the final. Bergh most likely thought he would be playing No. 1 seed Justin Gimelstob from UCLA in the second round. However, Gimelstob seemed so let down after his UCLA team lost in the team final to Stanford that he bowed out quickly in the first round to Phil Cooper of Wichita State 6-3, 6-2, leaving Bergh to play his way through the rest of the draw.

In the final, Mamiit broke Bergh twice in the first set to go up 5-1, but Bergh broke back. Mamiit broke back again in the following game to take the set 6-2. In the second set, Mamiit came out strong, taking a 4-1 lead, but Bergh broke him twice to surge ahead 5-4. After a rain delay, Bergh won the second set. "I remember that he served very well in the second set and I was getting tight," Mamiit said. "Coach Leach came over and just said, 'Breathe.' That calmed me down." Mamitt came back to take the third set and the match 6-2, 4-6, 6-3, becoming the first player to win the NCAA singles title as a freshman since Stanford's John McEnroe in 1978. He also reclaimed the men's singles championship for the Trojans, becoming the 13th player to earn the title in 16 years—and the first since Robert Van't Hof in 1980. That summer, Mamiit left USC for the pro tour where he attained a career high ranking of No. 72 in 1999. He also played on the Philippine Davis Cup team from 1996-2001.

Cecil Mamiit won the NCAA singles title as a freshman in 1996

In the doubles final, UCLA's Gimelstob

and Muskatiovic bounced back from their team tournament disappointment to win the doubles over Texas Christian's Ashley Fisher and Jason Weir-Smith 6-7 (3), 6-4, 6-4.

As the 1997 season began, Dick Leach was excited to bring in George Bastl, a native of Switzerland, who transferred in his junior year from the University of South Florida. Bastl was a standout Swiss junior player and was the No. 1 player for South Florida with a 47-7 record as a sophomore. "George Bastl was one of the best players I ever coached, and that's saying a lot," said Leach. "He is competitive with anyone in the country. He has an outstanding work ethic and comes every day ready to play."

Bastl joined newcomers freshman Patrick Gottelsleben from Germany, Roman Kukal from Slovakia and Jordan Walker from Canada, returning juniors Fernando Samayoa and Kyle Spencer, and sophomores Scott Willinski, Akram Zaman and Ryan Hollis. Coach Leach also brought in Glenn Michibata as his assistant coach. Michibata, a former All-American from Pepperdine, had won four career titles in doubles and achieved a career high doubles ranking of No. 5 in 1991. The Trojans finished 18-6, placing third in the Pac-10 with a 6-4 record.

The NCAA tournament season proved very disappointing for the Men of Troy. Said Leach, "In the Regionals, we played Fresno State in Fresno. Earlier in the season, we had beaten them but they played very well in this match, and we lost to them 4-3. This was the first time in 20 years that we didn't make it into the final sixteen of the NCAA tournament."

The Bulldogs, coached by future USC coach Peter Smith, came out of the gate fast with Kelly Gullett and Robert Lindstedt clinching the doubles point 10-8 in the tiebreaker, beating George Bastl and Kyle Spencer. Bastl posted a 6-1, 6-0 win over Fredrik Giers at first singles, and Samoya defeated

Andy Scorteanu 6-2, 3-6, 6-3 at No. 5. Fresno had wins from Eni Ghidirmic in No. 3 singles over Spencer 3-6, 6-4, 6-2 and Olivier LeJeune at No. 6 winning 6-4, 7-6 over Zaman. Lindstedt bested Patrick Gottesleben 6-4, 3-6, 6-4 to win at second singles. Said Peter Smith to the *Las Vegas Sun*, "Getting that first point was huge for us because so many of the singles matches figured to be close."

USC finished No. 15th nationally and Stanford, seeded No. 3, won its third national title in a row beating the University of Georgia 4-0 in the final at UCLA. While Stanford lost three of its top players, they had recruited some very good freshmen — including Mike and Bob Bryan from Camarillo, California.

Despite the disappointment of the team tournament, two bright spots occurred for the Trojans. Unseeded Bastl reached the NCAA singles final, losing to UNLV's Luke Smith 6-4, 6-3, and Bastl and Spencer teamed up to reach the doubles final, falling to the Rebels' team of Smith and Tim Blenkiron 6-4, 6-4.

Despite the poor finish in 1997, the Trojans were optimistic as they entered the 1998 season. Three All-Americans, Bastl, Spencer and Fernando Samayoa all returned, as did All Pac-10 first-team player Patrick Gottesleben, the No. 2 singles player from Germany. The team also consisted of junior Scott Willinski (Jamaica's No. 1 player); and sophomores Akram Zaman from Australia and Ryan Hollis. Three new players, Roman Kukal, No. 4 ranked junior doubles player in the world Jordan Walker from Canada, and German Christoph Poehler joined the team. The Trojans finished second in the Pac-10 with a 5-2 record and 17-7 overall.

At the NCAA Championships, which were once again held at Georgia, Stanford beat Georgia for the second straight year in the finals 4-0 with the Cardinal team consisting of Bob

Bryan, Mike Bryan, Paul Goldstein, Geoff Abrams, Ryan Wolters and Charles Hoeveler considered one of the best collegiate teams ever. The team finished with a 28-0 record and only lost three individual matches the entire dual-match season. "It will flat-out never happen again. It won't even come close to happening again. This is the best team I've ever had," Stanford coach Dick Gould told the *Stanford Daily*. With its fourth straight NCAA team title, Stanford joined the USC team from 1966-1969 under Coach George Toley as the only two teams to register an NCAA "Four Peat."

Cardinal Bob Bryan captured the rare NCAA triple crown by winning the team, singles and doubles championships. He beat USC's Bastl, 6-3, 7-6 (5) in the quarterfinals and teammate Goldstein 6-3, 6-2 in the final. Bryan and twin brother Mike won the doubles title, beating Pepperdine's Kelly Gullett and Robert Lindstedt 6-7 (6), 6-2, 6-4. Peter Smith, who had moved from Fresno State to Pepperdine, coached Gullett and Lindstedt. The Bryans became the first brothers to win the NCAA doubles title since Robert and Tom Falkenburg of USC did so in 1946 and went on to become one of the greatest doubles teams of all time.

At the beginning of 1999 season, Kyle Spencer, Fernando Samayoa and George Bastl graduated. Bastl went on to register one of the biggest upsets in Wimbledon history when he defeated seven-time champion Pete Sampras in the second round in 2002 6-3, 6-2, 4-6, 3-6, 6-4. It was the last ever match for Sampras at Wimbledon.

While Dick Leach was concerned with the turnover, he was looking forward to a very successful freshman class led by Andrew Park, the reigning USTA National Boys' 18 champion from San Marino, transfer Greg Hill, the No. 4 player from University of North Carolina, CIF Southern Section Player of the

Year Ryan Moore from Fullerton, and Nick Rainey, a graduate of the well-known Weil Tennis Academy in Ojai, California, who had won the USTA junior international grass court singles title in Philadelphia. Returning were Patrick Gottesleben, Roman Kual, Scott Willinski and Scott Merryman. The team had a 19-5 record and placed third in the Pac-10 conference.

"When deciding on colleges I had two great choices— USC or Stanford," said Park. "Both had great tennis coaches in Dick Gould and Dick Leach, as well as very strong tennis histories and academics. Growing up, my parents had always emphasized the importance of academics. My ultimate career goal was to become a physician, so when I learned that I was accepted into a combined baccalaureate/MD program at USC, that sold me."

The Trojans got off to a great start and were performing very well, despite having no All-Americans on the team. Andrew Park was playing with great confidence, and Ryan Moore surpassed expectations with a 7-0 record in singles and an 8-0 record—and No. 12 ranking nationwide—in doubles with partner Nick Rainey. But, in mid-February, Moore suffered a compression of a disk in his back resulting in severe pain in both hips. The injury sidelined him for the entire season and Coach Leach had to scramble to redo the doubles line-up with Scott Willinski filling in for Moore. By mid-April, the team was still doing very well, at 17-3 overall, and 4-1 in the Pac-10 conference.

The surprise of the season was Willinski's performance. After three years of undistinguished seasons at USC, Willinski played a critical role in many matches, including a victory over Arizona State that clinched the 1,000th team victory in Trojan tennis history. Leach told the *Daily Trojan*, "Scott's play has been totally unexpected. Who knows what would have happened this year if he hadn't performed the way he has."

USC entered the 1999 NCAAs ranked No. 15 and in the round of 16 faced Pepperdine. Coach Peter Smith had moved from Fresno State to Pepperdine and was now head coach of the Waves. Pepperdine took the doubles point and three singles matches to win the match 4-1. The Trojans' only win came at first singles when Patrick Gottesleben defeated Peter Luczak 6-0, 7-5. Peter Smith had now beaten SC in the NCAA tournament with two different teams.

Georgia won its third NCAA title, the first under coach Manny Diaz, beating UCLA 4-3 in the final. This was the third time they had beaten the Bruins in the national final, winning 5-1 in both 1985 and 1987.

The Trojan duo of Gottesleben and Kukal made it to the NCAA doubles semifinals, losing to Nenad Toroman and Gareth Williams from the University of Tulsa 6-2, 6-3. K.J. Hippensteel and Ryan Wolters from Stanford beat Toroman and Williams in straight sets to win the NCAA doubles title. Jeff Morrison, the No. 2 seed from the University of Florida, won the singles title upsetting top-seeded James Blake from Harvard 7-6 (2), 2-6, 6-4. At year's end, USC was ranked No. 17.

The Trojans began the 2000 season ranked No. 11. Returning to the team were sophomores Andrew Park, Nick Rainey, Scott Merryman and Ryan Moore, juniors Roman Kukal and Gregg Hill and senior Patrick Gottelseleben. Two freshman joined the team, Parker Collins from Newport Beach and Daniel Langre from Mexico City. Assistant coach Glenn Michibata was named to the head coaching job at Princeton and left SC. Rick Leach stepped in as assistant coach for one season. Langre had the best record of the year going 23-6 overall playing at No. 4 or No. 5 singles. The team had an 18-9 record overall and went 5-2 in the conference placing third in the Pac-10.

In the NCAAs, USC upset Fresno State, the No. 13 seed, 4-1 in the second round but lost in the round of 16 to No. 3 seed Florida 4-1. The Trojans won the first set in four of six matches and things were looking good. Unfortunately, sophomore Ryan Moore's win at No. 3 singles over Nathan Overholser 6-2, 6-3 was the only victory for the Trojans. "Our team came out there and played hard," said Dick Leach. "I think the key came early when we fell behind in doubles to them. We played well in the early sets and had some chances at the beginning of some of the matchups, but Florida did a very good job of out-playing us in the second and third sets of those matches." The team finished the season again ranked No. 17.

Stanford won the NCAA team title again defeating Virginia Commonwealth University 4-0 at the University of Georgia.

In the individual tournament, Stanford's Alex Kim beat Kentucky's Carlos Drada 6-1, 6-1 to take the singles title. Nick Rainey and Ryan Moore had the hallmark achievement for the Trojans for the year in doubles, reaching the NCAA doubles final only to lose to Graydon Oliver and Carey Franklin from Illinois 6-4, 6-2.

In 2001, junior standouts Andrew Park, Nick Rainey, Ryan Moore returned to the team as did sophomore Parker Collins. Daniel Langre, one of the top four players, tore his ACL and was out for the entire season. Fortunately, the team received a boost when two strong freshmen, Ruben Torres from Cali, Colombia and Damien Spizzo from Melbourne, joined the team. The team did not have a particularly strong season with a 15-9 record overall, tying for fourth place in the Pac-10.

Andrew Park was a key member of USC's 2002 NCAA
Championship team

At the NCAAs, USC traveled to the University of
Mississippi in Oxford, Mississippi to play in the first and
second round matches and started out strong with a 4-0 win
over Virginia. Rainey and Moore set the tone by knocking off
top seeds Brian Vahaly and Huntley Montgomery 8-5 to clinch
the doubles point. Ruben Torres beat Brian Hunter 6-1, 6-1 at
No. 5 and Nick Rainey dominated Mike Duquette at No. 4,
6-4, 6-1. Damien Spizzo clinched the match, taking out Tommy
Croker 6-3, 6-3 at No. 3.

In the second round, the Trojans faced ninth-ranked Ole
Miss. The score was tied up at three matches apiece as Ruben
Torres, who had won the first set, started his second set on court
five against Ole Miss Rebel Paul Ciorascu. Torres came into the

match with a 12-1 record at No. 5 singles. At 5-5 Torres broke to go ahead 6-5, but Ciorascu broke back to force a tiebreaker. After being down 4-1 in the tiebreaker, Ciorascu regained a 6-5 lead, but Torres would win the next two points to clinch the match and the 4-3 win for USC in a big upset over Ole Miss on their home turf. To celebrate the Trojan victory, Coach Leach left USC logo balls on the Ole Miss courts as a memento for their practices the next day.

In the round of 16, held at the University of Georgia, the Trojans faced Texas Christian University, who beat the Trojans 4-2, despite Andrew Park's win over Esteben Carril 7-5, 1-6, 6-1 at No. 1 singles. The Trojans finished the year ranked No. 20.

Georgia won its fourth national title beating the University of Tennessee 4-1 in the final. Top Bulldog Matias Boeker won the NCAA triple crown by also winning the singles title, beating Brian Vahaly of Virginia, 6-2, 6-4, and the doubles title with Travis Parrott, beating Johan Brunstrom and John Wallmark from SMU 6-4, 7-5.

The 2002 Trojan team had one of the deepest benches that Dick Leach can remember, "All the good teams have seven or eight solid players and a decent amount of experience," said Leach. "This is the first time in a long time where I've actually had seven players who are experienced at this level and I am excited."

Returning to the team were seniors Andrew Park, Nick Rainey, Ryan Moore, Damien Spizzo, Ruben Torres and Daniel Langre. Prakash Amritraj, a top junior player, joined the team while five other players, Christian Jensen, Garret Wong, Jeff Karzrian, walk-on Teige Sullivan and Daniel Tontz, rounded out the team.

"I started playing tennis when I could walk," said Prakash Amritraj. "My father, Vijay Amritraj, was a famous name on the worldwide professional tour in the 70s and 80s, so I grew up around the game. I have pictures of Jimmy Connors and Boris Becker holding me when I was in diapers. When I was nine-and-a-half, in the summer of 1993, I found myself sitting in the champions locker room at Wimbledon—between Boris Becker and Pete Sampras—and in that moment I knew what I wanted to do. I came to USC because of its amazing history. So many great professionals came out of SC. Also, I wanted to be coached by Dick Leach who had worked with so many of these players. And I was an LA boy, so I wanted to be close to my father who had such a big impact on my game."

Despite the strong team at the start of the season, Coach Leach was finding it hard to keep his own momentum. "In 2002, my diabetes was getting worse and I had to start using insulin," he said. "I grew very tired in the afternoons. I had a defining moment. We were playing Stanford the first week of April. My old Arcadia High School tennis coach Ray Pascoe, a Stanford graduate, came to see the match, as he had ever since I started coaching the team in 1980. Before the match started he came down to the fence and asked me when I was going to get out of this nerve-wracking business. I asked him how I would know when it was time to retire as I hadn't really thought much about it. Coach Pascoe said these simple, profound words, 'You will know.'"

The Trojans won a close match and then two weeks later traveled to the Farm for a rematch. Leach did not foresee that this would be the most dramatic match in his 22 years of coaching. "My daughter, Mindy, who played tennis for Minnesota and Alabama, came to watch with her family," he said. "We were down early and then caught up to 3-3. At No. 2 singles, Scott Lipsky from Stanford and Ryan Moore for the Trojans were playing the deciding match." Earlier in the season, Lipsky had defeated Moore 6-1, 6-2 at the Indoors in Kentucky. During this match, Moore lost the first set and started to cramp in the second. Leach told him that he could default and the team could all go home. Moore told him, "No way!" and somehow rallied to win the second set. Said Leach, "I didn't see much hope for him in the third. He was hurt. But Ryan was determined, so I told him just to go for winners since he wasn't able to run well especially during the long rallies. Remarkably, Ryan went up 6-5 in the third and needed to hold serve to win the match. He was fighting, 'like a Trojan.' After the changeover, the cramps took over and Moore's legs completely gave out. He double faulted three times in a row and lost the game to go into the third-set tiebreaker.

"What happened next was even more bizarre. Dick Gould, in my opinion, the greatest college tennis coach in history called a time out – something I had never heard of before. Immediately, Brett Hansen, my assistant, helped me put ice where Ryan was cramping."

Moore went back on the court and, amazingly, took the lead 6-4 in the third-set tiebreaker. At stake was one of the greatest points in USC tennis history— match point for his match and for the team win. "I thought he had hit winners on three occasions during that point, basically hobbling on one leg, but Scott Lipsky, a very talented player, ran them all down and then hit a scorching passing shot to win the point. The crowd went crazy! It was now Scott's serve at 5-6 and he had a *big* serve. I guessed he would hit his favorite serve to the backhand corner, and I ran across the court and told Ryan to take that serve away—just as Scott started his service toss. Ryan moved to his left, and guessed correctly, hitting a very hard return that Scott hit into the net." Moore had won the match and USC had defeated a powerful Stanford team for the second time that season.

"Right after the match ended, Mindy came down to the courts and told me that another match like that one might kill me," said Leach. "She knew how nerve-wracking all this was since she was a very accomplished college player. On the flight home I started thinking about retiring. I went to bed around 10pm after a long day and couldn't sleep. I got up and wrote my letter of resignation and then slept like a baby."

The next day, Dick went to see his boss and close friend Daryl Gross, the assistant athletic director at USC. Dick handed Daryl the letter. Gross looked at it and told Dick that he should sleep on it and come back the following day. "I knew nothing was going to change," he said. "It was time for a younger person to take over. I was 62 at that point. The 100-mile-a-day drive to and from Laguna Beach had also taken its toll. I estimated that, after 22 years and nine months, I had driven about 400,000 miles. I owned the 405 Freeway, or maybe it owned me…"

"Two weeks before the NCAA tournament, I had to remove our No. 3 player, Damian Spizzo, for breaking a team rule," said Leach. "Thus, I was short one player and Andrew Park had a sore shoulder and was playing hurt. I was getting very nervous."

Dick met with the team and told them that this would be his last year. He mentioned that the three seniors, Andrew Park, Ryan Moore and Nick Rainey, were three of best recruits he had ever had in the same year and yet they hadn't won an NCAA title together. This was the moment to prove themselves. The team was stunned by Dick's announcement.

"The guys decided to have a team meeting without me and came back to say that they had decided to go all out and train as hard as they could," Leach said. Shortly after that, the team left for the NCAA first and second round regionals in Tulsa for what Leach thought could be the last series of matches in his career at USC.

The four teams in Tulsa were Arkansas, Oral Roberts, Tulsa and USC. "The weather was awful—windy and rainy," Leach said. "Tulsa had a beautiful new indoor facility and after looking at the weather report for the next two days I had a hunch we would be playing Arkansas indoors in the finals. Arkansas played most of its matches indoors during the early season and our only indoor experience was in February at the National Collegiate Indoor Tournament in Kentucky. With this in mind, I asked the Oral Roberts coach if we could play our match indoors, since the weather was so cold and windy outside. He was a good guy and agreed. This gave us the indoor practice for our upcoming match with Arkansas the next day. We beat Oral Roberts 4-0 and then beat Arkansas, who had a very good team, 4-0 as well. Their coach Robert Cox was a good friend of mine and he told me after the match that his team had played very close matches with both Tennessee and Georgia and that USC was just as good. He also said he had never seen a more focused team than ours and wondered how I was able to do this. This got me thinking, I had received the NCAA information about the Sweet Sixteen in College Station, Texas before we had left for Tulsa and had thrown it in my filing cabinet as I thought we would lose in Tulsa."

On his way back to USC, Leach called his good friend Kent DeMars from the University of South Carolina (also known as USC) from the Salt Lake airport and asked him how he did in their regionals. DeMars told Leach that Georgia had beaten them 4-0 that day.

"Since he was on the way home to South Carolina, I asked where the teams were staying in College Station," Leach said. "Kent said the Hilton Hotel was the headquarters for the tournament, but that all the rooms were booked. Then he told me that I was in luck, as he had booked five rooms with double beds under USC (University of South Carolina). He told me that I could have them, since his team had lost. Could things be going any better? All the flights out of LAX to College Station were taken, so I found a flight out of Long Beach. We left for Texas just two days after getting home from Tulsa and a few days before the tournament started to get used to the heat.

"When I arrived at the airport in Long Beach I was dragging my golf clubs along and the team was waiting for me outside on the curb. This was the start of my using a few tricks to get my team motivated. I told them they would probably lose in the first round of the team event and because I had to stay for the individual singles and doubles tournament I thought I would play a few days of golf. They all looked at me and said that they were not going to lose in the first round so I would be keeping the clubs in the bag."

After arriving in College Station, the team checked into the Hilton Hotel under "USC."

"The hotel staff never questioned it!" said Leach. "It was really hot and humid, so I sent Ruben Torres out to buy all of the Pedialyte he could find. Under these conditions, I would mix the Pedialyte (an oral electrolyte solution) with Gatorade to help prevent dehydration and replace electrolytes and this would reduce cramping."

Said Torres with a laugh, recalling his special duty, "Look, if you want to know the truth, I was responsible for our success at the NCAAs! It was May and 120 degrees every day and we were all cramping. So Coach gave me his credit card and asked me go out to buy Pedialyte. I found the only pharmacy in College Station. At first, I was only going to get a few boxes, but then it occurred to me that the other teams might need Pedialyte as well. I asked the pharmacist how many boxes he had. He told me ten boxes—that was it. So...I bought them all. To this day, Coach and I laugh about my Pedialyte sweep. We were the only guys in the tournament who had this stuff. In the final, I saw the Georgia manager scrambling to mix powdered Gatorade with water and I just grinned."

The team practiced hard for two days in anticipation of playing Baylor in their round of 16 match. Baylor had lost only one match the entire year and had four German players who were very good, all of who played in the top-level German *Bundesliga* (team leagues). Baylor's top player, Benjamin Becker, (who later won the NCAA singles championship in 2004 and defeated Andre Agassi in his last match at the U.S. Open in 2006) was their star.

Park faced Becker at No. 1 singles and, to prep for the match-up, Leach asked other coaches about Becker's weaknesses. "Every coach I asked would think and then say, 'He doesn't have any,'" said Leach.

South Carolina's DeMars told Leach that sometimes Becker appeared bored during a match because tennis came so easily to him. This was the key Leach needed. He asked Park if he could remember his matches in the 14-and-unders when he would hit higher, off-speed balls to wear out his opponent. He told Park that he had to try different strategies on Becker and attempt to bore him with long rallies. If Becker got complacent, he might start coming to the net, and then Park, who had the best passing shots in the country, could pass him. At 5-5 all in the first set, Becker did indeed lose patience and Park quickly finished him off 7-5, 6-3.

"I remember returning serve very well that day," Park said. "I also hit a lot of angles and tried to slow down the pace with a few high balls. At the time, I believed that I had to win in order our team to win. I was glad I could play Becker before he peaked in his professional career! This was the biggest win of my collegiate tennis career."

USC handed Baylor only its second loss of the year in a 4-2 upset win to move into the quarterfinals.

Said Prakash Amritraj, "I remember playing in the round of 16 against Baylor. I lost my match against one of the German players and I was quite upset. At dinner, Coach Leach told me, 'That's the beauty of college tennis, you can have a bad day and your team can get through, and you have another chance to put the team on your shoulders tomorrow.' That made me feel great after having a tough loss and spurred me on."

The Trojans next faced a very good Illinois team that was seeded No. 3. USC lost the doubles point, but won at No.'s 3, 4, 5 and 6 singles and advanced into the semifinals against Tennessee with another 4-2 upset win. After the victory, once again, the team struck a wager with their coach.

"After the match we had a team meeting and the team asked me to dye my hair Cardinal if we beat Tennessee in the next round for the finals," Leach said. "Naturally, I said, 'Sure.'"

Tennessee had won the SEC Conference title defeating No. 1 seed Georgia. USC lost the doubles point again, putting pressure on to win four of the six singles matches. In the end, it all came down to No. 5 singles with Daniel Langre playing Tennessee's Simon Rea, a big lefty with a strong game. After a long battle, Langre was up 5-4, 40-30—match point for USC to make it into the finals. Rea surprised Langre by serving and volleying to fight off the match point to hold serve. As they entered a third-set tiebreaker that would decide which team would advance to the final, Langre started to cramp. Leach told him try to hide his cramps from his opponent and to get to the net on every point. He also reminded Langre that every time he came in on Rea's backhand, Rea hit his passing shot crosscourt.

"I also told Daniel that if Rea hit another backhand crosscourt passing shot by him I would never speak to him again," laughed Leach.

At 8-7, match point for USC, Langre hit an approach shot to Rea's backhand. Rea hit his passing shot crosscourt, Langre guessed right, covered the shot, and put the volley away to put USC, the 11th-seeded team, into the finals.

Amritraj said he had vivid memories of his singles match victory over Tennessee's Adam Carey with a unique source of inspiration.

"Tennessee's coach, Michael Fancutt, had recruited me very hard," said Amritraj. "He loved my work ethic and he loved serve and volleyers. Carey was coming into the match with a very long winning streak. In the third set, all the other matches had finished and I found myself playing against an opponent who was playing the best tennis of his life. I kept hearing Fancutt yelling to Carey, 'Keep him at the baseline! Don't let him get to the net!' Adam was playing out of fear; fear of me coming in. I used that to fuel me and just kept net rushing as my instincts always told me to do. It was during this match that Nick Rainey and the other boys really got behind the cheering as well. I had just watched Muhammad Ali's *When We Were Kings* documentary, which is still one of my most favorite films. My teammates kept yelling 'Prakash Bomaye' (The same Lingala chant Ali received in Zaire against Foreman meaning 'Ali kill him') while I was out on the court and I won the match 7-6 (5), 3-6, 6-3."

After the victory over Tennessee, Leach stayed at the stadium to watch the other semifinal between UCLA and Georgia.

"I took a lot of notes on both teams as I wasn't sure who would win," Leach said. "Our players knew the UCLA team very well as some had grown up in Southern California together and the great Billy Martin coached them. Georgia was the defending NCAA team champion and had the defending NCAA singles champion Matias Boeker at No. 1."

Georgia won the match 4-3 to set up the final match of Leach's career in the NCAA team tournament final.

"After dinner, I had the team up to my room at the Hilton to go over each player's game plan," said Leach. "I always gave them plan A and plan B, in case plan A wasn't working. After going over everyone's singles opponents I didn't say anything for over a minute. I just stared at the team. When I finally broke the silence, I said, 'I'm going to change the doubles teams for tomorrow's final match.' Of course this is unheard of at this time of year, but it was another of my ways of getting the team's blood boiling. Everyone looked at me like 'You are going to do WHAT?!' I told them all the other coaches have been asking me why our doubles play was so bad; they wanted to know if I had stopped coaching doubles. I told the team that we had to win the doubles point and then I pulled out my notes showing that over the course of the year, every time Georgia won the doubles point they had won 25 matches and lost none! In other words if we were going to win we had to make sure that Georgia did not win the doubles point. I then pointed out to every player what they were doing wrong. I also mentioned what they must do tomorrow to have any chance if they wanted to win their doubles matches."

Leach had a feeling his strategy might work. He was never planning to change the teams but he had to get the team agitated. He remembered Andrew Park coming to him, asking if they could have one more chance to keep the teams as they were. "Park told me that they wanted to show me what they could do," Leach said. "I didn't answer for about 15 seconds and then said, 'Okay.' The players all looked relieved. Then, they reminded me that I would have to dye my hair Cardinal for the final.

"Little did they know that my wife Sandy had already gone out and purchased some Cardinal-colored hair dye and later that evening she dyed my hair—did I ever look stupid. Our final was scheduled for 3 p.m. the next day. In the morning, Andrew called my room and said the team was ready to dye my hair for the match. I put on my USC cap and went down to meet them. When I met up with the team, I took off my hat and they team went crazy. They were having so much fun and were very relaxed."

Leach had another surprise to keep the team loose. In the A&M bookstore Sandy Leach had noticed the "12th Man" T-shirts. The "12th Man" is a regular student at Texas A&M who has the opportunity to play on the kick-off team. He is really the 11th man on the field, but they call him the 12th Man. If he makes a tackle on the return, the A&M student body goes nuts.

Said Leach, "Before the final, as the teams were warming up I had each player put the '12th Man' shirts over their USC team shirts. The crowd loved it and became USC fans for the final. The NCAA representative, Mark Bockelman, knew you could only wear your school's colors in a match and came looking for me. I knew the rule, too, and decided to hide under the stands. After the crowd saw us in A&M T-shirts, I asked the team to take them off. Mark knew what we were doing and he was not too upset with me. The team was having fun and, since this was my last year at USC, I thought 'What the heck?'"

Leach had to balance keeping the mood light with keeping the team motivated. "That morning, I decided that I had to light another fire under my doubles teams," Leach said.

Said Ruben Torres, "On the day of the big match, while we were driving in the van, Coach turned to me and said that I wouldn't be playing in the lineup because I wasn't listening to him and not playing well enough. He knew I had a hot temper in those days. And at first I thought he was joking."

"I was having a hard time getting Ruben to do what I wanted," said Leach. "For instance, when someone is playing the deuce court in doubles, if the ball is hit hard to the backhand, especially close to the body, the right shot is to hit the return directly at the player at the net, not cross court. Trying to hit an inside out backhand is a tough shot. Ruben kept trying to hit the inside-out backhand without much success. Also, on a short lob, the right shot is to hit the ball right at the person at the net not back to the player in the backcourt. Ruben kept hitting the ball to the backcourt player and the point would start again. Thus, the advantage would be lost. So I told Ruben these things."

Said Torres, "During the rest of the ride, Coach was telling me all that I was doing wrong. After we got out of the van, I realized that he wasn't joking about my not playing and my blood started to boil. I told him he was getting old, that he didn't know what he was doing. But he just walked away."

Everyone was stunned. Torres went over to talk with assistant coach Brett Hansen, who came to Leach telling him that Torres could do the job.

Ruben Torres, 2002 NCAA National Championship Team

"Coach let me stew and then came walking back," Torres said. "I started to protest again, getting louder and louder. Finally, he said, 'All right, Colombia, you are in the lineup.'"

To Leach's satisfaction, Torres went into the match like a man on a mission and Leach had to hope his strategy had worked.

"Remember, we were only seeded 11th, and in many ways we were not that good," said Leach. "I had to think of ways to motivate the team. My 'rejuvenated' doubles teams were really fired up when they took the courts, but I still I didn't know what to expect.

"Since Andrew Park had a sore shoulder, I kept him out of the doubles and substituted Teige Sullivan. Our No. 2 team of Sullivan and Torres was really ready to play. After every point, when Ruben did what I told him to do, he would look over at me and shake his fist. He was playing between the two other doubles matches and he was yelling, pumping his fist, and spreading his fire to the other courts. Everyone was so pumped up. They won 8-4.

"After the match, I told Ruben that I had always intended to play him, but I am not sure he believed me."

Said Torres, "I still remember how passionate I was during that match. Dick was very smart to do this because it worked. I think I played some of the best tennis of my career that day."

The No. 3 team of Langre and Amritraj won 8-3, and USC's No. 1 team of Nick Rainey and Ryan Moore were deadlocked at 6-6 against Bo Hodge and Matias Boeker, but the match was suspended since they had already won the doubles point. Leach's three teams had done everything he had talked about the night before in the hotel room. Leach was elated.

In the singles, USC went up immediately at No.'s 2, 3, 5 and 6 and only had to win three singles matches to win the NCAA title.

Said Leach, "Soon Langre at No. 5 won against Adam Seri 6-4, 6-4 and Torres at No. 6 beat Nicolas Boeker 6-2, 6-2. Prakash Amritraj, our freshman, was having a great tournament—clinching several other matches on the way to the finals. He was playing No. 3 and up 7-6 (3) and 6-5, serving for the championship."

Leach's team was within minutes of their championship goal.

"Prakash was up 40-15 with two match points," said Leach. "He mishit his serve and then double faulted on the first match point. I ran onto the court and told him to hit a high kicker to Bo Hodge's forehand, as his two-handed backhand was his best shot."

Said Amritraj, "I tried to smile it off but then stepped up and served a ball straight down the T to win the match, 7-6 (3), 7-5 and we were the NCAA champions. Right after the last point, I ripped off my shirt and flexed to the crowd—ESPN will never let me forget that moment. I didn't even know they had an MVP award, so when they announced that I had won the award, I was so proud. That proved to be the start of a pivotal summer for me, as it propelled me to my first ATP semifinal at the Los Angeles Open and to the Championship at Kalamazoo the USTA National Junior Championships, a title which earned me a place in the U.S. Open men's singles main draw.

Park said that Leach announcing his retirement before the end of the season was a strong motivation for the team and that every team member stepped up when it most mattered.

"I felt like I was just along for the ride," said Park. "My teammates played so well in the post-season. When we lost the doubles point against Illinois, I am sure Coach thought he was dreaming after we won the four singles matches. Then, we beat Tennessee after the losing the doubles point again. We were so deep on our singles lineup. I would go out there, try to hold my own against some very good players, but I always took comfort knowing that everyone else was matched up so well against our competition. I remember hurting my ankle at some point through the year. That's when Teige Sullivan, a talented walk-on player, filled in for doubles. He and Ruben clicked right away. Teige provided a new energy for their partnership."

In the singles tournament, Nick Rainey had a great win over Benjamin Becker in straight sets 6-2, 6-1 then lost in the quarterfinals to UGA's Matias Boeker 7-5, 6-2. Boeker went on to win the singles title for the second year in a row, besting Kentucky's Jesse Witten 7-5, 6-0. Boeker was the first person to win back-to-back singles titles since fellow Georgia Bulldog Mikael Pernfors did so in 1984-1985. In the doubles final, Andrew Colombo and Mark Kovacs of Auburn beat Stanford's Scott Lipsky and David Martin 6-2, 3-6, 6-2.

The 2002 Trojan team were the lowest seed at No. 11 to ever win the NCAA men's national title. Along the way the team beat six teams, including No. 1 Georgia, No. 2 Tennessee, No. 3 Illinois and No. 6 Baylor. Everything came together. Andrew Park, Ryan Moore and Nick Rainey, thought to be three of the top recruits in 1998 had never been able to get beyond the NCAA Round of 16 in three earlier seasons, but scored key wins to advance the team. Both Daniel Langre and Ruben Torres were stalwarts, never dropping a match throughout the tournament. And the ironman of the tournament was Amritraj, who clinched the wins for Trojans in the quarterfinals, semifinals and in the final.

Said Torres, "To this day, Coach Leach refers to our winning the NCAAs as the eleventh seed as the 'greatest heist in the history of college tennis!'"

Years later, Park summarized the team sentiment following their historic NCAA title.

"Ryan Moore, Nick Rainey and I all came in together, but I never felt that we lived up to our potential for the first three years," he said. "We had some difficult losses and some injuries, but in the end we felt vindicated. I feel very fortunate having played for Coach Leach. It was such a privilege. He kept the game simple and had the ability to convince

Prakash Amritraj clinched the 2002 NCAA title for USC

players to stay focused on the team. I think, with his amount of experience, he was able to figure out how to motivate each individual athlete. As a largely individual sport, tennis tends to foster many type-A personalities. Coach Leach would organize practice to keep things focused on improving as a whole, as opposed to creating an environment where we would be competitive with each other. There was a month where I was struggling at No. 1 and No. 2 singles. Coach had decided to put me at No. 4 singles for a big road trip. The way he worked things, nobody ever thought that was punishment or some type of demotion. I think that takes unique skill. Outside of tennis, Coach Leach is just such a great person. Some of my favorite memories of college tennis are when we were on road trips and just listening to the endless amount of stories he has about tennis. I'm sure I've heard hundred of stories through the years with the each story being funnier than the next."

Said Fernando Samayoa, "Coach Leach's honesty and understanding of his players were undeniable. He had an ability to motivate you and help you understand that getting an education was the most incredible gift you can receive; he was also the best doubles teacher ever. He not only taught us tennis, he taught us but what was important in life. I can say with certainty that he helped me and others become the men we are today. He had an immeasurable, positive impact on my life."

For Leach, the win was truly a family affair. Wife Sandy had been with him since the beginning of the tournament and both of his sons, Rick and Jon, were in the stands for his last match.

"Rick was going to be there anyway since he was getting inducted into the Intercollegiate Hall of Fame at the banquet following the Championship the next evening," said Coach Leach. "Jon was working for JP Morgan in Newport Beach at the time. His boss wouldn't let him leave for one day to watch the final. He finally checked out of the office, saying he was going to see a client and would be back later. He went to John Wayne Airport and took an early morning flight to College Station and arrived to see what was his Dad's last match. I took him to the airport the next morning for a 6:30 a.m. flight. He was back in the office that morning and no one was the wiser."

Dick Leach was awarded the Coach of the Year honors at the NCAA banquet the next night and Rick Leach was inducted into the Collegiate Tennis Hall of Fame.

"I must have looked stupid with my cardinal-red hair," Leach said. "But a bet is a bet. Looking back, I think I was able to create an atmosphere with the team where they were having fun—and just maybe, they were not playing only for an NCAA team championship, but also to send their retiring coach out a winner. It was a Hollywood ending for a wonderful coaching career at USC."

"The next day, I received a call from USC's President Sample congratulating us on being the lowest seed to ever win the tournament," Leach continued. "I appreciated this very much, as I really admired him. About an hour later, I received a call from football coach Pete Carroll. Pete was so excited about our win saying, 'I just want to win my last game and walk off the field being No. 1.' He got his wish in Miami in 2004 when the Trojans beat Oklahoma. I sent Pete a note that day asking him how it felt to finally walk off the field No. 1.

"Even though he accepted my resignation, USC's assistant athletic director, Daryl Gross, asked me to stay on staff to help onboard our new tennis coach Pete Smith. He offered me a stipend for another year if I would be around when needed. Peter was already a very successful coach and certainly didn't need any help coaching the tennis team from me. So I helped him with the newsletters I always sent out to our boosters."

Following the victory, the team was invited to the White House to be welcomed by President George W. Bush.

"The plane ride was unbelievable," said Leach. "The flight attendants announced over the intercom that the USC men's tennis team was on the flight and was going to meet the President. The President had invited all the NCAA champion teams for all the spring sports. After clearing security we were led to the 'Blue Room' and lined up for our group picture with President Bush. When he came into the room it was surreal. He shook hands with everyone and when he came to me, he said he had heard all about our big upset in winning the title. He knew Prakash Amritraj's Dad, too, from meeting him at other social events. During our photo op, President Bush stood between Sandy and me, so guess what photo we used for our Christmas card in 2002? We left the Blue Room for the East Room as a Marine quintet played the USC fight song. In the East Room, we joined with all the NCAA spring championship teams, and the President gave a wonderful ten-minute talk, congratulating all the student athletes and noting the difference they could make back home at their Universities and within their communities. One of the most meaningful parts for me was watching the awed expressions of all the young people in the room."

Dick Leach retired in 2002 after 22 years of coaching the team. His impressive record included four national titles, eight semifinals berths and three quarterfinals appearances. Leach said he not only valued the wins during his tenure, but the competition.

"I really enjoyed coaching at USC," he said. "We had incredible matches with two of the greatest teams to ever play the sport—UCLA and Stanford. I had a great relationship with both UCLA coaches, Glenn Bassett and later Billy Martin. Glenn and I had played against each other many times before our coaching days. And, of course, my dear friend Dick Gould at Stanford and I knew each other going back to junior tennis. Our other big battles were with cross-country-rival University of Georgia. I didn't know Georgia coaches Dan Magill or Manny Diaz before I started coaching. But I came to know them as really good coaches and good guys who fielded many great teams. While we never played them at USC, I must admit that finally winning in Athens in the 1991, 1993 and 2002 finals was very sweet."

8

Peter Smith: Ascendancy of a Championship Tennis Coach

eter Smith's office sits underneath the David X. Marks Tennis Stadium. Everyone can see him though the glass walls. The openness of the office is emblematic of Smith's approach to life and tennis.

Everything is transparent.

If he is in a good mood you know it; if he is not, you know that too. Smith can be disarmingly direct.

His office, part of the larger team room, is littered with rackets, gear, string, trophies, plaques, frisbees, oversized posters of his championship teams and a wide assortment of nuts and energy bars. Two of the people who buoy him up are Phil Siordia, the team's operations manager, who also serves an avuncular role for the players, and Associate Coach Kryzsztof (Kris) Kwinta, a very talented guy who always has a long "to do" list. One minute he is watching a YouTube tennis video, yelling to anyone who will listen, "You've got to see this," the next he is pantomiming to a player how he should hit a particular stroke. There used to be a stringing machine in the team room, but Michael Tang wore it out. Tang, a former player-turned-manager reckons he strung 2,000 rackets over the course of his four years at USC. His claim to fame was that he could string a racket in ten minutes; he was so good that the new stringing room bears his name.

The USC tennis facilities are nothing short of spectacular and commemorate the great achievements of the players and coaches who have contributed to the legacy of the men's and women's tennis teams. Donors have endowed almost every corner of the facility, named the Buntmann Family Tennis Center. There is the Lisa and Douglas Goldman Family Student-Athlete Learning Studio, the Michael Uytengsu Tennis Pavilion, the John and Gil Shea Men's Tennis Suite and the Peter Smith Locker Room, where former players like Kaes Van't Hof, Daniel Nguyen, Bob Lutz, Leonard Lee, Dennis Ralston, Bruce Manson, Chris Lewis, Robert Farah, Robert Van't Hof, Tim Pawsat, Steve Johnson, Stan Smith, Eric Amend and Ruben Torres have endowed every locker. Specific donors, including Phillip Sivolobov, Fritz B. Burns Foundation, Werner Buntmann, George Toley, Art Sanborn, and the Cancro Family have endowed each of the six courts.

Coach Smith was the driving force in getting the new facility built. Pat Haden, the athletic director at the time, didn't need much convincing after Peter took him on a tour of top facilities around the country. What started off as a relatively small renovation blossomed into a multimillion-dollar reboot. The center opened its doors in February of 2016.

The atmosphere in the team room is always lively, with a constant stream of players and visitors coming and going. Some appear to live there. When players first saw the new digs they were in utter disbelief. For years, everyone had gone about their business, accepting that they would train in facilities that had been state of the art in 1972, but 44 years later, had fallen behind the times. Ironically, even with those outdated facilities, the Trojans kept winning—illustrating that plush facilities and amenities aren't a necessary condition for greatness. There are other factors at work.

Even though Smith's new surroundings are spectacular, they do not reflect who he is. He doesn't stand on ceremony and seems uncomfortable when the center of attention. He is accessible to all-comers and only cares about fostering the development of each player's skills while finding ways to build team cohesion. Said Coach Smith, "I'm the luckiest guy in the world. I get paid for doing something I absolutely love."

Smith was born in Rome, Italy in 1964. His parents Evelyn and Ted moved the family to Weatherford, Connecticut shortly after he was born. The youngest of five children growing up in a household full of boys, Smith was a multi-sport athlete: hockey, baseball, football, basketball, soccer, swimming and diving. His brothers began teaching him the game when he was four. He played his first tournament at age 12. "Our driveway was the perfect dimension of a paddle tennis court and so we turned it into one. I used a two-handed backhand, which was very rare at that time. My mom didn't like that. She thought I should hit with one hand."

Yet, other top two-fisted players like champions Jimmy Connors and Chris Evert were already paving the way for what would become the most common way to hit a backhand, "I knew there was something to that two-handed stroke. It felt right to me," said Smith.

In 1977, when Smith was 13, the family moved to San Diego and he began to play at the La Costa Tennis Resort in Carlsbad where Pancho Segura, one of the world's top coaches, was the head pro. In addition to Segura, several other coaches, including Gary Young, who was Segura's stepson, helped Smith as he was coming up the ranks.

"Peter was incredibly curious about every aspect of the game," said Young. "He would hang around the tennis courts and listen to Pancho and me talking about all of our experiences in the sport. He was a very likable kid who wanted to learn everything."

Segura, the "Ecuadorian Guru," had been head pro at La Costa since 1971. For almost 20 years, La Costa was a Mecca of tennis. Great players from Rod Laver and Ken Rosewall to Andre Agassi and Jimmy Connors took the pilgrimage, and they all worked with Pancho at one time or another.

"All of the pros were very nice to me, but Pancho was the key person in my tennis life," said Smith. "Two other very influential people were Glenn Bassett and Dick Gould. I patterned my coaching style after them."

At La Costa, Smith's eyes were opened to another aspect of the game. While Bobby Riggs was well known in Los Angeles for his gambling activities, he also transported his antics to Carlsbad. And like John Shea, Ed Atkinson, Bob Lutz and others before him, Smith soon had first hand experience with Riggs and his reputation as a hustler. Riggs would bet on everything and Smith and Segura often got involved. "As a kid, I played many matches for money and it was an unreal education," said Smith. "Kids don't grow up like that anymore. I remember winning a set of doubles with Pancho for $2,000—a lot of money for a 16-year-old boy."

"Regarding my game, I didn't always know what to make of what Pancho was telling me. I was either going to be the next great player or a piece of crap. Neither of us knew. Was I a serve-and-volley-guy? A baseliner? My ranking in Southern Cal was around 20th—average at best. I grew up losing to a lot of future greats like Michael Chang, Rick Leach, Tim Pawsat, John Letts and Kelly Jones. I was surrounded by great competition but still couldn't figure out my game."

In 1984, Long Beach State gave Smith a $500 scholarship, which covered books and tuition.

"Coach Dan Campbell was a great guy and had a bunch of top So Cal kids on the team," he said. "I practiced constantly and my game really took off there. Dan retired after my sophomore year and Coach Larry Easley took over. He was a great volley coach. He had an 11-year-old student come to practice every Friday. His name? Pete Sampras. I would stay after practice and work in with Pete's lesson. He and I became practice partners and I have many fun memories of playing tennis and golf with him."

"As a young freshman, I grew up a lot at Long Beach State. My best win in college was beating Kelly Jones (who became the No. 1 doubles player in the world in 1992) in singles and doubles and that helped us beat Pepperdine. My teammates were my friends and my coaches. I learned a lot from them and they helped shape me as a coach. The upper classmen always drive a team and they need to be on the same page as the coach. When Larry retired suddenly, I was asked to continue playing while simultaneously coaching. My first team had six former teammates of mine on it. I viewed myself as a member of the team who was leading them. And, to this day, I still think that way."

Smith earned a bachelor's degree in Liberal Studies from Long Beach in 1987 and was a four-year letter winner for the 49ers. He played the satellite and challenger tours in 1987 and the qualifying rounds of the U.S. Open and Wimbledon that year.

"I was ranked 360 in the world," he said. "After fifteen months, I went back to get my degree and probably would have kept on playing, but Long Beach State offered me the coach's job."

Smith went back to Long Beach and became the youngest Division I men's tennis head coach at age 23, serving as the 49ers' head coach for four years from 1988 to 1991.

After Long Beach State, Smith took the coaching job at Fresno State and then moved again in 1997 to Pepperdine to coach the Waves. Smith was successful with every move and is the only men's coach to take four different men's teams to top-25 national rankings.

In 2002, Smith was offered the head coach job at USC. "There was no real interview," he said. "I knew that questions were being asked about me and then one day, I got a call and was offered the job."

Smith was chosen because of his strong credentials. Over the previous five years at Pepperdine, he had amassed a dual match record of 118-31 (79.2%), and was chosen as the West Coast Conference Coach of the Year for five years in a row in addition to winning many other awards. Said USC Athletic Director Darryl Gross in 2003, "We are very fortunate to have someone of this caliber replace legendary coach Dick Leach. Peter Smith is one of the best coaches in the country and he will keep the Trojan tennis tradition alive. He is an incredible teacher and motivator. It's just a perfect fit at USC. We couldn't be more pleased."

For Smith, coming to USC was a challenge, given the history and expectations of the program. Dick Leach had just completed his 22nd year at USC and had won his fourth NCAA team title. With the legacy of USC tennis and the knowledge that all coaches at USC were always under performance pressure, Smith knew he had a lot to live up to. At the same time, two of his teams, Fresno State in 1998 and Pepperdine in 1999, had beaten the Trojans in the NCAA tournament. He was clearly up to the challenge.

"I had a mixed welcome when I came to USC," he said. "Some former and current players welcomed me, but there were others who weren't sure about whether I was the right guy for the job. No one really said anything negative to me—it was just a feeling that I had. When I was hired, I had a lot of success, but not USC-level success. I always said that if a state school kid like me could get hired at USC, anything is possible. People weren't sure what to make of me. Let's be honest, I didn't have the playing credentials associated with USC. I felt very confident, but at that point, I really didn't think I had the necessary skills to win an NCAA Championship."

Hiring Smith as coach definitely broke the tradition of bringing back former Trojan players. The three previous long-term coaches, Harold Godshall, George Toley and Dick Leach, were all strong Trojan players who returned to coach.

After Leach retired, Athletic Director Mike Garrett sought advice for SC's next tennis coach from Ruben Torres. Torres opined that, without question, it should be Peter Smith since he had played with some of the guys on Pepperdine's team and saw how they had improved significantly under Smith's tutelage.

Smith was offered the job but initially turned it down. Puzzled, Torres paid Smith a visit. "It was late July and I jumped into my beat-up car and drove to Malibu to talk with Peter," said Torres. "I had my 2002 NCAA Championship ring tucked inside my pocket. Peter told me, 'Why would I leave Pepperdine? Tammie and I like our house, the views are stunning, the schools are convenient and the kids love it.' As he was talking, I pulled out my ring and told him 'Because USC is the place where you will get one of these.' A week later he took the job—and then, to my chagrin, two years later, in 2006, Pepperdine won the NCAA team title."

Smith's first season proved challenging. Andrew Park, Nick Rainey and Ryan Moore had graduated and Teige Sullivan decided to focus on academics and left the team. Returning were Prakash Amritraj, Ruben Torres and Daniel Langre. New players included Johan Berg, a talented Swede who transferred from Pepperdine, redshirted junior Parker Collins from Newport Beach (a guy who Torres characterized as, "the best looking guy to ever play for USC. He left Brad Pitt in the dust"), redshirted freshman Jeff Karzarian, Scott Patterson, a junior transfer from Glendale Junior College, Brian Wright, a sophomore transfer from Fresno, freshman Sumil Menon (Sashi Menon's son) from San Juan Capistrano, Whit Livingston from Sacramento, Aaron Badart from San Marino and redshirted freshman Daniel Tontz from San Diego. Brett Hansen started his second year as assistant coach and Jefferson Hammond joined him as volunteer assistant coach.

By his estimation, Smith got off to a good start, ending the 2003 season ranked No. 22 in the nation with a 14-12 record and tied with the University of Washington for sixth place in the Pac-10. In the first round of the NCAA tournament, SC beat UC-Santa Barbara 4-0 but lost to UCLA in the second round. Top players Amritraj and Langre lost in the first round of the doubles, ending the season ranked No. 35. Amritraj lost in the first round of singles and was ranked No. 46 at season's end.

The University of Illinois had an outstanding season in 2003, winning its first team championship beating Vanderbilt 4-3 in the final. Illinois player Amer Delic also bested Benedikt Dorsch of Baylor in straight sets to win the singles title while teammates Rajeev Ram and Brian Wilson beat San Diego State's Oliver Maiberger and Ryan Redondo for the doubles title 6-4, 5-7, 6-1.

"I learned from my failures and the team's failures," said Smith of his first season as USC's coach. "When the team loses, it is 100% my fault. I always believe that. There is always something that I could have done a bit better. I'm never going to blame my players. I am hired to recruit the players, train them and coach them. When they fall short, it is my fault. The first year I was hired we finished 21st in the nation and let me tell you all of us thought we had overachieved. This was a rebuilding year for us and I thought we did very well."

In 2004, Kyle Spencer entered his first season as assistant coach. Spencer was an All-American at USC (1995-1998) and a former Olympian for Great Britain. Joining the team were Jamil Al-Agba, a freshman from Camarillo, California and one of the top junior recruits in the country who possessed one of the best down-the-line backhands in the country; Drew Hoskins, a junior transfer from the University of Texas; Adriano Biasella, a senior from Rome, Italy; and Adam Loucks from Irvine, California. The team started the year ranked No. 4 and had a very successful season going

23-4 overall and tied for first place in the Pac-10 with a 6-1 record. Biasella got to the final of the Pac-10 championship only to lose to Sam Warburg of Stanford 7-6, 6-3.

The Trojans entered the NCAA Championship seeded No. 2 and beat Arkansas 4-1 in the round of 16 and then blanked Stanford 4-0 in the quarterfinals. Even though Smith's previous teams at other universities had made it to five quarterfinals, this campaign marked the first time that Smith guided a team into the semifinals.

"I think our team gained confidence in late February of 2004 when we played Baylor at home," said Drew Hoskins. "The Bears were ranked third in the country and had a very talented team that included powerhouses Benedikt Dorsch and Benjamin Becker. We were ranked 13th. Daniel Langre and I upset the No. 32-ranked team of Deutsch and Ivor Lovrak 9-8 (7) to win the doubles point. Johan Berg, who was playing 3rd singles, beat Matias Marin 6-4, 7-6 (1) to clinch the match for us 4-3."

In the semifinals, SC thought they stood a good chance against Baylor, based on their earlier win, but the Bears got their revenge by winning the doubles point and taking three singles matches to win 4-0 before a hometown crowd in Waco. Said Hoskins, "We lost at No.'s 1, 3 and 4 but were definitely in the other three matches when they were suspended. In the end, I think that both teams were evenly matched, but we played better mid-season and they ramped it up in the tournament."

Baylor went on to beat UCLA 4-0 for the championship. The USC-Baylor contests in 2004 illustrate just how closely matched many of these college teams are. Sometimes, a home court advantage, game-day jitters or a few points, one way or another, can turn a match in one team's favor. Given the equal physical talents of the teams, it is these psychological factors that help to heighten the drama and excitement of college tennis.

Baylor's Benjamin Becker won the singles title defeating Tulane's Michael Kogan 6-4, 7-6(8). Sam Warburg and KC Corkery from Stanford beat Bo Hodge and 6'10" and future pro star John Isner from Georgia 6-2, 6-7(3), 6-4 to win the doubles title.

"In 2004, I thought we were good enough to win the NCAAs," said Smith. "Looking back on it, I didn't have the necessary experience to take the team over the hump."

The season ended on some bright notes, though, when Ruben Torres won the Pac-10 award for the outstanding male athlete at USC and Coach Smith was voted Pac-10 Coach of the Year.

In 2005, seniors Torres, Langre and Biasella graduated. Returning were seniors Johan Berg and Drew Hoskins, juniors Jeff Kazarian, Whit Livingston and Brian Wright, sophomores Jamil Al-Agba, Aaron Badart and redshirted freshman Bruce Aiken from West Hills, California returned to the team. The only new freshman was Kaes Van't Hof, the son of USC great Robert Van't Hof, from Newport Beach, California. Kaes was ranked No. 4 in the USTA national junior rankings and had won numerous accolades at Mater Dei High School in Santa Ana, including the *Los Angeles Times* Player of the Year in 2004 by compiling a 43-1 record as a senior. Kyle Spencer continued as assistant coach, joined by volunteer assistant coach Brett Masi, who had coached previously at Santa Clara and was a four-year letter winner at Cal Poly San Luis Obispo.

"I started playing tennis against the wall when I was 3 or 4 years old." Van't Hof said. "My dad, Robert Van't Hof, who won the NCAA singles title in 1980, always encouraged me and as early as I can remember, I had a tennis racket in my hand. My first tennis memories are going to the local park and simply playing against the wall for hours. My grandmother always said, 'The wall never misses.' Both of my parents went to USC, so it was always the logical destination for me, although it didn't seem that way when I was growing up. For most of my early tennis life, I idolized the great Dick Gould at Stanford and his teams of the 1990s. I went to Stanford tennis camp for three or four summers and liked the school as well. But, during my junior year in high school, I got to know Peter Smith and the USC team. During my recruiting trip as a senior in high school, I was completely hooked and committed to USC on the spot."

The Trojans began the season ranked No. 8 in the country in the pre-season poll, but entered the NCAA tournament ranked 21st. The highlight of the year was an upset of No. 4 UCLA. In the first round of the NCAAs, the Trojans beat SMU 4-1, but then fell to No. 12 Washington, 4-3. The match was tied at 3-3 when Washington's Alex Slovic overcame Johan Berg 7-5 in the third set.

In the NCAA team final, No. 7 seed UCLA was down 0-3 in the match, but came back to beat No. 1 seed Baylor 4-3 and avenging their loss to the Bears in the previous year's final. Kris Kwinta, playing No. 3 singles, clinched the match for the Bruins, beating Lars Poerschke 4-6, 6-4, 6-4. The win, the first national title for coach Billy Martin, also snapped Baylor's 57-match winning streak, the longest in NCAA tennis history. In the singles tournament, Jamil Al Ag-ba lost in the second round to top seed Benedikt Dorsch of Baylor 6-4, 6-0. Al Ag-ba was named an ITA All-American, the first on the Trojan squad since 2002. In the NCAA singles final, Dorsch beat Pierrik Ysern of San Diego State 6-2, 7-6 (6).

Kaes Van't Hof, the NCAA doubles champion in 2008 with Robert Farah, serves against the backdrop of the David X. Marks scoreboard

USC's Al Ag-ba and Berg teamed up for the doubles tournament losing in the round of 16 to Harvard's Jonathan Chu and Ashwin Kumar in three sets. In the doubles final, John Isner and Alex Ruiz of Georgia beat LSU's Mark Growcott and Ken Scupski, 7-6 (4), 7-5.

In 2006, most of the team returned, except for Johan Berg and Drew Hoskins, who both graduated. Joining the Trojans were Garrett Snyder, a junior transfer from the University of Texas, Nathan Stadler who served as a team manager his freshman year, freshman Carlos Salmon from Greenwich, Connecticut and Chong Wang from Houston. Brett Masi, who was the volunteer assistant coach in 2005, took over assistant coaching responsibilities.

The 2006 season was almost Smith's undoing with the team posting a dismal 8-14 record.

"We had a great team but terrible outcomes," said Smith. "We had match points on the best team in the country (Virginia) at home, but we lost nine matches 4-3 and even though our doubles teams were great, we couldn't win that last point to take the match."

The team's performance wasn't even good enough to garner a spot at the NCAAs and the Trojans finished the season at No. 54. Smith knew that things had to change significantly.

"I thought that things went well during my first two years," he said. "We didn't have a very good team the first year, but we were still ranked 22nd in the country. The following year we made it to the semifinals of the NCAAs. In the third and fourth years, though, we really struggled, and in 2006 we didn't even make it to the tournament. I think I made some recruiting mistakes and people were questioning me. I felt hurt because I wasn't a rookie—I had done this for a long time already. But in sports, everyone wants to know 'What have you done for me lately?' and people have a really short memory."

In 2006, Pepperdine, Smith's former team won the NCAA team tournament beating the University of Georgia 4-2 at the Taube Tennis Center at Stanford. In the singles tournament, UCLA's Benjamin Kohlloeffel overcame Virginia's Somdev Devvarman 6-1, 6-4 to become the first NCAA singles champion from UCLA since his coach Billy Martin in 1975. In the doubles championship, Kevin Anderson and Ryan Rowe of Illinois beat Andre Begemann and Scott Doerner of Pepperdine 6-2, 6-4.

"When I came in I was a confident young coach," said Smith. "I was brash. I thought 'If I can do this at Fresno and Pepperdine, I could kill it here.' For those coaches who have won NCAA championships and big matches, they know that in every match there is that one moment when you must give confidence to the players and call the right play. At the end of the day, talent doesn't win, character wins, and I had to learn that. At other schools, I was used to having players come to play for me. But USC was much bigger than Peter Smith, and recruits came to play for USC, not me. Everyone thinks it's going to be easier than it is. It's not easy to win at USC. It's easy to be good, but not easy to win. The standard that was set at USC in every sport in the 1960's was unrealistic. It's very hard to keep up with the expectations that were set then. College athletics have changed so much in 50 years.

"After the worst season we ever had, I did some major soul-searching," Smith continued. "I knew I had to become a different kind of coach. I had to be able to truly inspire the team, create unity and train them in a way I hadn't before. I needed a totally new game plan."

Said Kaes Van't Hof, "I think the 2006 season was the experience that turned Peter into the coach he is today. As everyone knows the 2006 season was, by most metrics, the worst season in USC tennis history. We had a losing record, were beaten in so many very close matches, missed the NCAAs, and finished 54th. You learn more about your teammates and your coaches in a year like this than you will ever learn in a winning season. After going through every kind of tough loss imaginable, winning is easy, and being on the big stage is almost relaxing. I have noticed how loose Peter's teams are now, and how relaxed he is in the NCAA finals. Other coaches look so nervous they can't deliver. I attribute this ease to both Peter's personality and to going through those tough times just a few years earlier."

Just before the start of the 2007 season, Peter Smith enlisted the help of Sergeant Major Keith Williams of the Marine Corps to help in the team's mental conditioning and leadership. The team went down to Camp Pendleton in San Diego and spent the weekend at the base. "We did a bunch of teamwork and bonding exercises and then Keith offered guidance in various ways—both to individuals and to the team," said assistant coach Brett Masi. "He helped the team understand how they should look at us as coaches and how they should be disciplined in their lifestyles. If we wanted to make changes in the program we all needed to make sacrifices – in other words, make the team more important than oneself."

Smith wanted to create a team mindset that would help the players overcome any obstacle.

"We were fortunate to go down to Camp Pendleton and work on building our team," said Smith. "We participated in parts of basic training and did the Crucible course. The Marines are all about building a team around six people, so we split ourselves into two six-person teams."

The 2007 team lost only person, senior Jeff Kazarian, who graduated. The Trojans added three new freshman players, Robert Farah, a member of Colombia's Davis Cup team, Jason McNaughton from Futures International High School in Oceanside and Gary Sacks from Calabasas High School. Three redshirted freshman also came aboard: Jack Lewis from Palm Springs, Andrew Piotrowski from Ontario, and Abdullah Magdas from Kuwait. The team finished 6-1 in the Pac-10 and finished in second place. Eric Amend, the former four-time All-American who won the 1989 NCAA doubles title with Byron Black, came back to USC as the volunteer assistant coach.

Freshman Robert Farah came to USC at the recommendation of Ruben Torres.

"I was born in Canada, but was raised my whole life in Colombia," said Farah. "In my country we didn't know much about universities in the U.S. and people tend to only know and talk about Harvard because of the movies! Once I decided to go to college, I had a couple of offers from other universities. I was fortunate that one of my good friends, Ruben Torres, who had already gone to USC, talked to me about Coach Smith. Based on Ruben's experiences at SC, I was very excited to join the team. I wanted an experience far from home and I also wanted to immerse myself in a university setting where I had to force myself to speak English. Once I started doing my research about USC, I found out it was one of the best schools in United States in athletics and academics. I felt very fortunate for this great opportunity."

USC started the 2007 season ranked No. 43 in the country. In early February, the Trojans upset No. 19th-ranked Stanford and got off to a flying start by winning 11 matches in a row. By early March, the Trojans moved to No. 9 in the rankings entering their match with their archrivals, the UCLA Bruins, ranked No. 6. The No. 1 and No. 2 doubles teams split victories, and the doubles point was in the hands of freshman Gary Sachs and senior Garrett Snyder. With USC up 7-6, Sachs bombed three aces, leading to a Trojan victory and the doubles point. USC then won five of the six singles matches to beat the Bruins 6-1. Less than a week later, the Georgia Bulldogs, the No. 1 team in the country led by senior standout John Isner, snapped the Trojans winning streak with a lopsided 6-1 victory, with Gary Sacks scoring the only win for USC. Isner's most powerful weapon was his serve, clocked at over 150 mph, leading former Bulldog's coach Dan Magill to label it "Big Bertha."

Robert Farah, the 2008 NCAA doubles champion with Kaes Van't Hof, coils to unleash his forehand

In late April, USC faced UCLA in Westwood where the Bruins continued their home-victory streak against the Men of Troy with a 4-3 victory to take the Pac-10 title. In the Pac-10 singles tournament, freshman Jason McNaughton was victorious over the University of Washington's Derek Drabble, winning the title in three sets.

In the NCAA tournament, the No. 12th-seeded Trojans upset No. 5 Notre Dame 4-3 to reach the quarterfinals, but were eliminated there by Virginia 4-1 with Robert Farah notching the only win for USC. Peter Smith was again voted Pac-10 Coach of the Year.

In the NCAA team final, Georgia blanked the University of Illinois 4-0 with John Isner of Georgia beating Kevin Anderson at No. 1 singles 6-1, 7-6 (1). Isner was the No. 1 seed in the singles tournament but lost to No. 2 seed Somdev Devvarman of Virginia in the final, 7-6 (7), 4-6, 7-6 (2). In the doubles final, Middle Tennessee State's Marco Bom and Andreas Siljestrom beat Anderson and Ryan Rowe of Illinois 4-6, 7-6 (5), 7-6 (4).

In 2008, USC opened with a pre-season ranking of No. 6. Returning were senior Kaes Van't Hof, juniors Abdullah Magdas and Andrew Piortowski, sophomores Gary Sacks and Robert Farah and freshmen Jack Levis from St. Louis, Daniel Gliner from San Francisco, Matt Manasse from Boca Raton and Jaak Poldma from Estonia. Eric Amend returned to USC for his second year as volunteer assistant coach.

In early March, USC had a 9-2 record and was ranked No. 10 when they faced No. 6 UCLA at Westwood. Unfortunately, the Bruins continued their long winning streak against the Trojans at home beating them 5-2. Even though USC lost the doubles point, Farah and Van't Hof won their match for the Trojans at first doubles. Farah and Van't Hof, playing at No. 1 and No. 2, respectively, also registered the only two singles victories.

At the Pac-10 Championships at Ojai, Farah and Van't Hof squared off against each other in the singles final with Van't

Hof winning 6-3, 7-6 (2). The win made Kaes and his father Robert the only father and son duo to win a Pac-10 title, with Robert winning in 1978 and 1980. Farah and Van't Hof then teamed to beat T.J. Bellama and Matt Brooklyn from Arizona State 6-4, 6-4 for the doubles title marking the first time that USC swept both individual Pac-10 titles.

At the NCAA's at Tulsa, USC fell to UCLA in the quarterfinals 4-2. Despite Van't Hof and Farah's victory at first doubles, UCLA's Harel Srugo and Holden Seguso, playing first and second singles, overcame Farah and Van't Hof in singles to reverse the Trojan's fortunes. Poldman, Sacks and Magdas won at No. 3, 4 and 5 singles, respectively, but Piotrowski lost at No. 6. Georgia ended up beating Texas 4-2 for their second team title in a row.

In the singles tournament, Farah got as far as the round of 16 before being beaten by Baylor's Denes Lukacs in straight sets. Somdev Devvarman of Virginia won his second straight NCAA title defeating freshman J.P. Smith from Tennessee 6-3, 6-2 in the final. Devvarman became the fourth player since the early 1950s to win back-to-back singles titles.

Van't Hof and Farah had a great run playing doubles in 2008, and ultimately, their performance in the tournament would serve as a significant turning point for the Trojans in the years to come.

"I have said many times, Kaes set the program up for success," said Smith. "He was a larger than life player and no one realizes the role he played except for me. He had incredible character, a great work ethic and a charismatic personality. He was a true leader and a close friend. In 15 years, no one argued with me more than he did and I called him the defense attorney for the team. However, he also argued on my behalf and had my back when I wasn't there and taught everyone—including me—a lot."

Said Van't Hof, "Working with Peter was great because of the attitude he brought to tennis every day. He understood the process and knew that players didn't necessarily want to practice every day. And, he knew that there were always going to be issues in a team sport composed of individuals who are used to playing for themselves. He channeled all of this by bringing fun to the game. Every practice we always did something fun besides hit crosscourt backhands for two hours. We played ultimate football, ultimate frisbee, soccer and basketball. All these other activities kept us sharp and fit. We also joked a lot to keep things light. Peter and I had some huge fights but then we even joked about those after the fact. I was kicked out of practice for a week after an incident and we laughed about it two days later."

Van't Hof and Farah had an unusual situation in the NCAA doubles tournament, playing two teams from Ole Miss in the semifinals and the final. In the semis, they faced Jonas Berg and Erling Tveit, the Ole Miss No. 1 team, and Bram Ten Berge and Matthias Willerman, their No. 2 team, in the final. "So their coaches got a good look at our team," said Smith.

In the semis, the USC duo split sets, both in tiebreakers, and then won the third-set tiebreaker 12-10. The final score was 6-7 (5), 7-6 (5), 7-6 (10). The match was dramatic.

"I had other teams before—in the finals in doubles at Pepperdine and the finals in singles at Fresno," said Smith. "We were up in the third sets of both matches and we lost both times. I learned from those matches that I needed to have a bigger role in the match. So I stepped into that match and coached much more aggressively. "

Robert Farah and Kaes Van't Hof with their NCAA doubles title trophies flanked on left by Coach Peter Smith and on the right by volunteer coach Eric Amend

Farah and Van't Hof won the final 7-6(10), 7-6(6). At one point, the pair was down 5-6 in the second-set tiebreaker when Van't Hof held serve to tie the match at 6-6. The Trojans won the next two points to take the championship. This was the first time since 1989, when Byron Black and current volunteer assistant coach Eric Amend won the title for USC, that the Trojans had won an NCAA doubles title.

Said Farah, "Kaes and I had an incredible season with a 26-match winning streak. Playing five tiebreakers in the semis and finals was amazing. By the fifth tiebreaker in the second match we were loose. Overall, winning the championship gave us a big boost in confidence that would carry us into the next year."

Said Van't Hof, "The semifinal match was an absolute battle. After that match, I became ill and remember getting an

IV to help me recover for the next day. We had some really nerve racking points in the final, but having played with Robert for two years prior and being nearly undefeated in 2008, we had a lot of confidence going into those matches which allowed us to play so well during the big points.

"Peter's biggest gift to me, and I am sure Robert would agree, was his system of volleying and how to appropriately play doubles. He is very specific on the appropriate footwork for volleying. It is a two-step volley (e.g. on a forehand volley for a right-hander, the player's first step to the right with his right foot and then steps forward with his left), a concept that was unnatural to me coming out of high school and I think is unnatural to almost all junior tennis players as juniors don't truly learn how to volley these days. He also was very helpful in improving my return and figuring out 'go-to' plays that should be almost locks for winning points if executed properly -- most notably I-formation doubles. His system paid big dividends in the later years and I give Peter 100 percent credit for winning the NCAA doubles championship with Robert. Without learning to play doubles his way, I would never have been in that position. I carried this success onto the pro tour for a year and a half and was fortunate enough to play in two US Opens and win five tournaments."

After the match, Smith spoke at a press conference. He remembered what he said. "This year we are holding the small trophy (the doubles trophy). Next year we hope to be holding the bigger trophy." And then he remembered thinking, "What have I just said?"

In 2009, Smith had an optimistic outlook on his squad, calling his Trojan team "definitely my strongest recruiting class since I have been at USC." Smith may have seen the early potential of his team, but he could not have known that this class would step on the courts and write a new chapter in the history of college tennis. A strong group of returning players included Robert Farah, Jason McNaughton, Abdullah Magdas, Daniel Gliner and Jaak Poldma and the freshmen class included Daniel Nguyen (Dwin), Stevie Johnson, Matt Kecki, Ben Lankenau and Andrew Kells.

"I first picked up a racket when I was around two years old. I've loved the game ever since," said Stevie Johnson. "I had success as a junior and was at the top of the rankings in my age division, but I didn't know the importance and necessity of having a strong off-the-court work ethic and I was pretty lazy at times. I learned very quickly that if you wanted to be great, you had to develop on and off the court. We had a couple of talented upper classmen who worked very hard. They led by example and I was inspired. USC was an easy choice for me as it was my dream school. Peter, Brett Masi and our volunteer coach Eric Amend were great people that made it easy for me to decide to go to USC."

The late Steve Johnson, Sr., who passed away suddenly in May of 2017, recalled when his son first started to play tennis. "Stevie could rally and play points when he was four," he said. "When he was five, I took him to my good friend Rance Brown, UCLA's associate coach of the women's team, and asked him to evaluate Stevie. Rance fed him some balls and said 'This kid is good!'"

Steve Johnson, Sr. was a teaching pro and Stevie was always around the courts and hitting balls. He'd go with his father to tournaments and hang out with the kids he was teaching. He always wanted to be a part of everything.

"One time, Stevie won the first round in a tournament at six, and at seven won 10-and-under, and 12-and-under events," said his father. The next year, father and son traveled to Texas to play in a national-level tournament called "Little Mo," sponsored by the Maureen Connolly Brinker Tennis Foundation. Stevie took fourth place in his division. "That was the beginning of tournament tennis becoming a big part of his life," Stevie Johnson, Sr. said.

Steve, Sr. and Rance Brown took Stevie to the U.S. Open when he was eight years old, planting the seed that one day he could play there. At the Open, young Stevie met a lot of people, including some of the pros. But his father ensured that his athletic focus was broader than just tennis. "Stevie continued playing all sports, fitting tennis around them," he said. "I have always felt that you have to develop as an athlete *and* a tennis player. Luckily, Stevie is a gifted athlete. Giving him a balanced life growing up was a very important part of his success. Regular school, playing other sports and developing as a good human being with strong character was always the first priority for my wife, Michelle and me. Stevie has a strong internal drive. He also saw his mom, a college math professor at Mt. Saint Antonio College in Walnut, California, and me striving to be good at what we do. Stevie always wanted to do more drills and repetitions, and was always asking me to make it harder. In high school, he decided he wanted to go to USC and be a tennis player, so he dropped the other sports to focus just on tennis."

Stevie Johnson met Kaes Van't Hof in the juniors and Van't Hof encouraged Johnson to become a Trojan. "Stevie and I would go to watch USC play and he liked the atmosphere that Peter Smith had created," said Steve Johnson, Sr. "Stevie's dream was to play on a team that could win the NCAA tournament and possibly an individual title and USC was the place for him to realize his goals."

Steve Sr. first met Peter Smith at a USTA high performance training camp. Smith saw Stevie play when he was about 12. Steve, Sr. tells how he remembered joking with Peter that maybe in a few years Stevie would be good enough for him at USC.

"I liked the way Peter coached and the way he interacted with his players," Steve, Sr. said. "I felt Stevie would thrive in that environment. Stevie wasn't in great shape as a freshman and Peter and the staff really helped him develop a strong work ethic. When Stevie saw his results improve so rapidly, he wanted more. Peter also helped him with his mental game, understanding the importance of balancing winning and losing, and staying in the moment, rather than just winning. He told the guys that they would be making memories for their lifetimes so they should enjoy the process. This approach helped USC teams play so well in those championship finals as they were much looser than their opponents and weren't scared. Peter is as good a coach as you'll find."

Steve, Sr. said there were other coaches he thought could move Stevie's game to the next level, but Stevie really wanted to stay close to home, so that family and friends could be a part of his journey, and Smith was a big part of the decision as well.

"I really wanted Stevie's college coach to be a father figure," Steve, Sr. said. "So we had narrowed it down to a couple of schools. I felt very strongly about who I was going to be handing my son off to and now we all know it was the best handoff possible. My family owes so much to USC, Peter and the entire coaching and training staff that helped Stevie achieve all that he did."

Stevie Johnson flying high after hitting a backhand

The Trojans started the spring season ranked No. 6. Their first tournament of the season was the Sherwood Collegiate Cup, that brought together three of the top powerhouse teams on the West Coast – UCLA, Stanford and USC. USC freshman Stevie Johnson lost in the quarterfinals to Stanford's Alex Clayton in three sets but teammate Robert Farah avenged Johnson's loss by beating Clayton in straight

285

sets. Johnson and Farah teamed up in doubles losing in the doubles final to Stanford's Blake Muller and Richard Wire, 8-4.

In April, the No. 7-ranked Trojans took on No. 9-ranked UCLA at the Los Angeles Tennis Center. UCLA came out strong, winning the doubles point. Even though Farah and Johnson won their singles matches at No.'s 1 and 3, and despite very strong three-set efforts by Poldma and Magdas, at No.'s 2 and 4, the Trojans still lost 5-2, as the Bruins took the Pac-10 Team Championship.

In the Pac-10 singles championship, Farah ranked No. 7 and Johnson ranked No. 67 fell, consecutively to Stanford's Bradley Klahn in the semifinals and finals. Johnson scored a major upset victory in the semifinal beating Stanford's Alex Clayton in straight sets. In the doubles championship, USC's Magdas and Nguyen lost in straight sets to Klahn and Ryan Thatcher in the semifinals. There was no doubt that the Trojans had the talent and competitive drive, but both the Bruins and the Cardinal were proving to be formidable opponents.

The loss to UCLA proved to be a defining moment for the 2009 Trojans. "After that loss, we were in the locker room and I said, 'Does anyone have anything to say?'" Smith said. "Robert Farah spoke up and said, 'Don't worry it about it guys, we can still win the NCAA championship.' I remembered thinking, 'This guy is nuts. What an outrageous statement to make.' I didn't think it was too likely. We all felt badly about the loss to UCLA, but Farah's outburst really set things in motion for us."

At the NCAA tournament at Texas A&M, USC moved quickly through the first few rounds, with wins over UC-Santa Barbara and the University of Minnesota to advance to the round of 16, where they faced Stanford, coached by Dick Gould's successor John Whitlinger. During the season, the

Cardinal and the Trojans had split matches with one other. "We were the eighth seed and Stanford was seeded ninth and they had a great team with top players like Alex Clayton, Bradley Klahn and Ryan Thatcher," said Smith "I really felt, though, that we could out-tough 'em. We won the doubles point with Abdullah Magdas and Daniel Nguyen winning at No. 2 and Farah and Johnson at No. 1 coming from behind to win in the tiebreaker 9-8 (4)."

In singles, Jaak Poldma had a great win over Ryan Thatcher 7-5, 7-6 (4) at No. 3, followed by Nguyen beating out Blake Muller in three sets. Stevie Johnson lost at No. 2 singles to Bradley Klahn in three sets. Playing at No. 1 singles, Robert Farah toughed out a three-setter against Alex Clayton 3-6, 6-3, 6-4 to clinch the match.

"I think our discipline really came through, and we competed very effectively down the line," said Smith. "This was one of the closet matches we played over our four-year run."

In the quarterfinals, USC played top-seeded Virginia, who entered the match with a 32-0 record. The Trojans won the doubles point with Magdas and Nguyen, and Matt Kecki and Jaak Poldma, winning at No. 2 and No. 3 doubles. The match was then postponed until the next day due to rain. That evening at a press conference, Peter Smith made a comment about Virginia's coach Brian Boland that added fire to the USC/Virginia rivalry.

"I made the following comment: 'I don't know how Brian is going to sleep tonight but I am going to sleep well,'" said Smith. "I don't know why I said that. I didn't even know Brian. I can be very playful and a big joker. I guess I was very happy that we won the doubles point, but it was odd for me to say someone's name in a press conference. It was probably inappropriate. I suppose I was thinking that it would very difficult to sleep on a doubles loss and come back and win the next day."

The next day, Robert Farah lived up to his post Pac-10 outburst and played like a man possessed, screaming and yelling encouragement to the entire team. Farah and Johnson won their matches in straight sets, but it was Abdullah Magdas at No. 4 beating Houston Barrack 4-6, 6-2, 6-3 who clinched the match for the Men of Troy. The Trojans won the match 4-0 handing Coach Smith his 400th collegiate victory.

Abdullah Magdas clinched the 4-0 upset win over undefeated Virginia in the 2009 NCAA quarterfinals

In the semifinals, USC played Texas, led by their coach Michael Center, one of Smith's closest friends. "Every time we play them I always go up to Michael and say, 'I hope you beat me today,'" said Smith. "If I am going to lose to anyone, I hope it is to him. When I go out to compete and I don't focus on winning or losing, I just get loose. My attitude and behavior then affects the team. I remember calling one of my former players and telling him that I had a bad feeling about the match. We had won so many matches against Texas that we shouldn't have. I worried that this was the day that karma was going to smack me on the back of head. Sometimes you have these feelings, but you don't tell anyone on the team. On the other hand, we had Stevie, Dwin and Robert out there, and my gut told me they were all going to win."

The doubles point was very close. Farah and Johnson at No. 1 won their match 8-6, with Kecki and Poldma, the No. 3 team, clinching the doubles point 8-4.

"Stevie hit the best shot I have ever seen in that doubles match," Smith said. The Texas team hit a lob over Johnson's head. Johnson raced to the fence and, with his back to the court, made an incredible get, hitting a 100-foot lob back over the net. The ball bounced high on the opponent's baseline and, amazingly, the Texas player hit the ball into the net and USC clinched the doubles point. With the Trojans playing tough in singles that day, USC won the match 4-1.

In the final, USC faced the Ohio State Buckeyes, who were coming off a great 28-0 undefeated record and making their first appearance in an NCAA Championship match.

"What was important about the final was that you had two coaching staffs who had never played in an NCAA team final," Smith said. "When we played Ohio State, I had agreed to be filmed in the locker room before the match. That kind of stuff is important for college tennis. I really didn't want reporters in the locker room, but I thought it was more important for the sport to have them there. I was very nervous before the match and sometimes it is hard to think of the right thing to say. Jim Sweeney, who was the football coach at Fresno State, an amazing guy and a classic football coach once stated, 'There is not one speech that has ever won any game. Players forget it as soon as they hit the field, but a very bad speech has lost many a game.' A coach can't win a match, all he can do is lose it in the locker room.

"I had two speeches - one in front of the cameras and one once the media left. When the cameras were rolling I said just go out and focus and give 100%. Let the results take care of themselves. As soon as the media left, I joked that I was glad that they were gone and let's go out there and kick their ass. I

Jaak Poldma paved the way for the 2009 championship with his spectacular doubles play

was very nervous so I had to really psyche myself up to act as normally as I could in front of the team. If they sensed my nervousness they would feed off that.

"Our doubles teams split matches and Poldma put the team on his back and won the doubles point. For me, this was the single most important match in our run. When we won the doubles point, we knew we could win the NCAA title. We believed we could be successful with the singles match-ups."

"At sixth singles, Dwin was playing Chase Buchanan, the No. 1 recruit in the country. I thought Dwin would be mental about playing Chase, so I did something that I have never done before. I told him I would be on his court and that he wasn't allowed to hear any voices but mine and that he couldn't look at the scoreboard. I kept changing the score on him. So instead of being 5-0, I told him the score was 3-0. When he was up 5-2, I told him it was 3-2 and I told him we needed a break. Ninety-nine percent of all players wouldn't be able to do what I was asking. I wanted him just to listen to me and he really didn't know the score. Dwin was the best at following directions and he followed my lead to the letter. He was mentally free and just played amazingly well. The other thing to our advantage was that OSU's fourth singles player hurt his ankle in the quarterfinals, which helped our captain Magdas beat him that much quicker. When Dwin won his match we took the lead 3-0."

Farah, the No. 8 ranked player in the country, appropriately, clinched the title for Trojans when he won at No. 1 singles over Brian Koniecko, the No. 3 ranked player in the nation, 5-7, 6-1, 6-4. The first person Smith looked for in the crowd was Steve Johnson, Sr.

"I turned to him and yelled, 'Can you believe it!'" he said. "Steve, Sr. already had his arms up in the air celebrating. The 2009 championship was the most important one for us. We had never won one before and didn't know what it felt like. This title gave all of us so much confidence."

The title was the 17th NCAA team title for USC and the first time since Dick Leach's last season in 2002. Farah finished the year ranked No. 5 in the singles rankings and Johnson ranked

No. 35. As a team, Farah and Johnson finished with a No. 10 national ranking. Farah was named Pac-10 Player of the Year, the first Trojan to hold that honor since Wayne Black in 1994.

In the NCAA singles final, Devin Britton from Ole Miss defeated Steve Moneke from Ohio State 3-6, 6-2, 6-3, while Dominic Inglot and Michael Shabaz of Virginia bested John Patrick Smith and Davey Sandgren from Tennessee in three sets to win the NCAA doubles title.

"Looking back at my first NCAA final, I really believed that I had to win this tournament if I wanted to keep coaching at USC," Smith said. "Many coaches got fired at USC for not winning and I was very aware of the pressure that day. I thought to myself, 'Peter, you better not blow this. Do not blow this.' In the end, you have to make it all enjoyable. You shouldn't overthink it. Many coaches make it too important, over stress it, over play it, over plan it, and over coach it.

"With Virginia in the quarters, I sensed our team was uptight so I made them do their warm-up twice. The players told me later that they thought I was the one who was uptight. I knew that I had established a culture where everyone played off my energy…my lead. So I came up with an idea. I brought the team together and said, 'Here's the deal guys, we have three matches left, and we have three coaches on the team. For every match we win, one of our coaches will shave his head.' I will go first, then Brett, and then Eric. I didn't discuss this with them, but and Eric and Brett are my brothers for life and they said they were all in. I wanted to give the team something else to think about."

Said Brett Masi, "I remember this episode vividly. But the haircuts were only part of it. At the beginning of the season, Peter and I started this whole 'van war' thing when he put lotion on one of the handles of the van doors. From there, it escalated into a huge competition to see who could one-up the other with the vans. At a certain point in the year, the guys would stay with the same van just for fun and to see what would happen next. After we won the Virginia match, Peter shaved his head. I told my wife about what was going on and she wasn't too happy at first. The next day we beat Texas and sure enough I went to SportsClips to get my haircut. ESPN had heard about our antics and gave us a camera to film. When we were done, I told the girl to wrap my hair up because I had an idea. That night, we took the "van wars" to the next level. The guys in my van and I got some peanut butter and used it to write all sorts of stuff— like, *Fight On!, Trojans,* and *Mase's Hair*—on Peter's van's windows. Then we stuck the hair clippings on the peanut butter. The next morning, when we went to the courts, it was already so hot the peanut butter was running down the whole van. We took pictures and then drove to the courts with our vans looking like that."

Said Smith, "I could barely see to drive my car to the match with the windshield covered with peanut butter and hair. People don't put a lot of stock in this type of stuff, but it was a great way to start the day. Somehow I got to a gas station and cleaned off the van and we drove to the courts laughing. That's how it should be."

Said Masi, "The whole story still brings back chills. It was a special moment and just so much fun. In my opinion it might have been the greatest coaching move of all time. The whole thing was genius on Peter's part—it kept the guys loose and took their minds of what was in front of them. The team grew closer because of it and played harder for one another. To this day, it's the closest group of guys I've ever coached."

Continued Smith, "We had great coaches in Brett and Eric. Eric brought a toughness and cockiness and a USC swagger that we sorely needed."

Amend said the NCAA win in 2009 was truly significant for him. "For 12 years I lived with the disappointment of that very difficult loss to Georgia in 1987," he said. "That loss really haunted me. The team championship finally got that monkey off my back. It was a double win for me!"

In 2010, Robert Farah, who was ranked No. 14 in the nation in the pre-season rankings, and Jason McNaughton returned for their senior year. Abdullah Magdas had graduated, but juniors Daniel Gliner and Jaak Poldma came back and were joined by junior transfer Peter Lucassen from The Netherlands. Stevie Johnson, who incredibly was accorded with the pre-season No. 1 singles ranking in the country, led a very strong group of sophomores that included Ben Lankenau, No. 47th-ranked Matt Kecki and No. 78th-ranked Daniel Nguyen. Two new freshman, Joel Giger from Switzerland and JT Sundling from Thousand Oaks, California, also joined the squad. George Husack joined as associate coach when Brett Masi left to take the head coaching job at the University of San Diego. Husack had played at San Diego State and was the former associate head coach at Illinois and Santa Clara. Eric Amend returned for his fifth season as volunteer assistant coach.

"I felt an instant connection with Peter when I came on board, and I do believe that the differences in our personalities worked," said Husack of working with Smith. "We were always on the same page and wanted to do our best. We would joke around calling one another Ying and Yang. We also believed that no day was different from the next. Our routine was to get up, go to work, get things done and repeat that process over and over until the season ended. Peter and I spent a lot of time together each day, commuting from our homes and sitting at desks that were only a few feet apart. In addition to Trojan tennis, both of us had a lot of other things going on. I had an infant daughter when I moved to USC with my wife Kristina and just under a year later welcomed a twin boy and girl to our family. So that was brand new and kept me focused on family and work at the same time. Peter and Tammie were raising their three boys who were very active. Our wives were incredibly supportive and they usually don't get the credit they deserve but their emotional support was invaluable. Peter kept things structured and loose, serious and light, intense and humorous. We embraced the guys we had on the team and had fun with them and with what they were accomplishing rather than focusing on the goal of winning a national title every year."

The Trojans started the 2010 season ranked No. 1 in the nation. "The first thing that strikes me is that I think we're better than last year," said Smith in the Trojan media guide. "I think at some point our experience is going to make a difference, but guys like Daniel Nguyen and Steve Johnson are significantly better tennis players than they were a year ago and that's saying something."

In the fall season, Johnson won the ITA National Indoors, one of the major individual collegiate championships, beating Guillermo Gomez of Georgia Tech in three sets.

Daniel Nguyen clinched the 18th NCAA Team Championship for the Trojans in 2010

On March 3, 2010, USC created some program history with a 6-1 win over UCLA at Westwood, snapping a 19-match losing streak from the Trojans on UCLA's home courts. A USC-UCLA match, whether at Westwood or at Marks Stadium, has an electric atmosphere and the partisan crowd often lifts their team to new heights. Such was always the case with the Bruins at home, which made the win, their first at UCLA since 1991, even more important. During that 19-match span, USC had won four national championships, but could not beat the Bruins in Westwood.

The UCLA-USC rivalry began before players even stepped on the court, as both schools competed to enroll freshman talent.

Said Nguyen, "Originally, I had my sights set for UCLA since my best friend from high school was going there, and I had a lot of respect for their tennis team. However, during the end of my senior year, I received a late notice from UCLA that they were not interested. I was devastated and confused after hearing the news, since I had my heart set on spending the next four years as a Bruin. Fortunately, Geoff and Annette Grant, a family I was living with in Santa Barbara, knew a tennis player—Chase Muller (co-founder with Troy Pollet of the now defunct, 7th Man Club—a tennis booster group on the USC campus)—who had been on Peter Smith's team for four years. After graduation, Chase had worked for Geoff at his investment banking company in Santa Barbara. When I told Geoff the news about UCLA, he immediately contacted Chase and asked him if Peter could help me with acceptance at USC. Because I was a top player in Santa Barbara, Peter saw me as an asset for USC and rushed to get me into the university in July. I'm extremely grateful to the Grant family, Chase Muller and Peter Smith. Without these amazing individuals I probably would have attended a different university."

Smith was equally pleased with how things worked out. "The Grant Family legally adopted Daniel in high school. They put him on a course that completely changed his life—and therefore my own—and so many others. For me, Daniel's story has some parallels to *The Blind Side* football movie."

It took Nguyen some time to bond with Smith and the team, but things picked up once the season began.

"It was the tail end of my freshman year when the team really came together," said Nguyen. "Peter had really helped elevate my game by simplifying things on and off the court. Every day, he spends one-on-one time with the players to hone their skills and this sets him apart from other coaches.

During workouts, Peter gives it his all. When we see him work hard, we get inspired. He never tells the team to focus on winning but rather to improve our skills and conditioning. We practice this philosophy at every match and it really pays off at tournament time."

Lest anyone doubt that UCLA-USC rivalry results in some of the most competitive, seesaw battles in college tennis, consider these epic contests of the 2010 season leading up to the NCAA tournament. In February, USC beat the Bruins 4-0 at the ITA National Team Indoor Championships. It certainly appeared that the Trojans were the dominant team that year; however, in mid-April, the Bruins engaged the Trojans again at Marks Stadium, and this time the tables would turn. UCLA started out strong and won the doubles point—never a good omen. On the USC side, Farah, Johnson and Nguyen all won their singles matches—but the Bruins kicked things into high gear beating the Trojans at No.'s 3, 5 and 6 to give UCLA a 4-3 victory and USC's first conference loss of the season. With the loss to the Bruins, Stanford and USC ended up sharing the Pac-10 title.

The 2010 NCAA tournament was held in Athens, Georgia and the Trojans were seeded No. 5. McNaughton, who had played for most of the regular season, had sustained an injury that would keep him out of the NCAAs. In the first two rounds, USC beat Marist 4-0 and Fresno State 4-1 and then notched a 4-0 victory over No. 12 seed Kentucky in the round of 16. In the quarterfinals, the Trojans also shut out No. 4 seed Ohio State 4-0.

In the semifinals, No. 5 USC faced Virginia again. This time, the top-seeded Cavaliers had amassed a 36-match undefeated streak and they were even more anxious for its first team title. The top two Trojan doubles teams started strong, taking the doubles point with Farah and Johnson and Nguyen and Sundling winning 8-5 and 8-6, respectively. Farah won his singles match against UVA's Michael Shabaz 6-1, 7-6 (9), saving two set points in the second set to give SC a 2-0 lead. On court five, Trojan Matt Kecki lost 6-2, 7-6 (8) and Peter Lucassen at No. 6 closed out his match against UVA's Julen Uriguen 6-2, 6-3, giving USC a 3-1 lead. At No. 4 singles, Nguyen battled Drew Courtney to a win 7-6 (9), 6-4 and clinch the match.

In the final, USC faced No. 2 seed Tennessee and the match provided its fair share of drama. "The Tennessee match was very interesting," said Smith. "Steve had a bone on his pinky toe that needed to be shaved off in March, right before the NCAAs and had been having trouble walking. Not knowing how his foot was going to react, or whether it would take three days or a month to heal, we had put off the surgery until after the season. But on the day of the final, Steve was walking normally and said he felt great. I think his adrenalin kicked in because the day after that match, he couldn't walk!"

In the fall season, Johnson and Farah had faced Tennessee's No. 1 doubles team at the ITA Men's All-American Championships. In a first-round match, Farah hit what they believed was a shank winner to break serve, but the Tennessee team called it out. Farah and Johnson were stunned—and mad—and ultimately lost the match 9-7.

Smith remembered that a sense of déjà vu returned during their No. 1 doubles match in the NCAA final. "Stevie and Rob are playing the Vols again and thought they got another bad call," Smith said. "One person you don't want to piss off is Robert Farah. When he had something to play for, he was really dangerous. Rob was hot and he shoulder-bumped one of their guys on the changeover. Tennessee won the doubles point again 8-6. It was the first time we had lost the doubles point in that run for the title. In the locker room, the talk was not about winning the NCAAs, but about beating *those* guys. I didn't say a word. Their coach was so tight that he couldn't even speak. Sometimes when you can see the win, you can get tight and Tennessee thought they could see the win."

Johnson, Farah and Lucassen all won their singles matches but Jaak Poldma lost in three sets, bringing the score to 3-2 in USC's favor.

"Peter Lucassen struggled for the whole year until the NCAAs," said USC Associate Coach George Husack. "He had lost a lot of confidence in his game over the last four weeks of the season, doubting himself, his game and his ability. Peter Smith and I were seriously considering not playing him at all in the NCAAs. Eric Amend took Peter under his wing for the post-season and gave him no options. He had to win. Usually Lucassen is a complete grinder, but at NCAAs he used transitions and serve-and-volley plays with a massive impact on his results. Opponents didn't expect it and quite frankly didn't know how to respond. When Peter beat Matteo Fago at sixth singles in the final to put us up 3-2, I felt that was the final nail in the coffin. I was so pumped for him."

Said Smith, "Lucassen had joined the team ranked No. 541 in the world, but now he was playing No. 6 for USC. I know it was confusing for him. He did not lose a set in the entire tournament and without him I don't think we would have won."

The remaining two matches were Kecki playing No. 5 and Nguyen at No. 4. Kecki had split sets and was down 4-5 in the third. Nguyen was playing Tennys Sandgren and had served for the first set at 5-4 and then at 6-5, but lost both service games, and then he lost the tie breaker. Smith then pulled out a tactic that had been very effective the previous season.

Peter Lucassen got his groove back and didn't lose a set in the 2010 NCAA tournament

"Similar to the 2009 championship, I told Dwin, 'In the middle of the match, you don't hear the umpire and you don't look at the scoreboard," Smith said. "You hear nothing but me. And I kept changing the score on him again. He never lost another game. When he was up 5-1 in the second, I told him it was 3-0 and he had to break. He didn't know what the score was and then didn't know that he had won his match and the national title." The final score for Nguyen was 6-7 (3), 6-1, 6-0 with him winning the last 12 games in a row to hand USC the title by a 4-2 margin.

Said Nguyen, "It was an extremely tough match against Tennessee. We lost a tight doubles point against a very passionate Volunteers team. Coach Smith and the captains Robert Farah and Jaak Poldma gave a great inspirational speech after the doubles point in the locker room and then we were ready for the battle. During my singles match, I lost a very close first set tiebreaker after leading in the beginning of the set. I was very frustrated, and I remember Coach coming up to me while I was sitting on the bench on a changeover and telling me to not worry about the scoreboard and to just keep playing my game. I regrouped well after squandering the first set and finished strong winning the next two sets 6-1, 6-0. When I won my match point I didn't realize I had clinched it for the team until I saw my crazed teammates running towards me. It was a confusing yet exciting feeling. I was so focused on the moment and process, that I lost track of the score."

Said Smith, "It was a great win for us as I believe the Tennessee team was the most talented we encountered over our four-year run."

Bradley Klahn from Stanford won the NCAA singles title beating Louisville's Austin Childs in straight sets in the final and Drew Courtney and Michael Shabaz from Virginia won the doubles title beating John Patrick Smith and Davey Sandgren of the University of Tennessee 6-7(4), 6-2, 6-3. At the end of the season, Johnson and Farah were awarded ITA All American honors.

USC finished the 2010 season with a 25-3 record, winning back-to-back NCAA team titles. The 2010 win, the Trojan's 18th national title, was also significant as it moved USC into first place in overall NCAA team titles unseating Stanford, whose legendary coach Dick Gould had guided the Cardinal to 17 team championships.

9

The Second
Four-Peat

In 2011, Robert Farah graduated and joined the pro tour. Seniors Jaak Poldma, serving as captain, and Peter Lucassen both returned, as did juniors Steve Johnson and Daniel Nguyen. Emilio Gomez, a top South American junior from Ecuador, also joined the team. Emilio was the son of Andres Gomez, the winner of the 1990 French Open. The elder Gomez had thought about coming to USC to play for George Toley, before deciding instead on a professional career. Sophomore JT Sundling and three freshmen, Michael Grant, Corey Smith and Ray Sarmiento, completed the 2011 roster. George Husack returned as associate tennis coach and was joined by volunteer assistant coach Jeff Tarango—a three-time All-American at Stanford who had been on two NCAA championship teams for the Cardinal.

Early in the season, the Sherwood Cup final between Stevie Johnson and Stanford's Bradley Klahn foreshadowed an intense and historic season. Even though Klahn won the match 6-4, 6-2, Johnson would not lose another singles matches in his college career, running the table with 72 victories in a row.

The Trojans started the season ranked No. 2 behind Virginia. They amassed seven straight wins before suffering two losses in quick succession to Duke and Stanford in February. For the rest of the season USC was on a tear, with Johnson winning the Ojai singles tournament against Klahn, who was becoming his main rival and a player who he called, "a great competitor who always gave me the toughest matches over my college career." Johnson noted that Klahn was, "a phenomenal player—left handed, with a huge forehand. He is also a very smart player, so even on his off days I knew he was going to do his best to try and figure out a way to win."

The Trojans also were twice victorious over the Bruins—both at home and at Westwood, ending the regular season with a perfect 6-0 record against Pac-12 teams to take the Pac-12 title. In 2011, the Pac-10 had changed to the Pac-12 with Colorado and Utah admitted to the conference. The Trojans finished the regular 2011 season 23-2.

In the quarterfinals of the NCAA tournament held at the Taube Tennis Center at Stanford, USC faced Kentucky on a very windy day. The Trojans scored a decisive 4-1 victory. In the semifinals, the Trojans crushed Georgia 4-0 to advance into the NCAA final for the third straight year. Smith once again was creative in how he kept his team pumped up but loose.

"In 2011, we started a great tradition," he said. "USC was having a fundraiser in San Francisco and (Athletic Director)

Pat Haden told me he was planning to send the Trojan band, the Spirit of Troy, to our match. I loved the idea but didn't tell the team. To psyche the guys up, I said to them, 'Tomorrow we are going to act as if we are playing on our home turf at Marks Tennis Stadium.' The team came out onto the court and the band was playing. And we played really well and beat Georgia. Now the tradition is that if the team makes it to the NCAA semifinals, the band travels to the match."

In the final, No. 2 USC once again faced No. 1 Virginia. In 2009 and 2010, UVA had been seeded No. 1 in the NCAA tournament—only to be denied by the Trojans. In 2011, USC was on a roll, entering the final with an 18-match winning streak. Just before the final with Virginia, Smith did an interview with Whitelaw Reid of the *Green Country Record* and addressed Virginia's losses to USC. "I think they have to get over some demons and I think the Trojans are their demons," he said. "They'll have to exorcise those demons. It will be interesting. I don't know if we're in their head but I think this tournament is. When you're the No. 1 seed and you don't win...I don't think it's the Trojans *per se*. I think we're just the team that's done it."

Smith kept the tone playful, but at the same time, he was calling Virginia out and intending to ratchet up the pressure. "In the finals, I think I made too big a deal about winning three titles in a row," he said. "No one had done that for years. I got ahead of myself but at the same time the press kept asking me leading questions. This is a slippery slope."

Sundling and Poldma and Johnson and Gomez won their doubles matches to give the Trojans the doubles point. Gomez won at No. 5 singles beating Justin Shane and Johnson beat Michael Shabaz handily in straight sets at No. 1. The

Trojans were up 3-0 but the Cavaliers surged back, winning three three-set singles matches at No. 2, No. 4 and No. 6.

All eyes then turned to the No. 3 singles court where Daniel Nguyen, who had acquired the nickname "Mr. Clutch," was battling Sanam Singh.

Smith had decided to coach on courts 4, 5 and 6, while having assistant George Husack take the first three singles courts. "Before the National Anthem the Cavaliers looked so nervous," said Smith. "I figured if we won the doubles point, Stevie would win and we would be up 2-0. Fortunately, we played a great doubles point and won. I had told Daniel that I couldn't be on his court as I had the previous two years and that George, who I trusted so much, would be there with him. I also told Daniel that if he saw me on his court he would know he was the last match—and of course that is what happened."

Nguyen had two match points at 5-2 in the third. At 5-3 he served a terrible game and lost his serve. At 5-4, Smith went out on court and could see that Nguyen was in his own world. "Dwin looked up and saw me and said, 'Oh s...t,'" Smith said. "I told him to just breathe. He was in good shape as he was returning with the wind rather than serving against it. I reminded him, 'We have been here before and you're OK.' In the next game Nguyen got some help. Up 0-15 on Singh's serve, Nguyen dived for a ball and managed to get it over the net but then fell to the ground. Singh's next shot, which should have been an easy put away, clipped the top of the net and went out. Singh won the next point. With Nguyen up 15-30, Singh hit a forehand that again grazed the top of the net and careened out. Dwin now had two championship points. Singh stayed in the match hitting a drop volley to win the next point. At 30-40, after a long rally Singh came to the net but Nguyen hit a tough forehand that caused Singh's volley to just clear the tape. Nguyen had followed his forehand to the net and hit a ball high to Singh's backhand side. Singh stretched for the backhand volley and Nguyen, who was now on top of the net, put the ball away. At the end of the match Smith said to Nguyen, "You did it. And you knew the score this time.'" Nguyen had won the match 7-5, 0-6, 6-4 in a dramatic finish to give the Trojans their third straight national title.

By all accounts, Virginia was super tough that year. It was the closest match the Trojans had played against them. In a YouTube video posted shortly after the 2011 victory, Stevie Johnson was effusive, "Daniel is unbelievable. There is no other person I would rather have out there in the last match of the day. He is so big in the NCAAs. I would rather have him out there than me in these situations."

As in the previous year, Nguyen made a half-hearted attempt to mimic 2002 champion Prakash Amritraj by pulling off his shirt, but the intensity of the moment got the better of him and the shirt stayed on. It was the second straight year that Nguyen had won the deciding match for the title for the Trojans and USC's 19th NCAA team title.

"For me the third NCAA title was very special as all of my family and close friends and USC fans came to Stanford to support me," Nguyen said. "It really felt like a home match. On one side of the stadium, Trojan fans were cheering for USC, and on the other side, the Virginia fans were in full force. The atmosphere was electric. In the beginning of the match, our team started strong by winning the doubles point. Going into singles, we knew that every position in singles was going to be tough. My goal was to focus on my match and to keep playing as if I was going to be the last match on. My match against

Sanam Singh from Virginia was epic. I started well in the beginning of the set, then lost focus in the second set. I raced to a 5-3 lead in the third set, and had chances to serve it out, but missed my opportunities. I remember in that 5-4 game, I kept repeating to myself, 'One point at a time and fight hard.' I could hear Peter Smith and George Husack on the side telling me to stay calm and focus on getting it done. When it was match point I knew I had to fight for it and leave everything out there. It was a long rally in which I came to the net. He hit the ball right at me and I hit a backhand volley winner. My racquet dropped out of my hand, and before I knew it, all of my teammates jumped on top of me. What a feeling to clinch the match for my team, my family and friends and the university!"

Added Smith, "Two of Dwin's former coaches, Ben and Zibu Ncube, kept playing DJ Khaled's song, "All I Do Is Win," behind his court the entire match. Classic!"

Smith's focus may have been on coaching the team to take the 2011 NCAA title, but he also believed that there was much more on the line than their final fight against Virginia.

"Before the match, I also told George, 'Today is really big. We either lose, and Stevie turns pro, or we win and Stevie comes back for his senior year," Smith said. "We've got two NCAA titles on the line—this year and next year."

Smith soon learned that the chance to be a part of USC history was on Stevie Johnson's mind as well. "After the match, Stevie came running up to me screaming, 'We frigging won and I'm coming back and we're winning four,' and he jumped on me," Smith said. "I had had knee surgery during the season and my leg was weak. We both fell to the ground. Now that made me smile!"

Daniel Nguyen and Coach Peter Smith embrace after "Mr. Clutch" clinches the 2011 NCAA title

Said Husack, "For me, the really fun part that night occurred at dinner. We were watching TV and Dwin made ESPN's Top Ten List. I will never forget his reaction when he saw himself on television!"

The championships for USC didn't end with the team title as Johnson also won the singles title defeating Rhyne Williams of Tennessee 4-6, 6-2, 6-1 in the final. In doubles,

Austin Krajicek and Jeff Dadamo became the first Texas A&M national champions in tennis beating Stanford's Bradley Klahn and Ryan Thatcher 7-6 (4), 6-3 in the final.

In 2012, Smith began his tenth season at USC, having been named the Pac-12 Coach of the Year for the 2011 season. Smith was riding a tidal wave of success: three consecutive NCAA team titles and his No. 1 player Stevie Johnson was the 2011 NCAA singles champion. George Husack, Smith's highly trusted associate head coach, also returned along with volunteer assistant coach Jeff Tarango.

Stevie Johnson, Daniel Nguyen and Ben Lankenau all returned for their senior year—although Johnson would take the fall season off to play as an amateur on the pro circuit. The rest of the team was young but talented and included sophomores Emilio Gomez, Michael Grant, Ray Sarmiento and Corey Smith. Six new freshman were also on the roster, including Yannick Hanfmann, ranked No. 39 in the men's rankings in Germany, Eric (EJ) Johnson from San Jose, California, John Meadows from Melbourne, Australia, Roberto Quiroz, a standout player from Ecuador, Jordi Vives from Barcelona, Spain and Johnny Wang from San Marino, California.

To no one's surprise, the Trojans were ranked No. 1 in the pre-season rankings and by the end of February the team had a 14-0 record, having won its last 34 consecutive matches, dating back to the previous year. The 14th win of the season came when USC beat UCLA 6-1 at Westwood. Johnson, Sarmiento and Nguyen continued to play at the top three positions with Gomez, Hanfmann and Quiroz at Nos. 4, 5 and 6.

On March 15, 2012, Steve Johnson notched his 50th straight singles victory beating Texas A&M's Alexis Klegou 6-2, 6-1. In late April, the No. 5 Bruins halted USC's 45-match winning streak on Trojan soil. USC won the doubles point and

Johnson and Nguyen won at No.'s 1 and 3, but UCLA proved too tough on this day, winning the other four singles matches in tight contests.

In 2012, the Pac-12 championship used a new team tournament format, and USC was victorious, beating the Bruins 4-2 to claim the tournament title.

The Trojans entered the NCAA tournament as the top seed. They beat Fairfield and Texas A&M 4-0 in the first two rounds to reach the round of 16.

"This was the year of Stevie," said Smith. "We wanted to win the fourth title for us—but probably more for Stevie. We all felt it and knew he had given up so much to go for the fourth NCAA championship—we just didn't want to let him down."

In a highly unusual move, Johnson called a meeting of the coaches before the round of 16. He told them, "I am dying. I gave up the last year of my life to pursue this fourth championship. If we lose, I'm going to feel like I've wasted a year of my life."

Smith told him, "Then prepare to lose. You have to accept losing to free yourself up to play. We have all done everything we could and we are all great competitors."

"Stevie took it well," said Smith. "He had faith in me."

USC blew through Illinois 4-0 in the round of 16 and then moved past Duke, coached since 2008 by Stan Smith's son Ramsey, 4-1 in the quarterfinals.

In the semifinals, the Trojans battled UCLA once again, this time winning decisively 4-1. "Mr. Clutch," Daniel Nguyen, once again earned his nickname by beating Dennis Novikov in three tough sets. Both the USC men's and women's teams both made the semifinals in 2012 with the women's team scoring a key victory over Stanford 4-2 in the quarterfinals before falling to the Bruins in the semifinals. During an interview at the tournament, in which Johnson and women's team All-American Danielle Lao were interviewed, Lao, with her arm around Johnson, presciently announced, "I'm just happy to see this guy play. He's history in the making."

On May 21, 2012 at 5:00 p.m., USC's men's tennis team took the courts at the Dan Magill Tennis Complex in Athens, Georgia to defend their three previous NCAA team titles, again against Virginia. Writing in the *Richmond Times Dispatch*, Whitelaw Reid described the contest between the Trojans and Cavaliers as "the biggest in the sport." After losing to USC in the last three tournaments, most notably in the 2011 final in which they were the No. 1 seed, Virginia, who had never won a national title, was aching to win. The Trojans got off to a slow start, and uncharacteristically, lost the doubles point to give the Cavaliers a psychological edge. Just as the teams were switching from doubles to singles matches, a mid-afternoon Georgia thunderstorm drenched the courts and play was suspended. It was almost as if the Trojans' coach Peter Smith, summoned the rain to allow his team time to regroup.

"The 2012 NCAA final was very challenging," said Smith. "Overall it took ten hours. Virginia played a great doubles point. Their team had done a 180-degree turn from the year before. They were loose and wanted it and Mitchell Frank, their new freshman, played without fear. It was going to be a different match."

After a delay of close to three hours, the match was finally moved indoors. Since there were no cameras inside the facility, anxious fans around the country, intent on watching online, were now denied any real access. Instead they had to follow the match via a web-based scoreboard that was updated only intermittently. Said Husack, "We weren't really used to playing indoors—even though we were national indoor champions. There were only four courts inside, so not everyone was playing at once. The facility was hot, there was no air conditioning and people were packed in like sardines."

Once indoors, Johnson, the nation's No. 1 player, and sophomore Sarmiento played inspired tennis at No. 1 and No. 2 singles, respectively, dispatching their opponents in straight sets and giving the Trojans a 2-1 lead.

Said Smith, "Ray played superbly at No. 2 that day. I don't think I have seen him play better."

From an aesthetic point of view, Sarmiento was a pure joy to watch. Not only did he have every shot in the book, but his strokes were clean, he was always on balance and was as graceful as they come. Growing up as a top junior in Southern California he was always ranked in the top five in the 14, 16 and 18 age brackets. Early on, his coach Harout Khachatrian at the Burbank Tennis Center gave him a piece of advice that he never forgot – 'Crush the ball!' which is exactly what he did that day.

Daniel Nguyen, no doubt exhausted from his previous decisive victory, suffered his first ever singles loss in four years of competing in the NCAAs, leveling the team score at 2-2. Said Smith, "We came back after the delay and Dwin lost for the first time in 16 matches in the NCAAs."

USC gained more momentum when sophomore standout and No. 4 player Emilio Gomez posted an impressive win just after 1:00 a.m. local time to give the Trojans an encouraging 3-2 lead.

The championship was then in the hands of two talented freshmen, Yannick Hanfmann and Robert Quiroz, both facing off against seasoned competitors from Virginia. Winning only one of the two matches would send the Trojans home with their fourth consecutive NCAA title. Quiroz, the talented Ecuadorian, was down 4-1 in the second set after losing the first to Julen Uriguen of Virginia. On the next court, Hanfmann and his opponent Justin Shane split sets, but Hanfmann was up 4-2 in the third.

Smith positioned himself on Hanfmann's court to provide support. In a post-match interview, Smith said, "When the guys get nervous, I like to talk. For me, it's a conversation. In this case, Yannick was my doubles partner and I was his."

In a gritty comeback, Quiroz won the second set in a tiebreaker, then fell behind 3-0 in the third. He continued, however, to fight back and won three of the next four games. He was continuing to claw his way up, but was still down 4-3. Said Quiroz, "I knew I had to stay in it and keep fighting," Quiroz said. "I saw that Yannick was doing well but in tennis matches things can change very quickly so you can't assume that anyone is going to win. As I was thinking these things, I saw the crowd's attention turn to Yannick's match."

Justin Shane, Hanfmann's opponent, had tied the score at 4-4 and then rallied even further to break Hanfmann to take the lead at 5-4 in the final set. But Hanfmann, who was remarkably calm, had been in a similar situation indoors several months earlier when he was instrumental in winning the ITA National Team Indoor tournament for the Trojans, beating Devin McCarthy of Ohio State in three tense sets. Fighting back with big groundstrokes, he broke Shane to level the score at 5-5.

Two weeks of intense tennis, however, was taking its toll on Virginia's players and Uriguen was cramping badly against Quiroz. In fact, play had to be halted up to the time limit so that the Virginia trainers could attend to their player. Meanwhile, Hanfmann and Shane went into the deciding third-set tiebreaker. Leading 6-4 in the tiebreaker, Hanfmann, the freshman from Karlsruhe, Germany, engaged in a long baseline rally. With the crowd on their feet, he hit a forehand deep into the court to force the error. He threw his hands up in the air in victory. With that point, Yannick won his match, the team match and a fourth straight and 20th overall NCAA title for USC. Pat Haden, USC's Athletic Director at the time and a football legend who has seen it all, was in Athens to support the team. Said Haden, "We were all sitting about 20 feet from the players and it felt like we were in the match. It was the most tension-filled sports event I have ever experienced. It was so intense that I had to keep closing my eyes."

Down but not out, Roberto Quiroz kept fighting back until the bitter end in the 2012 Championship match

With the win, Quiroz, who no longer needed to finish his match, together with the other Trojans, burst onto the court chanting, "Four-peat, Four-peat!" This dramatic ending to the team's quest will go down in Trojan lore as one of the truly great moments in USC sports history.

"It was definitely the most exhausted I've been after a match," said George Husack. "I didn't play a point, yet had been so engaged with the courts I was on that if felt like I had played every point with the guys. I remember running to Yannick's court after he clinched, jumping up and down, and within seconds, I couldn't jump anymore. I literally had no power in my legs...maybe it was from squatting in a catcher's position while coaching Roberto Quiroz."

Quiroz recalled how fatigued he was as well. "The end was a combination of nervous exhaustion and excitement," he said. "It was completely surreal."

Asked in a post-match discussion about what was the deciding factor in the match, Peter Smith (who, for the first time seemed truly spent), said it was his players' mental attitude, conditioning and team focus that propelled them to victory. "A lot of Virginia fans were screaming at us," he said. "They were heckling Daniel and Yannick, too, but Yannick has a bit of a hearing problem and didn't hear one word! Look, in college tennis heckling is just part of the game. You have to prepare your team for anything. What I determined with Yannick is that he is very good under pressure. The bigger the moment, the better he played. If you could inspire him, you would get his best."

Said Hanfmann, "To win the two national championships (Indoors and NCAA) in one year, especially as a freshman, was amazing for me. It has taken me a few years for this to really sink in. In 2012, our team was really

Yannick Hanfmann, overcome with emotion, is rushed by teammates seconds after he clinched the four-peat for the Trojans

stacked and it felt like we were supposed to win everything, but as in all sports, that feeling doesn't guarantee you anything. Winning the Indoor title gave me a mental boost for the NCAAs. I remember being down in the third set and just telling myself to keep having faith that things will work out. And, in the tiebreaker, I felt like I had a slight edge. It made a huge difference that Coach Smith was on my court helping to guide me and I could see the team and our fans cheering in the background.

"I also have to say that being on the same team as Stevie was something. He was the guy you would notice whenever he was around. He has a very uplifting personality and off the court he is very funny and an easy person to be around.

But, when he steps on the court, you can see something come over him. You can feel his intense desire to win no matter what and would know that he would give everything he had. Often I would tell myself that I needed to adopt the same kind of attitude on the court, but when I tried I couldn't duplicate it. He's simply unique."

Said Daniel Nguyen, "Winning that fourth title was a storybook closure to my collegiate tennis career. I couldn't have scripted it better if I tried. The hard work and sacrifices I made throughout my college career made that fourth title even more rewarding. It was the culmination of the extra gym and tennis time that finally paid off during that championship week and it was one of my greatest life accomplishments. I don't know if I'll ever experience anything like that again in my tennis career. It's amazing becoming close with a group of guys and winning four straight national championships. In the end, we won not just for ourselves, but also for our families, coaches, mentors, friends and fans. We played as individuals, but we won as a whole. I will remember it forever."

Winning four championships in a row meant that the Trojans had won 24 consecutive matches over all four NCAA tournaments. In college tennis today, the competition is so fierce that upsets occur all the time. In every tournament, the Trojans faced the best tennis players in the nation, sometimes teetering on the brink of defeat. Many feared that they couldn't sustain their incredible streak and yet they were victorious time and time again. Interviewed by the NCAA's Scott Treibly after the four-peat victory, Smith talked about the feeling of winning a title victory. "Think of the best thing that can ever happen to you—for me it was as good as the birth of my kids—it's that good," said Smith. "Now when you watch the NBA and see

Kobe or LeBron win it, you know exactly how it feels. It's an explosion in your brain!"

"And how did you win four in a row?" asked Treibly.

Smith replied, "Every season is different. We have great leadership and talent. The captains and coaches are on the same page. That's the only way you can win. And of course, Steve Johnson has a golden right arm, Daniel Nguyen has ice water in his veins."

Co-captains Stevie Johnson and Daniel Nguyen hold the 2012 NCAA Team Championship Trophy, the fourth time the two won the national title together.

In the NCAA singles tournament, Johnson repeated as singles champion by beating Eric Quigley of Kentucky in straight sets. It was Johnson's final collegiate match and his 72nd straight singles match victory, a record unlikely to be toppled any time soon.

"Stevie is a one-in-a-million competitor," says former world No. 1 Tracy Austin Holt. "He is wired very differently than most and has an inner drive, a raging fire, that cannot be put out."

"The streak is something I can enjoy a little more now than back in the day, but still something that I don't bring up often," Johnson said five years later. "My personal winning streak meant nothing at the time if we didn't go out and win those NCAA titles as a team. I think I played my best in the 2010 and 2012 NCAA titles in particular, and I look back at all of those championships so fondly as they were the most important part of my collegiate career."

In the doubles tournament, Chase Buchanan and Blaz Rola from Ohio State beat Raony Carvalho and Gonzalo Escobar of Texas Tech 7-6 (4), 6-3 to win the title. The duo became the first men's doubles team in collegiate tennis history to win all three major collegiate championships in a single season, also being victorious in the ITA All-America Championships and the ITA National Indoor Championships earlier in the year.

The Trojans entered the 2013 season ranked No. 2 in the nation, with six team members having national rankings. Junior Ray Sarmiento (No. 10), sophomores Roberto Quiroz (No. 24), Emilio Gomez (No. 27), Eric Johnson (No. 64), Yannick Hanfmann (No. 84) and Johnny Wang (No. 121) all returned. Max de Vroome, a top player from the Netherlands (No. 78) also joined the team. Michael Tang, a former standout player at University High School in Irvine, California, moved on to the roster for his senior year. Previously, Tang had served not only as manager, but also as stringer extraordinaire for the team. Former Trojan player Peter Lucassen returned as volunteer assistant coach.

Kris Kwinta, a former member of Poland's Davis Cup team, joined the Trojans as assistant coach after graduating from UCLA in 2008 with a degree in political science. Playing for the Bruins for two years, he was an All-American in doubles in 2004, and had a distinguished career playing for UCLA coach Billy Martin. In 2005, Kwinta clinched the NCAA title for the Bruins in their 4-3 final-round upset over Baylor. After graduating, Kwinta stayed on as assistant coach to Martin for several years. Some thought it unusual that Kwinta would take a position at an archrival school, but Kwinta explained, "I loved my time at UCLA and working with Billy but thought it was time to move on. I really respected Peter Smith and thought that I could learn from him."

Said Billy Martin, "We hated to lose Kris, but in the end I thought it was a good move for him. I do have to admit that I still cringe at times, knowing he is now a Trojan. Kris will always be a very special person to me and I wish him the best." And, Martin added with a smile, "Even though USC and UCLA have a very healthy rivalry, we are all connected in one way or another in Los Angeles. For instance, I have a graduate degree (EMBA) from USC, and my father-in-law, the late Larry Greiner, was a professor in the Marshall School of Business."

Kwinta brought a very particular and competitive coaching philosophy to USC. "My coaching style is very aggressive and intense. As a player, you shouldn't question your commitment to the team, and your ego has to come second. If you fail, we fail. This is an enterprise that is bigger than any of us. You have to be mentally and emotionally ready every day to improve. We are in the most competitive environment there is in college tennis. To play with us, you may have to sacrifice other parts of your social and academic lives. That's not something that we demand, but all players have to decide for themselves. Stevie is the best example of someone who rose up to the highest level of commitment and sacrifice. On the other hand, Peter and I know that tennis is just a game—but the way that you develop and improve mimics just about everything in life. When we scout recruits, we are trying to assess attitudes and habits. We are trying to figure out, 'Will this player crack under, or rise up to, the intense pressure we face?'

"All of the training climaxes when players are put into these super high-pressure situations. And as a coach, your job is to make these situations appear normal. You don't try to make these moments bigger than what they are, or your players will get tight and choke. My approach in these situations is to tell players to be more aggressive and that will help you win more often than not. Those who are competitive in everything they do will have a better chance in the clutch. If you and I are bowling or playing ultimate frisbee, I want to win. When one competes all the time, facing any sort of pressure becomes second nature. Those who shy away from pressure will just not be prepared. Their bodies will not respond well. When we train, we are developing mental discipline and habits. True champions are ultra competitive and want to win. Because Peter and I can still bang balls with our guys, we get respect on the court. You can sell the knowledge quicker if they know you can play.

"The toughest thing about my transition to transfer to USC was competing against my former Bruins' players. I sort of justified it by thinking if I coached hard against UCLA that they would have to play better, too. You may think it odd that I moved to USC, because all I wanted to do for years was to beat the Trojans; but now my feelings are the opposite.

"There is so much competitiveness across all sports at the two schools and the UCLA guys always give me a hard time. When UCLA beats USC in basketball, my phone doesn't stop ringing! The rivalry pushes both of us to be better—it's like Roger Federer and Rafael Nadal."

The Trojans opened the 2013 season well going 12-0 through mid-February. Their 12th victory occurred when they beat the Bruins at home 4-3. The Trojans suffered their first loss to Virginia 4-2 in the championship match at the ITA National Indoor Championships. On March 29th, USC beat Stanford 6-1 giving Coach Peter Smith his 500th victory. The Trojans' third and fourth losses of the season came at the hands of the Bruins, 4-3 at Westwood, and again at the Pac-12 Championships in Ojai, 4-2.

In the round of 16 of the NCAA team championship at the University of Illinois, USC beat Baylor 4-1. Gomez and Quiroz (who happen to be cousins) won at No. 2 doubles, but Baylor rallied to win the other two doubles matches to take the doubles point. Gomez, Quiroz and Johnson won their singles matches with Hanfmann at No. 3 singles beating Mate Zsiga in three sets to clinch the match.

The quarterfinal against Ohio State was another matter. Once again, the Trojans lost the doubles point 2-1 with de Vroome and Johnson being the sole victors beating Blaz Rola and Hunter Callahan. While Eric Johnson, Max de Vroome and Yannick Hanfmann all won their matches in straight sets, it wasn't enough to fend off a very tough Buckeye team who ultimately beat the Trojans 4-3. The loss to Ohio State broke the Trojans' streak of 27 consecutive wins in the NCAA tournament and USC finished the season with a 26-5 record.

"In 2013 our team just wasn't as cohesive as it had been in the previous years," said Smith. "I know that the guys felt a lot of pressure to succeed, especially after Stevie left, but sometimes you just can't get everyone on the same page. For me, it highlighted how strong Stevie and Dwin were as leaders as they put aside their egos to lead the team."

Virginia finally won its first national title by beating UCLA 4-3 in the final. UCLA actually had team match point at No. 3 singles in the decisive match. Adrien Puget of UCLA hit a volley to Mitchell Frank's backhand and Frank hit a lob that sailed out and the Bruins thought they had won the title. However, the chair umpire ruled that Puget's right foot had touched the net and awarded the point to Frank. Frank went on to win the next four games, the match, and the title for the Cavaliers. It was a heart-breaking loss for the Bruins. In the singles final, Blaž Rola, the four-time All-American from Ohio State, beat Virginia's Jarmere Jenkins 7-8 (8), 6-4 for the title. Rola became the first NCAA singles champion in Ohio State's history. In doubles, Jenkins and Matt Styslinger of Virginia defeated Chris Camillone and David Holiner of Texas in three sets to win the doubles title.

In 2014, Michael Grant, Yannick Hanfmann, Eric Johnson, Roberto Quiroz and Ray Sarmiento all returned to the team. Emilio Gomez left USC for the professional ranks. Four new freshmen joined the squad, including Rob Bellamy – a top player from the Pacific Palisades – whose father, Steve Bellamy founded the Tennis Channel and whose mother Beth Herr Bellamy was the NCAA women's single champion for USC in 1983. Nick Crystal, a top-20 recruit from Waccabuc, New Jersey, Connor Farren from Foster City, California and redshirted freshman David Laser from New Trier High School in Illinois also joined the team.

Starting the season ranked No. 4, USC showed some early signs that they were in for another strong season. At the beginning of February, the Trojans hosted the first Pac-12 - SEC Showdown with USC, UCLA, Georgia and Florida competing in the two-day event. On the first day, USC beat No. 3 Georgia 4-0 and No. 2 UCLA toppled No. 11 Florida 4-1. On day two, the Trojans were victorious in a 4-0 win over Florida, and UCLA inched past Georgia 4-3. At the ITA National Indoors, Ohio State showed some muscle, beating the Men of Troy 4-1 in the final, with Hanfmann notching the only win for USC at second singles.

On March 25, USC ranked No. 1 in the nation with an impressive 18-2 record. In the Pac-12 title match, the Trojans fell to No. 5 UCLA 4-2. UCLA came out quickly garnering the doubles point. Hanfmann and Sarmiento won their singles matches, giving USC the edge at 2-1, but the Bruins fought back handing de Vroome, Johnson and Michael Grant straight-set losses to give the title to UCLA.

With the USC band playing *Fight On!* and *Conquest*, the Trojans took the courts at the Dan Magill Tennis Complex at the University of Georgia to battle Virginia in the NCAA semifinal in 2014. The Trojans had advanced to the semifinal with a 4-1 victory over the University of Texas. USC fans were ready and raucous. Over the years, as the popularity of tennis had grown, USC had become very adept at strategically positioning its managers, team members and fans on the various courts to very loudly cheer the Trojans on.

Despite the fan support, it was not an easy match. The weather was oppressively hot and humid. Said Michael Grant, "I broke out my senior year after not doing too much my first three years on the team, playing well throughout the tournament, and winning my matches against Columbia and then Texas. In the semifinals, we were facing Virginia for the fifth time in six years and I was up against a very tough player, J.C. Aragone. I won the first set, but J.C. took the second. Early in the third set at 3-2, my left foot was cramping and Virginia noticed.

"The match score was 3-1 in our favor with Max, Yannick and I still playing. Yannick and I were both very close to finishing. I remember I had a very long 50-ball rally, which I won. Then, I heard a lot of cheering and looked up. Yannick had finished just seconds before me to clinch the match. I sank to the ground and the next thing I knew everyone piled on top of me… and then my leg really started to cramp! I knew I was going to be in big trouble the next day."

Michael Grant soldiered on despite severe leg cramps

Both Sarmiento and Grant were dehydrated and exhausted and, by 11:30 p.m., both were in an ambulance with IVs in both arms. Said Smith, "We have a lot of respect for Virginia. They are a great team. That day we brought our A-game and Virginia didn't play their best. I think we were still in their heads."

In the final, USC was up against the University of Oklahoma Sooners, a formidable team coached by John Roddick, the former four-time All-American from Georgia and the older brother of U.S. Open champion Andy Roddick. While Oklahoma was ranked No. 2 in the country, they had never been to the big show, so this match would test their mettle. The weather in Athens continued to be very hot and humid.

At the start of the match, Oklahoma came out guns-a-blazin' to overcome Connor Farren and Roberto Quiroz at No. 2 and de Vroome and Johnson at No. 3 doubles to take the doubles point. In singles, Quiroz could not get his sea legs and fell quickly to Dane Webb in straight sets. USC was down 2-0 and things were not looking good. On court one, Hanfmann fought very hard and got the first point for the Trojans, besting Guillermon Alcorta 7-5, 6-2.

On court two, Ray Sarmiento was struggling. "My final match against Oklahoma is a match I'll never forget," he said. "I was down 4-1 in the first set against Alex Alvarez, a guy who hits very big... and he just wasn't missing. I remember thinking 'He can't keep this up.' I slowed the match down a little and started to play my game. I scrapped my way back and won five games in a row to steal the first set 6-4. I got down early in the second set 4-1 again. I knew I didn't want to go to a third set."

Kris Kwinta, who was coaching on Sarmiento's court, was clapping very loudly every time he won a point. "At one point I realized that every time I clapped for Ray, someone else in the stands was also clapping. I looked up and it was Andy Roddick. I think he was mocking me. Maybe I was getting on his nerves," laughed Kwinta.

Said Sarmiento, "I needed to pick up my energy, so I started yelling to my teammates hoping that they could feed off my energy and vice versa. All these thoughts were racing through my head: 'This is my last year, my last NCAA tournament and my last match.' I didn't want to lose, but at the same time I told myself to enjoy the moment and play for my teammates, play for the coaches, and for USC. I started to play more aggressively and relaxed more and then caught up to 5-5. I was able to win the second set tiebreaker 7-6. My teammates told me later that my win took a lot of pressure off them. I have to say that this was one of the best matches that I played in college."

Ray Sarmiento crushing his forehand. Ray came from behind in both sets to tie the championship match against Oklahoma

With the match score now tied at 2-2, Max de Vroome, Michael Grant and Eric (EJ) Johnson were dueling it out on the three lower courts. Johnson was known as one of the most tenacious, aggressive players on the team. "When I did my interview for a spot on the team, the coaches knew I was a hard-working guy," said Johnson. "I was never the quickest player and I didn't have the best feel, but no one was going to outwork me. My approach was always to keep fighting, to be aggressive and to believe in myself. I also really listened to what the coaches told me. Why would I come to a top school like USC and not do what Peter and Kris thought I should do?"

Said Peter Smith of Johnson, "I always had great confidence in EJ. He is a proven winner who simply never gives up."

Johnson won his match 6-1, 7-6(2) at No. 5 and the Trojans took the lead for the first time 3-2. If either de Vroome or Grant was victorious, the Trojans could claim their 21st NCAA title. In addition to the IV that Grant had the night before the final, Drew Morcos, the USC fitness trainer, did rehab on his legs with pads that circulated freezing cold water and compressed the muscles at the same time.

"Once I stepped on the court, the pain just went away," said Grant. "I am sure the adrenaline took over. We were so close as a team that I was willing to die out there if I had to. Similar to the semifinal, I lost the set, but I was pacing myself and won the second set. At the start of my third set, Ray, Roberto and Yannick were off the court. Eric won in straight sets. Then everyone came down to the lower courts. I figured if I was still on the court, we were still in the match. I also didn't want Max to be out there alone. I had to stay out there with him. Then my left quad started cramping.

Max de Vroome seems to launch himself off the ground as he hits his massive topspin serve

"On a break, I remember calling to Drew, 'Please bring me the nectar of the Gods!' – which of course was pickle juice. Coach came to my court and I told him I was tired. Peter said, 'No you are not!' I was serving at 4-2 in the third and I could feel the tension building in the stadium, but it wasn't for me. I looked up at the scoreboard and Max had two match points. 'Crap, I thought! Max lost his first match point.' But I knew I couldn't stand around and watch."

On court four, de Vroome lost the first set 6-4 to Oklahoma's Andrew Harris, but came back strong taking the second set 6-3. In the third set, de Vroome broke to take a 5-4 lead. If he could hold serve, he would win the set, match and the championship for the Trojans. As they were changing sides, de Vroome picked up a bottle of Gatorade and promptly spilled most of it down his shirt. From two courts away you could see how much his hands were shaking.

After going up 40-15, de Vroome lost his first match point. Just before serving into the ad court at 40-30, Peter Smith approached him and whispered something into his ear. de Vroome nodded and went back to serve. Coiling his 6'5" frame, he delivered a monstrous 130 mph serve to the Harris backhand. Harris wound up and launched a blistering cross-court backhand return, but de Vroome had charged the net and was already at the service line. He lunged and stretched for a backhand volley that he hit down the line for an untouchable winner. Game, set, match—and USC had just won its 21st NCAA title.

As has been his trademark when his teams win a national championship, Smith threw both arms up into the air as de Vroome ran across the court to hug him. Later, he revealed what Smith had told him: "Kick serve to the backhand, volley and let's get the hell out of here."

Said de Vroome, "I have never felt so happy and overwhelmed. The tension was nerve-wracking but incredibly

Eric Johnson, the backbone of the team and a consistent winner winds up for a serve

exciting. I am not sure I will ever experience anything quite like the feeling of winning that match and the championship for the team. I remember turning and hugging Peter and then out of nowhere all of my teammates descended on me. To this day, I remember the feeling.

"Throughout the match, a million thoughts crossed my mind at one time or another: strategies, scores, realizing we are in the final, realizing we might win it. The most important thing was to stay focused on the strategy. You can't think too long about the score or how other courts are doing. You don't even really have time to realize you're in the final of the NCAA championship. You've got to be focused on how you can beat that guy on the other side of the net. Everything else is simply a distraction. So I kept telling myself to keep it simple, serve to his backhand, make the first shot and start attacking the net as soon as possible. It was a simple strategy and I had talked about it with coach and Kris.

"Because I knew Andrew Harris from the junior tournaments, had played him a couple times and always had very close matches, I knew what I was up against. I must have visualized beating him a 100 times the day before, but nothing compares to really being out there and doing it. I thought about all the matches I had played against him, how I wanted to beat him for the team, how badly I wanted the NCAA ring, how it would prove that I made the right decision to play college tennis, how there might only be one chance to win the NCAA, how cool it is that the band came out, how you appreciate all the people around you, how amazing the atmosphere is. Ninety-nine percent of the thoughts racing through my brain were just crazy stuff in the middle of an awesome experience as I tried to take it all in and really enjoy it.

"When I saw the players around me finishing, and the crowd circling in on the court, I realized that I could potentially have the honor of clinching the whole thing. We were told not to look at the scoreboard, but that is easier said than done—since there's a massive scoreboard right above your head. So yes, I watched the scoreboard and noticed that Mikey just started his third set. I was up 4-3 with a break so at that point you realize you've just got to do it... but instead of focusing on strategy I had all these jumbled thoughts racing through my brain, and then Andrew broke back to get us to 4-4.

"I remember looking at the crowd, seeing all the familiar faces who had been part of this hard but beautiful journey and I remember thinking, 'I am pretty lucky that I can actually control the outcome.' Everybody out there can only cheer, scream, be nervous, but they cannot play these games for me. I needed to focus on what I was supposed to do. So I broke back and then that last changeover before having to serve it out was probably the most nerve-wracking break I have ever had.

"I knew I had to serve a big serve, being up 5-4 going in to my service game. I realized what the expectations were and that Oklahoma was going to do everything to break my rhythm. I also knew I should hold my serve, but again, that was easier said than done. At those moments it is great to have a coach talking you through. It doesn't matter what is said, it is just nice to not be alone in an otherwise very individual sport. Realizing that the whole team was behind me no matter what definitely helped me to focus on that simple strategy: 'Serve to his backhand, make the first shot and start attacking the net as soon as possible.'

"Peter and I had discussed the strategy over and over again and the goal was for me to hit a high kick serve to Harris' one-handed backhand, then close in aggressively. We practiced that shot every day and that's what I focused on. In contrast to the rest of the match, my mind was very clear and I knew exactly what to do. I knew it was tough for Andrew to hit a one-handed backhand from out wide, above his shoulder under a lot of pressure. And I thought he must be nervous, too. So I figured it would come down to hitting a good serve. Andrew hit a really great return, which I wasn't expecting, but we had practiced this situation over and over, so I was ready. I felt I was on autopilot, knowing the muscle memory and a belief in myself would kick in. I'm still not entirely sure how I made that backhand volley but somehow it worked.

"It took me a while to realize that it was over because I wasn't sure that I made the backhand volley," de Vroome continued. "I was so focused on what to do next that it took me a little bit to grasp that it was over. Part of me was getting ready to play the next point, but then in slow motion I became aware of everybody around me celebrating. My teammates were cheering and running to the court and then it hit me: We did it, we won. While you want to enjoy the entire tournament it's hard because everyday you have to focus on staying healthy, recovering after a match, practicing a bit more, getting enough rest, eating well and hydrating and then suddenly there is nothing to worry about anymore. It took me a couple of weeks to realize it all and it is just the best feeling in the world to be able to celebrate with your teammates. It was one of the greatest moments of my life."

Said Grant, "I was in the middle of a point and heard the crowd cheering. All I could see was coach's arms go up high. I knew what that meant! I fell to the ground. It was over and we had won. It was the best feeling that I had had the whole year. No one can take this away from us. No one can say that we didn't earn this. We earned it everyday. It was a huge team effort."

Said Smith on the year-end USC Trojan Tennis highlight video, "Many coaches asked me, just before the Oklahoma match, 'How do you guys do it? How do you play this hard? How do you come through?' I told them, 'We are just playing our butts off—and we let the scoreboard take care of itself. It's always surreal. To win one championship is so special and so hard. Every year you try to visualize winning and try to get your team to a certain point, but there are so many great players, great teams and great coaches…it's just very special."

Sarmiento was emotional. "There are no words to explain it," he said. "It's the greatest feeling ever. Ending my career this way on a high note and winning the championship for my coaches and the team is so amazing."

The 2014 season was about many of the guys who had won with Johnson and Nguyen wanting to show that they could win without them.

"Losing in 2013 drove us forward," said Smith. "Once we got to the NCAAs, it was time to win. Ray really came through. Ray had never beaten Mitchell Frank at Virginia and it was a great win for him. Michael Grant was a rock, and of course Yannick and Eric played so well. And Max, well he was just like Stevie. He listened to me and trusted me. The win was an incredible moment for our team."

When asked to compare the 2012 and 2014 team championships, Hanfmann responded, "Those two championship years were really different. In 2012, we had that super team, with Stevie winning every singles and almost every doubles match. This gave us a huge advantage in that

Associate Coach Kris Kwinta hoists the 21st NCAA National Team Championship Trophy for the Trojans

we could have a good sense that we would be up 2-0 in most matches because Stevie was such a sure thing. That also meant that we only had to win two of the other five singles matches to win a match. Thus, 2012 was all about keeping it together and not getting ahead of ourselves. We felt like we could only get beaten if we fell to the pressure and couldn't handle it. The finals were super close, since we lost doubles, but once we changed our mindset to play to win rather than not to lose, we played really well. In every match, you need to be out there and giving it your absolute best, no matter how good your best is that day. If you show up, but are scared to lose, I think it really shows and you get punished. In 2014, we didn't have Stevie, but we still had a great team. But we didn't have that feeling that we were the team to beat. In the championship, we got rolling in the early rounds and started getting better and better. In the quarterfinals against Texas, we lost the doubles point but won the first four singles matches, with Roberto clinching. That match was key for us, as we had our backs against the wall. I think this created a different mentality for the team in the next rounds. The semifinal and final matches are still etched in my memory. In 2014, every player in our lineup played to the best of his ability when it mattered most. We were an incredibly close-knit group of guys and it felt like we were in combat together. Thinking back to that time I am just so grateful it happened."

The Trojans ended the season 32-3 overall. Between 2009 and 2014, they won three NCAA Championships at the Dan Magill Tennis Complex in Georgia (2010, 2012, 2014), one at the Mitchell Tennis Center in College Station, Texas (2009) and one at Taube Tennis Center at Stanford (2011). This was not only the 21st national team championship for the

USC men's tennis team but also their 100th all-time NCAA Championship.

During the awards ceremony, the NCAA selects the most outstanding players at each position across all teams. These All-Tournament Team honors went to five of the six USC team players including Yannick Hanfmann (No. 1 singles), Ray Sarmiento (No. 2 singles), Max de Vroome (No. 4 singles), Eric Johnson (No. 5 singles) and Michael Grant (No. 6 singles). Sarmiento was named the Tournament's Most Outstanding Player. Peter Smith was also honored by the USPTA as College Coach of the Year. Smith also won the award in 2011.

Marcos Giron from UCLA, the No. 2 seed, won the NCAA singles title by beating Alex Sarkissian from Pepperdine 6-4, 6-1. The unseeded Sarkissian was the first player from Pepperdine to play in the NCAA singles final since Robbie Weiss was victorious in 1988. Mikelis Libietis and Hunter Reese from Tennessee became the NCAA doubles champions, beating the No. 4 seeds Peter Kobelt and Kevin Metka from Ohio State in a nail-biting match 7-6 (4), 6-7 (3), 7-6 (8). The last time Tennessee had won the NCAA doubles championship was in 1980 when Rodney Harmon and Mel Purcell captured the title.

For the 2015 season, Rob Bellamy, Nick Crystal, Max de Vroome, Johnny Wang, and Eric Johnson all returned. In addition, five freshman joined the team; Henry Ji, the CIF San Diego Player of the Year, Tanner Smith, a top player from Servite High School in Anaheim, Laurens Verboven, a decorated junior from Belgium, Jens Sweaney from Australia and Thibault Forget from Rennes, France—the son of top professional player Guy Forget. The Trojans began the season ranked No. 1 in the nation, based on their NCAA victory the year before. In the ITA National Indoor Championship, the second-ranked Oklahoma Sooners got their revenge on USC, beating them 4-2 in the final. Only Nick Crystal and Eric Johnson won their matches.

On February 22, 2016, the new Buntmann Tennis Center, an awe-inspiring facility, was unveiled at USC signaling a new era for Trojan tennis. The facility includes a complete renovation of David X. Marks Stadium as well as all of the locker room facilities. In addition, new home and visitor locker rooms, a large team room, study wing, and new offices for the coaches as well as a and physical therapy facility were added. An additional court was added to the facility and a huge awning covering the seating area was constructed.

Yannick Hanfmann's powerful groundstrokes won many matches for him

At the end of February, the Tulsa Golden Hurricanes beat the Trojans, who were still ranked No. 1. Tulsa, ranked No. 51, came out of nowhere to stun USC 4-3 at home. While USC won the doubles point, only Johnny Wang and Max de Vroome won their matches.

"We had a very difficult loss to Tulsa," said Smith. "Our team was complacent and didn't come to play…but Tulsa did. There was no sense of urgency. The team did this to themselves. That being said, losses are vital to any program. The lesson is that you have to go out there everyday and compete. Everyone wants to beat us. It was good to find out where we were weak early in the season. We spent a lot of time working through that match and we got back on track."

For USC, Roberto Quiroz had a strong start to the season by beating Dennis Mkrtchian from UCLA 6-2, 6-0 to win the Sherwood Cup. Quiroz's big weapon is his huge lefty topspin serve that wins many points outright for him. Quiroz and partner, Max de Vroome, weren't quite so fortunate, losing to Tom Fawcett and Maciek Ramowicz from Stanford 9-4 in the doubles final.

In mid-March, the No. 5-ranked Trojans overcame No. 14-ranked UCLA, 4-1 at Marks Stadium. The Trojans won the doubles point with de Vroome and Crystal winning in straight sets. Johnny Wang at No. 4 singles clinched the match for USC, beating Karue Sell 6-4, 7-6 (4)

In April, the No. 5 seed Trojans were upset by No. 36 Stanford 4-3 in Palo Alto, but bounced back to beat UCLA again on their home court at the Los Angeles Tennis Center 4-2. Two weeks later, USC extracted their revenge on Stanford with a 4-3 victory to win the Pac-12 Championship at Libby Park in Ojai. Even though the team lost the doubles point, No. 3 Quiroz, No. 4 Wang and No. 6 Crystal won their singles matches. Eric

Johnny Wang prepares to hit his deadly two-handed slice forehand

Johnson at No. 2 singles also won a very tough three-set match (6-2, 4-6, 6-2) against the Cardinal's John Morrissey to clinch the title for the Trojans.

In May 2015, Johnny Wang was voted the ITA National Most Improved Senior. Wang started to play tennis when he was four. His first coach was Kal Moranon, who started him out with an adult size racket.

"I was too weak to hold the racket with one hand so I started using two hands on both my forehand and backhand," Wang said. As a result, he developed the ability to effectively hit topspin and underspin groundstrokes on either side. One of his most formidable strokes became his two-fisted forehand slice down the line that veered sharply off the court, staying so low that it pulled his opponents off the court. If a player was able to get it back, he was so out of position that Wang then quickly put the ball away on his next shot.

"My strategy is usually to use a lot of different spins to soften up a tentative groundstroke and then punish any short balls and sometimes come to the net," Wang said in 2017. "I am always looking to see if my opponent's forehand or backhand tends to break down on big points. If a player has a very strong or favorite shot, I don't want to allow him to get into the groove. By mixing things up so much, I try to keep my opponents off balance. The no-ad format in college tennis today creates an immense amount of pressure. You have to concentrate so much on those big points, otherwise it is over before you know it."

At the 2015 NCAA Championship in Waco, Texas, the No. 7-seeded Trojans fell to No. 2 Baylor 4-2 in the quarterfinals. While Nick Crystal and Thibault Forget were in a battle at No. 3 doubles, Baylor's first and second doubles teams won to give the Bears the doubles point. Eric Johnson and Roberto Quiroz and Eric Johnson won at No. 2 and No. 3 singles, respectively, but de Vroome, Crystal and Wang, at No.'s 5, 6 and 3, all lost in straight sets to give the Bears the win.

"Baylor was just too good today. You don't win all the time and today we lost to a better team," Smith said following the loss. "We put ourselves in a position to extend the match but Baylor really came through when it counted."

Virginia won its second NCAA team title by beating Oklahoma 4-1 in the final, while their top singles player Ryan Shane won the NCAA singles title, defeating Noah Rubin of Wake Forest 3-6, 7-6 (4), 6-1 in the final. In the NCAA doubles final, Soren Hess-Olesen and Lloyd Glasspool from Texas were victorious over Diego Galeano and Julian Lenz from Baylor 2-6, 6-3, 7-6 (3).

Nick Crystal "snapping the neck" of an opponent

In 2016, there was a major shift in personnel on the USC team. Johnny Wang, Eric Johnson, Yannick Hanfmann and Robert Quiroz graduated. Coming back were senior Max de Vroome, juniors Rob Bellamy and Nick Crystal and sophomores Thibault Forget, Henry Ji, David Laser, Tanner Smith and Laurens Verboven. Forget led the team with a 31-9 overall record and also posted an 11-match singles winning streak in the spring. These veterans were joined by three exceptional freshman, Jack Jaede, a top junior from Queensland, Jake Devine and Logan Smith. Devine was the No. 1 junior in the country in 2013, and Smith achieved a No. 1 nationwide ranking in 2014.

The Trojans began the season ranked No. 8 with Crystal being the leader of the team at No. 1 singles.

A talented player with a wide variety of shots, Crystal would often disarm seemingly stronger players with his versatility and ability to come from behind.

"One thing that helped me a great deal is that before each match, the coaches would develop a game plan with you," said Crystal. "The plan is designed to reduce the amount of thinking that you have to do while you are in the heat of battle, and this becomes really important when nerves kick in. The key is not to get ahead of yourself…just stick to the plan. When you are leading in the match, Coach Smith told us that you have to 'Snap the opponent's neck,' like a lion with its prey. I know it sounds dramatic but when you're up, you have to close out the match and not give your opponent any opportunities to come back. But closing out a tennis match is one of the hardest things to do since your opponent is trying not to let that happen -- so the coaches stress that you have to play aggressively. The other thing that both Peter and Kris do in these situations is to keep their players as calm as possible. Peter is so calm out there even in the most tense situations, his players are able to relax and focus on the next point.

"When you are behind in a match the approach is actually similar. Stick to the plan but play even more aggressively. I have always been a slow starter and I would often find myself being down by several games or even a set. Since I am a competitive person I had to get myself into a groove and fight back. Tennis is so much like a chess match… you have to wait for your move to attack and take control. The other highly motivating factor that pushed all of us forward was that coach stressed that you had to play your guts out for the team – this was not an option."

In mid-March, the Trojans took a road trip to Tulsa for a return match with the Golden Hurricane. This time, the outcome was different, with the Men of Troy winning 7-0. Nevertheless, DeVine, Logan Smith and Forget were all stretched to three-set matches. Towards the end of March, the University of Washington Huskies dealt a blow to the Trojans with 4-3 upset victory, winning the doubles point and the Nos. 3, 4 and 6 singles spots.

In mid-April, the USC and UCLA men's and women's tennis teams faced each other in a double header. In the morning, all three men's and women's doubles teams from each school played simultaneously. In the first part of the afternoon, the men's teams played each other, followed by the women's teams. The Trojan men lost 4-2 while the women won 4-1.

In the Pac-12 tournament, the No. 8-ranked USC fell in an upset loss during the semifinal to No. 16 ranked California 4-1. The Trojans had reached the conference title match during the previous four seasons winning the tournament twice in that time period.

At the NCAA Championships, after defeating UNLV and Georgia Tech to reach the round of 16 at Marks Stadium, USC faced No. 7-seeded Georgia. USC won the doubles point with Verboven and Crystal, and Jaede and Tanner Smith winning their matches. Verboven caused gasps from the crowd when he unleashed his beautiful one-handed topspin backhand. Forget and Jaede won at No. 4 and 5 singles, but Trojans Crystal, Smith and Bellamy lost at Nos. 2, 3 and 6. The match came down to a battle between Georgia's Austin Smith and de Vroome at No. 1 singles. Smith ended up breaking de Vroome in the third set and then held to win 7-6 (5), 1-6, 7-5, and give the Bulldogs the 4-3 victory.

In the final, Virginia won its second team title in a row, beating Oklahoma again 4-1. It was the third year in a row that Oklahoma reached the finals without taking the crown. In the singles tournament, No. 6 seed Mackenzie McDonald won the title by upsetting No. 1 seed Mikael Torpegaard of Ohio State 6-3, 6-3. McDonald made it a sweep as he and Martin Redlicki won the doubles title as the No. 2 seeds beating No. 8-ranked Arthur Rinderknech and Jackson Withrow of Texas A&M 6-4, 6-1.

In April of 2016, a panel of 20 players, coaches, members of the media and administrators determined the Pac-12 All-Century Men's and Women's Tennis Players. Of the 12 awardees on the men's side, USC had the most players with six. Stevie Johnson (2009-2012) was named Player of the Century and Alex Olmedo (1956-58), Rafael Osuna (1961-63), Dennis Ralston (1962-64), Stan Smith (1966-68) and Bob Lutz (1967-1969) were awarded the All-Century designation. In the women's category, Barbara Hallquist DeGroot (1976-1979) was the only Trojan to make the list. The Bryan Brothers of Stanford were voted Doubles Team of the Century and Stanford's Dick Gould was the Men's Tennis Coach of the Century.

For the 2017 season, the roster remained very similar to 2016, with the big loss of Max de Vroome. Everyone else returned to the team with the addition of two outstanding freshmen, Brandon Holt (the son of two-time U.S. Open champion Tracy Austin) and Peter Smith's middle son, Riley. Just before joining USC, Holt and Smith had won the $10,000 USTA Pro Circuit "Futures" pro tournament in Laguna Niguel, California and were runners up in the U.S. Open junior championships. Holt was the No. 1 high school recruit in the nation.

Peter Smith had two of his sons on the team. "What's it like having two boys on your team? It's 95% the best and 5% the worst of all worlds," said Smith. "You can't take the father out of any father. I have been very fortunate to win several USTA National Father-Son tournaments with Riley and Tanner.

The 2017 USC men's tennis team at David X. Marks Stadium, Buntmann Family Tennis Center. Front Row: Thibault Forget, Manager, Juan Granizo, Manager Dylan Holt, Manager Rae Lan; Second Row: Coach Peter Smith, Associate Coach Kris Kwinta, Operations Manager, Phil Siordia, Brandon Holt, Jens Sweaney, Nick Crystal, Laurens Verboven, Logan Smith; Third Row: Jake Devine, Henry Ji, Rob Bellamy, Jack Jaede, Tanner Smith, David Laser; Last Row: Volunteer Assistant Coach Deiton Baughman, Riley Smith.

Colter's next! I rely on Kris to coach my boys. I am concerned about any decision that I make with my kids. Being on the team can be hard on them, and hard on me. In the 2017 match against Georgia, Bulldog fans kept yelling to Riley, "Where's your daddy?" We all have to take that in stride. Tammie and I encouraged both Tanner and Riley to go to other schools but both wanted to be Trojans and Colter wants to follow in their footsteps."

Deiton Baughman, a standout player who was taking a break from the pro tour, signed on as the volunteer assistant coach. Dylan Holt (Tracy Austin's older son), Rae Lan and Juan Granizo assumed positions as team managers. Numerous staff members including Whitney Rotrock (academic advisor), Darcy Couch (tennis sports information specialist), Brian Crouser (athletic trainer), Tim Ojeda (strength and conditioning coach) and Philip Siordia (Director of Operations) supported the team.

Before the regular season began, the Trojans scored some great victories. Rob Bellamy won the "Battle in the Bay" tournament in San Francisco, winning four matches and besting Ben Donovan from Cal Poly, San Luis Obispo in three sets. Bellamy hits the ball with ferocity and has one of the biggest forehands on the team. In a harbinger of great things to come, Brandon Holt beat seasoned teammate Nick Crystal in straight sets to win the 60th Annual Southern California Intercollegiates.

USC opened the year ranked No. 8, but lost its first match of the season to No. 11 Florida 4-3 at the Pac-12/SEC Challenge, putting their record at 5-1 and setting the Men of Troy on course for a roller coaster of a season. Right after the loss to Florida, the team upset Georgia 4-0, but then suffered a 4-3 loss to UCLA two weeks later. Several weeks after losing to the Bruins, the Trojans gained revenge with a lopsided 4-1 victory. After winning the doubles point, No. 5 Forget beat Austin Rapp 6-2, 6-1, No. 1 Holt bested Martin Redlicki 6-4, 6-3 and No. 3 Logan Smith clinched the match by beating Evan Zhu 6-4, 7-5.

Logan Smith, one of the most tenacious players on the team, started off the season playing No. 1 singles and did an admirable job, but by mid-February, Coach Smith decided to move freshman Brandon Holt into the top position. On March 31, 2017, Smith celebrated his 600th team victory as the No. 5-ranked Trojans overcame the Oregon Ducks 5-0. In early April, UCLA gained revenge over the Trojans with a 4-1 win on their home turf in Westwood. The Bruins won the doubles point with No. 3 Logan Smith, and No. 4 Jack Jaede, losing in straight sets. Thibault Forget provided a glimmer of hope beating Austin Rapp at No. 5, 6-2, 6-4, but shortly after his win No. 2 Nick Crystal fell to Martin Redlicki in two very closely contested sets, 7-6 (9), 7-6 (2).

In May, David Laser was given a Tommy Award (USC's version of the Excellence in Sports Performance bestowed by ESPN which started in 2005) in the category of Unsung Hero of Trojan athletics with the emcee of the ceremony saying that, "His energy and spirit were unmatched on the team." Laser is as spirited a Trojan as you will find. He is the guy that you always want on your side because of his intense passion. At the beginning of every match, it is David who is in the center of the huddle, galvanizing the team. Other previous winners have included Robert Farah (2011), Jaak Poldma (2011), Male Trojan of the Year, Stevie Johnson (2012) for Male Athlete of the Year, Max de Vroome (2014) as a Rising Star and the USC Men's Tennis Team (2014) as Team of the Year.

David Laser, chief motivator for the team, incites the boys before a home match

On April 29th, USC and UCLA played for the Pac-12 title at Ojai. USC started well by winning the doubles point. Logan Smith and Thibault Forget both won their matches at No. 3 and No. 5, respectively, but Crystal, Jaede and Riley Smith lost at No.'s 2, 4 and 6. Riley Smith was riding a 14-match winning streak before losing to Maxime Cressy 7-6 (2), 6-4 at the No. 6 position. With the score tied at 3-3, the decisive match was No. 1 singles where Brandon Holt was in a dogfight with UCLA standout Gage Brymer.

For most of his freshman season, Holt played No. 1 singles—something that rarely happens in Division I college tennis. Holt had a great season, winning 34 singles matches and 24 doubles matches with partner Riley Smith. What many didn't know was that, in the final and deciding match against the Bruins, Holt was playing against his former idol, Gage Brymer. Holt and Brymer split sets. Brandon had followed Brymer's career as he was coming up the ranks. The third set turned out to be an epic battle with each player holding serve. Finally, at 5-4, Holt broke Brymer's serve to win the match 7-5, 3-6, 6-4 and the title for USC. Holt was later named ITA Southwest Rookie of the year.

As Darcy Couch reported from Ojai in her interview with Coach Smith, "It was a very special environment that the Ojai tournament and our rival UCLA provided, and the match did not disappoint."

Brandon Holt clinched the Pac-12 Championship for the Men of Troy in 2017

Said Smith, "We fought like Trojans. The scoreboard doesn't say it, but today was a complete and total team victory— each and every one of the guys provided a platform for their teammates to shine. I'm very proud of the environment we created. Each day throughout the tournament, a different Trojan stepped up—and today was no different. Brandon didn't act like a freshman today. He was as cool as the other side of the pillow. He came through when it mattered the most, which is a very difficult thing to do. He won a real barnburner on the way to winning us this conference title. It's a really special night for the team."

After such a heart-thumping finish, the NCAA tournament was disappointing for the team. Even though the Trojans entered the tournament ranked No. 4 in the nation, they succumbed in the round of 16 to the host Georgia Bulldogs 4-3. Holt and Smith clinched the doubles point for USC, and then both won their singles matches for three USC victories.

At the end of the season, Brandon Holt became an ITA All-American, ending the season ranked No. 17. He and Riley Smith finished their first season together ranked No. 11 in the nation and missed receiving All-American honors by just one spot. USC finished the season ranked No. 6 in the nation, having notched a 27-6 overall record.

Virginia won their third straight national title, beating first-time finalists North Carolina 4-2. Virginia's Thai-Son Kwiatkowski beat freshman William Blumberg of UNC 6-4, 7-6 (5) to win the NCAA singles title and the doubles title was won by unseeded Andrew Harris and Spencer Papa from Oklahoma, beating No. 1 seeds Robert Loeb and Jan Zielinski of Georgia 4-6, 6-2, 10-6 (tiebreaker).

Epilogue -

Lessons Learned and Looking to the Future

W hat lessons can be learned from the history of the USC tennis team and what does the future hold for the Trojans as they continue to battle to hold their place in the record books?

In surveying the panorama of USC tennis history, several themes are evident. The team's major coaches, George Toley, Dick Leach and Peter Smith were—and are—very accomplished players and driven men. Each has studied the game with a keen eye and learned a great deal about stroke production, strategy and fostering competitive drive. Toley, Leach and Smith all found their coaching calling early and devoted their lives to nothing else.

Another common thread among the coaches is that all set much higher goals for their players than just winning tennis matches. Each felt a responsibility to transform their groups of 18-year-olds into successful young men. There is no doubt that competing and succeeding on the tennis court at the highest levels of college tennis requires discipline, talent and maturity. Peter Smith has stated many times that talent doesn't win matches, character does. Thus, instilling a stable pattern of thinking and feeling, moral strength and integrity into an individual's life, will determine a person's behavioral responses to the many and varied circumstances they may face.

The three coaches together have won 19 national team titles (the two other titles were won by William Moyle and Louis Wheeler), the most of any university in the country, and garnered innumerable awards and accolades. Many of the world's greatest tennis players have emerged from the Trojan ranks. Surely this can't be a coincidence. The aphorism, "success breeds success" is applicable because, from the beginning, tradition and reputation were built and nurtured—first by Harold Godshall, then carried on by George Toley and Dick Leach and then resting in the hands of Peter Smith. No doubt there is enormous pressure to maintain the dominance of the men's tennis program, and every coach must feel they are up to the challenge of being strong leaders.

So what does Smith do to get the very best out of his teams? "We have had great players on our teams, but all of the top teams have great players," he said. "In some years, other teams may have had even more talent than us, but it is our training methods, teamwork and mental preparation that give us the edge and allows us to win national titles."

To this end, Smith is wide open to helping players on the physical, psychological and technical sides. "Both Kris and I do a lot of one-on-one individual coaching," he said. "We will spot a weakness in a player and then find ways to correct it."

Said Logan Smith, "I came to USC because of the reputation of the coaching staff. I knew there were some things that I really needed to improve if I was going to take my game to the next level. For example, I wasn't happy with my forehand. So the coaches overhauled it considerably and also changed my footwork in the process. It took several months for these changes to take hold and I lost quite a few matches before things got better. But, I was willing to listen to and learn from the coaches and my forehand improved and elevated my game significantly."

But not everything is about the technical. "I believe that the strongest team consists of the strongest athletes—both mentally and physically," Coach Smith said. And so he brings in sports psychologists, motivational speakers, state-of-the-art physical therapists, former players and the latest training tools. Smith also emphasizes the importance of meaningful in-depth bonding experiences that lead to team cohesion and higher performance.

Said Tanner Smith, "Not only do we always train with each other, but we live together—meaning we eat, socialize, and chill together. At home, we let our guard down with activities like playing Super Mario Kart, all night, or arguing over whose turn it is to clean the dishes. I believe that teams have the most opportunity to grow together off the court and that shows up when we play. You play the game your whole life, so playing tennis with a group of guys isn't really anything out of the ordinary; but living together is how best friends are made and how family develops." Said Henry Ji, "It's true, you can play together on the court and feel like you have bonded but it's the times when you are living together during the highs and the lows when real bonding takes place.

Jens Sweaney concurs, "You can't fake how you feel in these types of situations."

"Knowing your teammates on such an intimate level, let's you know how they are going to think and act in many situations, and information is very helpful," said Riley Smith. Said Aussie player Jack Jaede, "That's right, so when we see one our teammates down in a match we know what to say to them to ease the pressure or motivate them to get back in the match. It has certainly helped me many times when I hear my teammates yelling the Australian chant, 'Aussie, Aussie, Aussie, Oi, Oi, Oi.' I know they have my back and it gets me back on track."

Jake Devine, who was sidelined by injuries in the 2017 season said, "What makes our team unique is that our sense of family extends beyond the locker room. It is never lost on any Trojan athlete how much work has gone towards establishing our reputation as one of the greatest athletic powerhouses in college sports. Coach Smith regularly uses former players as a resource during the season to help inspire us and remind us that we carry a legacy. The commitment to uphold that prestigious legacy is, without question, one of the biggest reasons why our team performs so consistently."

Said Brandon Holt, "Our team is super close, and I think Coach does a great job of building our team spirit. In my freshman year, we went down to Mexico with Homes for Hope, an organization that fights global poverty. This was an unbelievable bonding experience and it brought us all together. During that trip we worked very hard side by side, slept together, traveled together and just hung out. We built a home for an underprivileged family and everyone cried when we gave the house to the family. Most teams don't cry together, but our team also seemed incredibly happy with each other and we were all really moved by the experience."

Said Peter Smith, "We were the first college team to build a home in Mexico. I saw Homes for Hope on the internet and checked out the company. We were there for three days and it was the best experience of their lives and I know we will go back. I think I do two things well. I can bring a team together and I can help individuals become better tennis players. I am not afraid to lose today to win nine months from now. I have to always ask myself the question, 'Are we making the boat go faster?' There can't be a change in the cadence and the course. There can't be any dissension, as that tears our culture apart. I am constantly thinking about ways to improve our program. I can tell you, immodestly, that we are the gold standard of college men's tennis."

Smith continued, "People often ask me to compare Stevie Johnson and Brandon Holt as freshmen. It's very difficult to compare them, as they have different playing styles and physical makeup. Stevie started at No. 4 singles and didn't play No. 2 until the NCAA tournament. Brandon played a good part of the year at No. 1. Stevie showed real growth by winning the national indoors as a sophomore and being ranked No. 1. Brandon also showed enormous growth with his victory at the Pac-12 tournament. Both are exceptional, but different, players. I do believe that Brandon has the ability to win an NCAA title while he is at USC.

Since 1929, USC has had an incredible rivalry—across all sports—with the UCLA Bruins. Darcy Couch, the USC information specialist, calculated that USC and UCLA played each other 204 times through the end of the 2017 season. "The Bruins are in the lead with 109 wins to our 95," said Smith. "We have to do something about that!" Clearly, the greatest rivalry in men's tennis history will continue to fuel great tennis at both schools.

"One of the reasons why we have arguably the greatest rivalry in college tennis is because both teams are in the same city," said UCLA coach Billy Martin. "It's similar to Duke and the University of North Carolina in basketball. Look, we recruit the same players and have long traditions of excellence in the sport. We each make the other team better."

Those who have played under Peter Smith, those who have worked alongside him, and those who knew him as a young man, believe that Smith is a truly formidable coach. Said Justin Gimelstob, former UCLA standout and commentator on the Tennis Channel, "Peter Smith is a truly superior coach who runs his tennis program with the same intensity as any major football coach in the nation. Producing an amazing player like Steve Johnson takes a very high level of commitment on the part of the coaching staff."

Said former player Ruben Torres, "Peter is a modern day John Wooden and my prediction is that he will retire as one of the greatest tennis coaches in NCAA history."

Trojan tennis fans and players alike no doubt hope that Smith's tenure as coach lasts through many more championship seasons. But the core values that are the legacy of the coaches and players going back to the turn of the 20th century are ingrained in the DNA of the USC men's tennis program, and it seems certain that those who follow in the footsteps of coaches Godshall, Toley, Leach, Smith, and players Mako, Osuna, Olmedo, Ralston, Smith, Lutz, Leach and Johnson will ensure that Trojan tennis remains worthy of the history books.

Origins of the Book

I am a life-long tennis fan. Born in Sydney, Australia, I learned classic Aussie strokes on red clay from my father, the late Dr. Sydney Young. Back then, Australian tennis players like Rod Laver, John Newcombe, Roy Emerson, Evonne Goolagong and Ken Rosewall were already national heroes and they served as inspiration for kids like me. When I was 12, I began to take group lessons with 20 others on a single court. The pro made us pantomime hundreds of forehands and backhands and serves before we were allowed to hit balls—and then chaos erupted.

In 1967, my family moved to Columbus, Ohio, where my father helped start the Department of Genetics at The Ohio State University. I played at Thomas Worthington High School and then at Oberlin College (under Coach Bob Piron) and captained both teams. I got my doctorate at the University of Pittsburgh and my wife, Sarah Bonner, and I joined the Leventhal School of Accounting in 1992. We've raised our two children, Nathaniel and Kaylee, in Southern California. As is so often the story, work and family consumed me, leaving little time for tennis. And I played so infrequently that my game kept sliding to the point where it just wasn't fun anymore. But I always held out hope that one day I would find a way back to the sport.

In early 2012, after years of being on the periphery of tennis, Alexandra Bitterlin, assistant athletic director at USC, asked if I would contribute an article for a publication called *The Trojan Way*, a book that Athletic Director Pat Haden, had commissioned to celebrate notable contributions to USC athletics. Alexandra let me choose the topic and I jumped at the chance to write about the men's tennis team who were heading into their fourth consecutive national championship. I reestablished contact with Peter Smith who I had met some time before, and he suggested that I talk to the players and watch some matches.

In doing research for the article, I became fully immersed in USC tennis. Through this process I discovered that some of the greatest players of all time—like Dennis Ralston, Bob Lutz

and Stan Smith, names that I knew well growing up—were Trojans. I was surprised to find that George Toley's book, *The Golden Age of College Tennis*, covering his years as a coach, was the only one I could find that discussed college tennis. I decided to write a book that would examine the entire history of USC tennis going back to its earliest roots.

Very quickly, it became clear that writing this book was going to push the limits of my knowledge

The author playing at Oberlin College, 1973

of the game. Tennis had changed dramatically since I learned to hit those classic strokes. Racket and string technology had changed; stroke production and grips were completely different, as were conditioning, nutrition, athleticism, and the level of talent of the players. How was I going to write about a sport that I was so passionate about again, but didn't fully comprehend? I asked Peter Smith if he could show me how the contemporary game was played. Peter got together with me for a few sessions and then turned me over to Kris Kwinta, his all-knowing associate coach, and other members of the team to school me in the modern game. I will always be grateful to Peter for providing me with this incredible, "George Plimptonesque" experience.

Over the course of my interaction with the team, I had the rare opportunity to face down Max de Vroome's monstrous kick serve, tried in vain to connect with one of Stevie Johnson's massive top spin forehands, watched Alex Olmedo's groundstrokes scream past me, scrambled to reach one of Rick Leach's pinpoint accurate volleys and watched helplessly as Johnny Wang's irretrievable two-handed, slice-sidespin forehand screamed down the line and veered off the court. How lucky can one guy be?

The most rewarding part of the process of writing *Trojan Tennis* has been the opportunity and privilege to talk directly to many individuals who played on, or were connected to, USC tennis teams, going as far back as 1943. There is no substitute for this kind of oral history in telling the story of USC men's tennis and I am honored to be able to capture these detailed reminiscences.

In May 2014, while watching the Trojans win their 21st NCAA team title in Athens, Georgia (their fifth title in six years), I found myself wondering why the team was so successful. What was it that led to this level of dominance when the competition in American college tennis has never been tougher? It would be presumptuous to say that I have discovered all of the answers, since the basis of developing a championship team involves so many intangibles. But, after five years of being close to the team I am confident in advancing some informed hypotheses. And, on a personal note, I am back to loving the game again. I just wish that I had more time to play and could master the windshield wiper forehand.

—*S. Mark Young*

Appendix I

Photos of USC's 21 NCAA Men's Team Champions 1946 - 2014

1946 NCAA Championship Team on the Hoover courts with the Shrine Auditorium in the background. Front Row: Martin Veselich, Jack Tunnell, SC Voges, Gene Fiegenbaum, Stanley, Alpert, Harold Guiver, Robert Perez. Back Row: John Piers, Keith Roberts, John Shea, Robert Falkenburg, Dick Odman and Tom Falkenburg.

1951 NCAA Championship Team. Front Row: Bob Blackmore, Chuck Stewart, Ray Love, Don Eisenberg. Back Row: Willis O. Hunter, Director of Athletics, Earl Cochell, Jack Kerr, Van Grant, B. Werner, Hugh Stewart and Coach Lou Wheeler.

1955 NCAA Championship Team. Front Row. Ray Levanthal, Alan Call, Francisco Contreras, Al Cleveland, Jacque Grigry, Joaquin Reyes, Jim Perely, Jim Nelson. Back Row: Coach George Toley, Stan Winston, Kevin Tichenor, Steve Anderson, Jim Munson, Rich Haskell, Lee Human, Warren Suzaki and Louis Wheeler.

1958 NCAA Championship Team. Front Row: Coach George Toley, Ed Atkinson, Ernest Follico, Jim Buck, Gordon Davis, Athletic Director Jess Hill. Back Row: Team Manager (unknown), Martin Schiller, Eduardo Guzman, Alex Olmedo and Coach Louis Wheeler.

1962 NCAA Championship Team. Front Row: Charles Rombeau, Jay Colden, Dave Blankeship, John Wheeler (manager), Don Greenberg, Bill Bond, Jr. Back Row: Athletic Director, Jess Hill, Jerry Hurst, Rafael Osuna, Ramsey Earnhart, Howard Lee, Harold Valentiner, Mike Lappin, Coach George Toley.

1963 NCAA Championship Team - The greatest men's college team ever?
Left to Right: Ramsey Earnhart, Tom Edlefson, Dennis Ralston, Rafael Osuna,
Chuck Rombeau and Bill Bond.

No known photo of the 1964 NCAA Championship team exists. Members
of the team included Bill Bond, Jerry Cromwell, Tom Edlefsen, Osamu
Matsumura, Leon Mayberg, Dennis Ralston, David Ranney, Horst Ritter,
Chuck Rombeau and Kent Schick. Pictured above are George Toley, Dennis
Ralston and Tom Edlefsen.

1966 NCAA Championship Team at the LATC. Left to Right: John Tidball, Dave Ranney, Jerry Cromwell, Tom Edlefsen, Stan Smith, Coach George Toley, Bob Eisenberg, Horst Ritter, Jim Hobson, and Joaquin Loyo-Mayo. Not pictured: Bob Lutz.

1967 NCAA Championship Team. Front Row: Bob Lutz, Larry Davidson, Joaquin Loyo-Mayo, Tom Leonard, Steve Avoyer. Back Row: Bob Eisenberg, Coach George Toley and Stan Smith.

1968 NCAA Championship Team. Left to Right: Tom Leonard, Bob Lutz, Bob Eisenberg, Coach George Toley, Stan Smith, Steve Avoyer and Larry Davidson.

1969 First Four-Peat NCAA Championship Team. Front Row: Marcello Lara, Joaquin Loyo Mayo, Tom Leonard. Back Row: George Taylor Fernando Gentile, Coach George Toley, Steve Ayorer and Bob Lutz.

1976 NCAA Championship Team that tied with UCLA for the title. Front Row: Chris Lewis, Andy Luchesi, Earl Prince, Mike Newberry and Bruce Manson. Second Row: Coach George Toley, Charles (Buzz) Strode, Stan Franker, Hans Gildemeister,and Butch Walts.

1991 NCAA Championship Team. Front Row: Andras Lanyi, Manager Brian Carr, Byron Black, David Ekerot. Back Row: Assistant Coach Carl Neufeld, Chad Rosser, Jon Leach, Donny Isaak, Brian MacPhie, Phil Whitesell, Coach Dick Leach.

1993 NCAA Championship Team. Front Row: Assistant Coach Carl Neufeld, David Ekerot, Coach Dick Leach, Pierre-Andre Genillard. Second Row: Lucas Hovorka, Leonard Lee, Chad Rosser, Adam Peterson. Back Row: Brian MacPhie, Chris Swortwood, Andres Lanyi and Jon Leach.

1994 NCAA Championship Team. Front Row. Bill Middleton (Volunteer), Chad Rosser, Coach Dick Leach, Wayne Black, Christian Foster. Back Row: Phil Whitesell, Brett Hansen, Chris Swortwood, Jon Leach, Lucas Hovorka, Adam Peterson and Assistant Coach Matt Anger.

2002 NCAA Championship Team. Front Row: Kneeling Ryan Moore, Prakash Amritraj, Daniel Langre; Second Row: Coach Dick Leach, Ruben Torres (holding photo of his former coach), Andrew Park; Back Row: Assistant Coach Brett Hansen, Darryl Gross, Teig Sullivan, Parker Collins and Nick Rainey.

2009 NCAA Championship Team. Front Row: Stevie Johnson, Matt Kecki, Andrew Kells, Daniel Nguyen, Robert Farah, Daniel Gliner, Jaak Poldma. Back Row: Abdullah Magdas.

2010 NCAA Championship Team. Front Row: Daniel Nguyen, Robert Farah, Eric Amend (kneeling), Associate Coach George Husack, Matt Kecki. Second Row: Michael Tang, Jason McNaughton, Stevie Johnson, Coach Peter Smith with trophy, Daniel Gliner, Jaak Poldma. Back Row: Peter Lucassen, Ben Lankenau, and JT Sundling.

2011 NCAA Championship Team. Front Row: Emilio Gomez, Daniel Nguyen, Peter Lucassen, Jaak Poldma, Michael Grant. Second Row: Stevie Johnson holding trophy, Coach Peter Smith, Michael Tang. Back Row: JT Sundling, Ben Lankenau and Corey Smith.

2012 Second Four-Peat NCAA Championship. Front Row: Roberto Quiroz, Daniel Nguyen, Emilio Gomez. Second Row: Johnny Wang, Peter Lucassen, Michael Tang, Ray Sarmiento holding trophy, Eric Johnson. Back Row: Jordi Vives, Yannick Hanfmann, Ben Lankenau, Coach Peter Smith, Stevie Johnson, Zach Friedman, Associate Coach George Husack.

2014 NCAA Championship Team. Front Row: Robert Quiroz, Eric Johnson, Ray Sarmiento, Michael Grant, Trainer Mia McCarthy, Trainer Rachel Thundat. Second Row:Coach Peter Smith, Yannick Hanfmann, Connor Farren, Associate Coach Kris Kwinta, Max de Vroome, Nick Crystal, Greg Labonowski, David Laser, Johnny Wang, Rob Bellamy and Head Trainer Drew Morcos.

Appendix II

USC Men's Tennis - Alphabetical List of Players 1899-2017

A

Abbott, Bion (1942)

Adler, Doug (1977, 78, 79, 80❖)

Agate, Jim (1980, 81, 82, 83)

Aiken, Bruce (2005)

Al-Agba, Jamil (2004, 05❖, 06, 07)

Alber, Arthur (1914, 18)

Albert, Antisdel (1952)

Allen, Mr. (1909)

Alpert, Stan (**1946✻**, 47, 48, 49)

Amend, Eric (1985, 87❖, 88❖, 89★★❖)

Amritraj, Prakash (**2002✻**, 03)

Anderson, Robert (1945)

Anderson, Steve (**1955✻**)

Andrews, John (1971, 72, 73❖, 74❖)

Anger, Matt (1982❖, 83❖, 84❖)

Antisdel, Albert (1952)

Arnett, Leonard (1959)

Arnold, Paul (1917)

Atkinson, Ed (1957, **58✻ ★★**, 60❖)

Avery, R.W. (1989, 99)

Avoyer, Stephen (**1968✻**, **69✻❖**, 70)

B

Badart, Adam (2003, 04, 05, 06)

Bagley, Bob (1926, 27, 28)

Baker, Mr. (1915)

Baker, Ben (1916, 18)

Baker, Douglas (1916)

Barr, Harold (1929, 30, 31)

Bartelt, Kenneth (1938)

Bastl, George (1997❖, 98❖)

Bastues, Wilfred (1939)

Bellamy, Rob (**2014✳**, 15, 16, 17)

Ballou, C.E.D (1898, 99)

Bengston, Ric (1982, 83, 84, 85)

Benyebka, Mehdi (1990)

Berg, Johan (2003, 04, 05)

Berry, Edward (1922, 23, 24, 26)

Bessent, Neil (1970)

Best, Oliver (1908)

Biasella, Adriano (2004)

Biedebach, Doug (1956)

Bingham, R. (1913)

Black, Byron (1988❖, 89★★❖, 90❖, **91✳❖**)

Black, Wayne (1992, **1993✳❖, 94✳❖**)

Blankenship, David (1962)

Blatz (1929)

Blackmore, Bob (1950, **51✳**)

Bleicher, Howard (1956)

Borgfeld, Paul (1930)

Bohrnstedt, Richard (1970, 71❖, 72❖)

Bond, Bill (**1962✳❖, 63✳, 64✳ ★★❖**)

Bonelli, William (1917)

Borelli, David (1970, 71, 72)

Bradhsaw, Dick (1959)

Brandt, Paul (1987, 88, 89, 90)

Bradley, Floyd (1918)

Brawley, Sean (1979, 80, 81, 82❖)

Bridwell, Josh (**1994✳**)

Bridwell, Walter (1908)

Broberg, Jack (1945)

Brokop, Robert (1949)

Brown, Fred (1898, 99)

Brown, Linus (1914, 17, 18)

Browne, Nat (1909)

Brownell, Corlis (1918)

Brownsberger, Scott (1985, 86, 87, 88)

Buck, Jim (1957, 58)

Buese, Sherman (1938)

Buckmaster, Guy (1908)

Buntman, Jake (1952, 53, 54)

Burroughs, George (1934, 35)

Buttner, Tom (1960)

Burt, Keith (1945)

Butler, Henry (1908)

C

Call, Joseph (1923, 24)

Call, Alan (1952, 53, 54, **55✳**)

Camm, Bill (1945)

Canada, Rocky (**1942**)

Carl, Kent (1994)

Carlock, Marvin (1939)

Carr, Charles (1935, 36)

Carr, Timothy (1963)

Carras, John (1985, 86, 87, 88❖, 89)

Carnes, James (1908)

Castlen, Phil (1933, 34★★)

Chadil, Bob (1933)

Chaffee, Frank (1912, 13)

Chavers, John (1952)

Cherry, Brad (1981, 82, 83, 84)

Chick, Bill (1942)

Clark, Straight (1943, 47, 48, 49)

Cleveland, Allen (1953, 54, 55)

Cleveland, David (1924)

Cochell, Earl (1942, 43, 50, **51**❋ ★★)

Cochrane, Burt (1944, 45)

Cone, Gladys (1915)

Collins, Parker (2000, 01, 02, 03, 04)

Collins, Jack (1943)

Contreras, Francisco (**1955**❋★★, 56★★)

Coogan, Jack (1947)

Cooper, Jarryd (2005, 06, 07)

Corekin, Sam (1956)

Cornwall, Chester O. (1909)

Crames, Bobby (1981)

Crane, Robert (1931, 32)

Creamer, Jack (1936)

Crippen, R. E. (1908, 09)

Crist, R.H. (1898, 99)

Cromwell, Jerry (**1964**❋❖, 65❖, **66**❋)

Connolly, Michael (1961)

Crooker, Leon J. (1909)

Crow, Charles (1953)

Crystal, Nick (**2014**❋, 15, 16, 17)

Cukierman, Daniel (2017)

Cullingham, Earle (1923, 24, 25)

Cvetkovic, Dejan (2005, 06, 07)

D

Dammeyer, Tom (**1991**❋, 92)

Davenport, Mr. (1915)

Davenport, Alfred (1942, 43)

Davidson, Larry (**1967**❋, **68**❋)

Davis, Gordon (1957, **58**❋)

Decker, Russ (1989)

DeLara, Jack (1930, 31, 32)

Delgado, Bob (1960❖)

DeVine, Jake (2016, 17)

Dickson, Ralph (1913, 14)

Dionne, Martin (1990)

Dixon, C.A. (1913, 14)

Donker, Bob (1950)

Donnell, Ellsworth (1944, 45)

Dundas, Chris (1986, 87, 88)

E

Earl, Carl E. (1909)

Earnhart, Ramsey (1961★★ ❖, **62**❋★★❖, 63❖)

Edlefson, Tom (**1963✻❖**, 65❖, 66✻❖)

Eichel, Berkley (1954)

Eisenberg, Donald (1950, **51✻**, 52)

Eisenberg, Robert (**1966✻**, **67✻**, **68✻**)

Ekerot, David (**1991✻**, 92❖, **93✻❖**)

Ellis, Mr. (1914, 15)

Emerson, Antony (1982, 83, 84❖, 85)

Everett, Leon (1938, 39, 40)

Ewens, George (1952, 53, 54)

Ewing, Jeff (1985)

F

Failla, Greg (1989)

Falkenberg, Bob (**1946✻ ★ ★★**)

Falkenburg, Tom (**1946✻**)

Farah, Robert (2007, 08★★❖, **09✻❖**, **10✻❖**)

Farren, Connor (**2014✻**, 15)

Faulkner, Kenneth (1927, 28)

Fazakerly, Jack (1925, 26)

Feigenbaum, Jean (**1946✻**, 47, 48, 49)

Fleitz, John (1948, 49, 50)

Flum, Arthur (1930, 31)

Flynn, Thomas (1930)

Follico, Ernie (1956, 57, **58**)

Forbes, Kevin (1979)

Forget, Thibault (**2015, 16, 17**)

Foust, Emil (1930)

Fowler, John (1930)

Fox, Bob (1938)

Franker, Stan (**1976**, 77)

Franklin (1909)

Freese, Leo (1922)

Fullerton, Bob (1950)

G

Garbutt, Fred H. (1909)

Gates, Austin (1908)

Gates, Bernard (1943)

Gates, Robert (1928, 30)

Gentil, Fernando (**1969✻**, 70, 71)

Genillard, Pierre-Andre (1990, **93✻**)

Georgi, Boyd (1935)

Giger, Joel (**2010✻**, **11✻**)

Gildemeister, Hans (1974, 75, **76✻**)

Gliner, Daniel (2008, **09✻**, **10✻**)

Godshall, Harold (1924)

Godshall, Leon (1917, 18)

Gomez, Emilio (**2011✻**, **12✻**, 13❖)

Gopaoco, P.J. (1996)

Goss, James (1959)

Gottesleben, Patrick (1997, 98, 99❖, 2000)

Grant, Gregory (**1955✺**, 57, 59❖, 60❖)

Grant, Michael (**2011✺**, **12✺**, 13, **14✺**)

Grant, Van (1950, 52, 53)

Greene, Paul (1922, 23)

Grieve, Jessie (1914, 15, 17)

Grigry, Jacque (1953, 54, **55✺**)

Griner, John (1952)

Guiver, Harold (**1946✺**, 48)

Guzman, Eduardo (**1958✺**)

H

Haase, Karl (1938, 39)

Hall, Mr. (1914)

Hall, Jack (1935, 36, 37)

Hall, Claybourne (1979)

Hamer, Hiram (1915, 17)

Hanfmann, Yannick (**2012✺**, 13✺❖, **14✺❖**, 15❖)

Hansen, Brett (**1994✺**, 95❖)

Hansen, Lloyd (1936, 37)

Hardy, Francis (1927, 28, 29)

Harris, Don (1947, 48, 49)

Harris, John (1930)

Harris, Lester (1934)

Harris, Russell (1947, 48)

Hart, Bell (1908)

Haskell, Richard (1952, 53, 54, **55✺**)

Heegar, Mickey (1942)

Heinisch, Al (1957)

Henning, Fred (1960)

Herbst, Jack (1929)

Hill, Gregg (1999)

Hiller, Mike (1957)

Hobson, James (**1966✺**, **67✺**, 71)

Hockett, Harold (1908)

Hochwall, David (1972)

Holder, Edith (1908)

Holladay, John (1973, 74)

Hollis, Ryan (1996, 97, 98)

Holt, Brandon (2017❖)

Hori, Tatsue (1922)

Hoskins, Drew (2004, 05)

Hovorka, Lukas (**1993✺**, **94✺**, 95, 96)

Hughes, Andrew (1995, 96, 97)

Hughes, Kenneth (1934)

Human, Lee (**1955✺**)

Hunt, Joseph (1938★★)

Huntington, Harold (1914, 15)

Hurst, Jerry (1962)

Huston, Dick (1952, 53, 54)

I

Ibanez, A (1953)

Ignatius, Joe (1944)
Irwin, Wendell (1924)
Isaak, Donny (1988, 89, 90, 91✳❖)

J

Jaede, Jack (2016, 17)
Jensen, Christian (2001, **02✳**)
Jensen, Luke (1986❖, 87❖)
Jensen, Murphy (1988, 89)
Ji, Henry (2015, 16, 17)
John, Vernon (1934, 35, 36)
Johnson, Cliff (1932)
Johnson, Eric (**2012✳**, 13, **14✳**, 15)
Johnson, J. (1952)
Johnson, Lamar (1947)
Johnson, Leonard (1947)
Johnson, Robert (1952)
Johnson, Steve (**2009✳❖**, **10✳❖**, **11✳★❖**, **12✳ ★❖**)
Jones, Charles (1950)
Jones, Philo (1898, 99)
Jorgenson, Frank (1941)

K

Kanaster, Louis (1930)
Karleson, Toby (1959)

Kayden, William (1942)
Kazarian, Jeffrey (2003, 04, 05, 06)
Kecki, Matt (**2009✳**, **10✳**)
Keeley, Bill (1929)
Kelchovist (1925)
Kells, Andrew (**2009✳**)
Kepler, Rick (1986, 87, 88, 89)
Kerr, Jack (1947, 49, 50, **51✳**, 52)
Kerr, Red (1927)
Kimbrell, Bob (1943, 44)
Kineade, Lily (1914, 15)
Klein, Jack (1959)
Knapp, Roger (1979❖, 80❖, 81, 82)
Knemeyer, Jack (1935, 36, 37)
Ko, Al (1943)
Kortlander, Jack (1937)
Krueger, K (1953)
Kruger, Jack (1978, 79, 80, 81)
Kukal, Roman (1998, 99❖)
Kunkell, George (1943)

L

Langre, Daniel (2000, **02✳**, 03, 04)
Lankenau, Ben (**2009✳**, **10✳**, **11✳**)

Lanyi, Andras (1990, **91✹**, 92❖, **93✹❖**)

Lara, Marcelo (**1969✹❖**, 71❖, 72❖)

Laser, David (2015, 16, 17)

Lawrence, Al (1948)

Leach, Jon (**1991✹**, 92❖, **93✹❖**, **94✹❖**)

Leach, Dick (1959, 60, 61❖)

Leach, Rick (1984❖, 85❖, 86★★❖, 87★★❖)

Leavens, Donald (1938)

Lee, Howard (1960, 61, **62**)

Lee, Leonard (1992, **93✹**, **94✹**, 95)

Lemaitre, Yves (1956, 57)

Lemon, Gary (1983)

Leonard, Thomas (**1968✹**, 70❖, 71)

Levanthal, Roy (**1955✹**)

Levand, Jack (1942)

Levine, Henry (1938)

Lewis, Jack (2008)

Lewis, Chris (1975, **76✹❖**, 77★★❖, 78❖)

Lindsay, Roy (1933)

Lipshultz, Irv (1950)

Little, Bob (1932)

Livingston, Whit (2003, 05, 06, 07)

Long, Wilbur (1918)

Loucks, Adam (2005, 06, 07)

Love, Ray (1949, 50, **51★**, 52)

Lo, Joaquin (1961)

Loyo-Mayo, Joaquin (**1966✹❖**, **67✹❖**, **69✹ ★ ★★❖**)

Lowe, Ed (1952)

Lowell, Maude (1915)

Lower, William (1917, 18)

Lozano, Jorge (1983❖, 84❖, 85❖, 86)

Lubin, Ronald (1939, 40, 41)

Lucassen, Peter (**2010✹**, **11✹**)

Lucchesi, Andy (**1976✹**, 77❖)

Lutz, Bob (**1967✹★ ★★❖**, **68✹★★❖**, **69✹❖**)

Lynch, Paul (1940)

M

MacCormick, Edwin (1917)

MacDonald, Wallace (1947)

Machette, Micheal (1970, 71, 72, 73❖)

MacPhie, Brian (**1991✹❖**, 92❖, **93✹❖**)

Magdas, Abdullah (2008, **09✹**)

Mako, Gene (1934★★ ★, 36, 37)

Malatesta, Mark (1990)

Mamiit, Cecil (**1996★❖**)

Manasse, Matt (2008)

Manson, Bruce (1975★★❖, **76✹❖**, 77★★❖)

Margolin, Mike (1972, 73, 74, 75)

Martin, A.O. (1898, 99)

Martini, Ranie (1974)

Marvin, Henry (1957, 59)

Marx, Kurt (1947, 48, 50)

Matsumura, Osamu (1964)

Mattman, Charles (1941★★)

Matsuo, Gene (1960)

Mcallep, W.R. (1898, 99)

McCarty, F.D. (1898, 99)

McCormack (1915)

McFadyen, Dwight (1918)

McGinnis, Roy (1928)

McMillan, William (1923, 24)

McNamara, Myron (1940)

McNaughton, Jason (2007, 08, **09✹, 10✹**)

Melville, Scott (1987★★✧, 88✧)

Menon, Sashi (1971✧, 72, 73✧, 74✧)

Merryman, Scott (1999, 2000, 01)

Meyberg, Leon (1963, 64, 65)

Michaels, Gary (1987)

Michaels, Greg (1988, 89)

Miller, Don (1949, 50)

Miller, E. H. (1898, 99)

Miller, Everett (1926, 27, 28)

Millman, Jess (1932, 33, 34, 36)

Moore, Richard (1944, 45)

Moore, Ryan (1999, 2000✧, 01✧, **02✹✧**)

Montgomery, Wayne (1908)

Morris, Steve (1959)

Morrow, Ray (1912, 13, 14, 15, 16)

Moy, Fred (1944)

Mucks, Robert (1925)

Mueller, Johannes (1997)

Munson, Jim (**1955✹**)

Murdock, George (1908)

Murphy, Howard (1925)

Murrel, Lester (1924)

N

Naamami, Henry (**1946✹**)

Nathan, Robert (1917, 18)

Nealon, Billy (1979, 80✧, 81, 82)

Need (1939)

Nelson, David (1937)

Nelson, Gordon (1941)

Nelson, Jim (1955✹)

Nelson, John (1937, 38)

Nelson, Lawrence (1939)

Newberry, Mike (1975, **76★**, 77)

Newell, Kenneth (1912, 13, 15, 16, 17)

Newell, Mabel (1915)

Nguyen, Daniel (**2009✳, 10✳, 11✳, 12✳**)

Nordahl, H. A. (1909)

Norton, B. N. (1898, 99)

Novelo, Marco (1978, 79, 80, 81)

O

Odman, Dick (1941, **46✳**)

Olerick, Charles (1922)

Olewine, Ted (1941✳, 42, 43)

Olmedo, Alex (1956★ ★★, 57❖, **58✳★ ★★❖**)

Olyphant, Andy (1987, 88, 89)

O'Reilly, Tim (1975)

Osuna, Rafael (1961★★❖, **62✳★ ★★❖, 63✳★★❖**)

Osuna, Rafael-Belmar (1983, 84, 85, 86)

Ouwendyk, Bob (1957)

Owen, Festus (1917)

Oxnam, G. Bromley (1912, 13, 14)

P

Park, Andrew (1999, 2000, 01❖, **02✳**)

Parmalee, Warren (1924)

Patterson, Scott (2003, 04)

Pawsat, Tim (1983❖, 84❖, 85❖, 86★★❖)

Perez, Bob (**1946✳**, 47, 48, 49)

Perley, James (1954)

Perley, Jim (1953, 54, **55✳**)

Peters, Charles (1943, 44)

Peterson, Adam (**1993✳, 94✳**, 95❖, 96)

Petrovic, Glenn (1976, 77, 78❖)

Philip, Mr. (1925)

Piers, John (**1946✳**, 47)

Piotrowski, Andrew (2008)

Poehler, Christopher (1998)

Poldma, Jaak (2008, **09✳, 10✳. 11✳**)

Posson, Harry (1917)

Prince, Earl (1975, 77, 78, 79)

Q

Quiroz, Robert (**2012✳❖**, 13, **14✳, 15❖**)

R

Rager, Robert (1921)

Rainey, Nicholas (1999, 2000❖, 01❖, **02✳❖**)

Ralston, Dennis (**1962**✺✦, **63**✺★ ★★✦, **64** ★ ★★✦)
Ramirez, Manuel (1995, 96✦)
Ramirez, Raul (1972✦, 73✦)
Ranney, Dave (**1964**✺, **66**✺, **67**✺)
Real, Richard (1949)
Reed, William (1956)
Reedy, William (1939, 40, 41, 42)
Reyes, Joaquin (**1955**✺★★, 56)
Richardson, Grant (1909)
Riskind, Morris (1930)
Ritchie, Gerald (1917)
Ritter, Horst (**1964** ✺, 65✦, 66)
Roberts, Keith (**1946**✺, 47)
Roberts, Warren (1952)
Roberts, William (1932, 33)
Robertson, J. (1952)
Robinson, Malcolm (1924, 25)
Robinson, Stern (1925, 26)
Rodriguez, Sean (1981)
Rombeau, Charles (1962, 63, **64**✺)
Roomie, Beatrice M. (1908)
Rosser, Chad (**1991**✺, 92, **93**✺, **94**✺)
Roth, Fred (1941)
Rowley, Robert (1934, 35, 36)
Rudy, Mr. (1978, 79)
Runston, Mr. (1939)
Runyon, Kenneth (1943, 44)
Russell, James (1949)

S

Sacks, Gary (2007, 08)
Samayoa, Fernando (1995✦, 96, 97, 98)
Sarmiento, Ray (**2011**✺✦, **12**✺✦, 13✦, **14**✺✦)
Saul, Arnold (1947, 48, 49)
Schiller, Martin (1958, 59, 60)
Schick, Kent (1964, 65)
Schlotte, Neleitta (1914, 15)
Schroeder, Frederick (1940)
Schulman, Steve (1957)
Scott, Edward (1945)
Scott, Hugo (1981)
Sellschop, Ryan (**1994**★)
Seto, Adrian (1996)
Seton, Kent (1989, 90✦, 92, **93**✺✦)
Shea, Gilbert (1948, 49 50, 53)
Shea, John (**1946**✺, 48, 49)
Sherman (1925)
Simerson, John (1985, 86, 87)
Sindorf, Ralph (1918)
Skleners, Joe (1922, 23)
Slattery, Reid (1996)
Smith, Dennis (1956)
Smith, Choi (1943)
Smith, Corey (2011✺, **12**)

Smith, Stanley (**1966✱**, **67✱★★✧**, **68✱ ★ ★★**)

Smith, Logan (2016, 17)

Smith, Riley (2017)

Smith, Marion (1917, 18)

Smith, Tanner (2015, 16, 17)

Smolicki, Mateusz (2017)

Snyder, Garrett (2006, 07)

Spencer, Kyle (1995, 96, 97✧, 98)

Spero, Stanley (1942)

Spizzo, Damien (2001, **02✱**)

Stabler, Professor L. J. (1898, 99)

Stadler, Nathan (2006)

Stannard, Ronald (1916, 17, 18, 21)

Steiner, Harold (1932, 33)

Stelle, Stanley (1928, 29, 30)

Stephens, Tom (1933)

Stewart, Chuck (1950)

Stewart, Hugh (1950, **51✱★★**, 52★, 53)

Stocks, James (1930, 31, 32)

Stoddart, Kling (1924)

Stoebe, Roy (1931, 32)

Strode, Charles (**1976✱**, 77, 78)

Sullivan, Teige (**2002✱**)

Sundling, JT (**2010✱**, **11✱**)

Swain, Ray (1929, 30)

Sweaney, Jens (2015, 16, 17)

Sweet, Donald (1940, 41, 42)

Swortwood, Chris (1990, **93✱**, **94✱**)

T

Tanbara, George (1942)

Tang, Michael (2013)

Tarna, Gary (1968)

Taylor, George (**1969★**, 70, 71)

Taylor, Venorris (1918)

Teal, Jack (1943, 47, 49, 50)

Terborg, Jack (1948, 49)

Tichenor, Kevin (**1955✱**, 56)

Tidball, John (1965, 67)

Toley, George (1940, 41)

Tong, Allen (1959, 60, 61)

Tong, Edgar (1942)

Tontz, Daniel (2003)

Torres, Ruben (2001, **02✱**, 03, 04)

Townsend, Richard (1974)

Transchel, Milton (1935)

Tunnell, Jack (**1946✱**, 47, 48)

Turner, Harry (1950)

U

V

Van Dillen, Erik (1970❖)

Van't Hof, Robert (1977, 78❖, 79❖, 80★❖)

Van't Hof, Kaes (2005, 06, 07, 08★★❖)

Van Oertzen, Fernando (1978, 79, 80, 81)

Verboven, Laurens (2016, 17)

Veselich, Martin (**1946✹**)

Vives, Jordi (**2012✹**)

Voges, SC (1943, **46✹**)

de Vroome, Max (2013, **14✹**, 15, 16)

W

Waldman, Robbie (1995, 96, 97)

Walker, Benny (1952)

Walker, Jordan (1998)

Wallgard, Jonas (1986, 87, 88)

Walts, Kenneth (Butch) (1974, 75★★❖)

Wang, Chong (2006)

Wang, Johnny (2012✹, 13, 14✹, 15❖)

Warren, Eugene (1914, 15, 16, 17)

Warren, Robert (1952)

Washer, John (1985, 86, 87)

Wayman, Micheal (1973, 74❖, 75)

Weiner, Roger (1960)

Welch, Stanton (1922, 23)

Wellborn, Maida (1913, 14, 15)

Weller, Earl V. (1913, 14)

Weller, George (1956)

Werner, Mr. (1950)

Wetherell, Lewis (1936, 37, 38★★)

White, Howard (1923, 24, 25)

Whitehall, Bob (1960)

Whitesell, Phil (**1991✹**, 92, **93✹**, **94✹**)

Williams, C. A. (1898, 99)

Williamson, Harold (1922, 23, 24)

Wiles, Bill (1952)

Willebrands, Jack (1956)

Willett, Hugh (1917)

Willinski, Scott (1997, 98, 99)

Willner, Robin (1945)

Wilson, James (1956)

Wilson, Jason (1995, 96)

Wilson, Theron (1927, 28, 31)

Winkenhower, Edward (1949)

Winkler, Bill (1959)

Winston, Stan (1955)

Witman, Roy A. (1898, 99)

Witsken, Todd (1982, 83❖, 84❖, 85❖)

Wong, Garrett (2001, **02**✶)
Woodbury, Doug (1942)
Wooledge, Philip (1933, 34, 35, 36)
Wright, Brian (04, 05, 06)

X

Y

Yamada, Henry (1956)
York, James (1967, 68, 69)

Z

Zaman, Akram (1997, 98)
Zellhoefer, Robert (1942)
Zertuche, Henry (1942)
Zotter, R. (1953)

Legend:

✶ = **NCAA Team Champion**

★ = **NCAA Singles Championship**

★★ = **NCAA Doubles Champion**

❖ = **All-American Player**

Appendix III

USC Men's Tennis - Honors and Achievements

National Team Championships (Most in the Nation)

William Moyle (1946)
Louis Wheeler (1951)
George Toley (1955)
George Toley (1958)
George Toley (1962)
George Toley (1963)
George Toley (1964)
George Toley (1966)
George Toley (1967)
George Toley (1968)
George Toley (1969)
George Toley - Tie (1976)
Dick Leach (1991)
Dick Leach (1993)
Dick Leach (1994)
Dick Leach (2002)
Peter Smith (2009)

Peter Smith (2010)
Peter Smith (2011)
Peter Smith (2012)
Peter Smith (2014)

National Singles Championships (15)

Gene Mako (1934)
Bob Falkenburg (1946)
Hugh Stewart (1952)
Alex Olmedo (1956)
Alex Olmedo (1958)
Rafael Osuna (1962)
Dennis Ralston (1963)
Dennis Ralston (1964)
Bob Lutz (1967)
Stan Smith (1968)
Joaquin Loyo-Mayo (1969)
Robert Van't Hof (1980)

Cecil Mamiit (1996)

Steve Johnson (2011)

Steve Johnson (2012)

National Doubles Champions (21) Most in the Nation

Gene Mako/Phillip Castlen (1934)

Joseph Hunt/Lewis Wetherell (1938)

Ted Olewine/Charles Mattman (1941)

Bob Falkenburg/Tom Falkenburg (1946)

Earl Cochell/Hugh Stewart (1951)

Francisco Contreras/Joaquin Reyes (1955)

Alex Olmedo/Francisco Conteras (1956)

Alex Olmedo/Ed Atkinson (1958)

Rafael Osuna/Ramsey Earnhart (1961)

Rafael Osuna/Ramsey Earnhart (1962)

Rafael Osuna/Dennis Ralston (1963)

Dennis Ralston/Bill Bond (1964)

Stan Smith/Bob Lutz (1967)

Stan Smith/Bob Lutz (1968)

Joaquin Loyo-Mayo/Marcello Lara (1969)

Butch Walts/Bruce Manson (1975)

Bruce Manson/Chris Lewis (1977)

Rick Leach/Tim Pawsat (1986)

Rick Leach/Scott Melville (1987)

Eric Amend/Byron Black (1989)

Robert Farah/Kaes Van't Hof (2008)

USC Athletic Hall of Fame

Gene Mako

Bob Falkenburg

Alex Olmedo

Rafael Osuna

Dennis Ralston

George Toley

Dick Leach

Bob Lutz

Stan Smith

Rick Leach

Bryon Black

Wayne Black

International Tennis Hall of Fame

Gene Mako
Ellsworth Vines
Bob Falkenburg
Joe Hunt
Alex Olmedo
Rafael Osuna
Dennis Ralston
Stan Smith

Intercollegiate Tennis Association Men's Collegiate Hall of Fame

Gene Mako
Bob Falkenburg
Alex Olmedo
Rafael Osuna
George Toley
Tom Edlefsen
Ramsey Earnhart
Bill Bond
Dennis Ralston
Bob Lutz
Stan Smith
Raul Ramirez
Dick Leach
Rick Leach
Robert Van't Hof

Wayne Black
Bryon Black
Bruce Manson
Matt Anger

All-Americans

Alex Olmedo (1957)
Alex Olmedo (1958)
Gordon Davis (2nd team) (1958)
Gregory Grant (2nd team) (1959)
Robert Delgado (2nd team) (1960)
Gregory Grant (2nd team) (1960)
Ed Atkinson (3rd team) (1960)
Ramsey Earnhart (1961)
Rafael Osuna (1961)
Dick Leach (3rd team) (1961)
Rafael Osuna (1962)
Ramsey Earnhart (1962)
Bill Bond (1962)
Dennis Ralston (2nd team) (1962)
Tom Edlefsen (1963)
Rafael Osuna (1963)
Dennis Ralston (1963)
Bill Bond (2nd team) (1963)
Ramsey Earnhart (2nd team) (1963)
Dennis Ralston (1964)
Bill Bond (1964)

Jerry Cromwell (2nd team) (1964)

Tom Edlefsen (1965)

Jerry Cromwell (2nd team) (1965)

Horst Ritter (2nd team) (1965)

Stan Smith (1966)

Tom Edlefsen (1966)

Joaquin Loyo-Mayo (2nd team) (1966)

Stan Smith (1967)

Bob Lutz (1967)

Stan Smith (1968)

Bob Lutz (1968)

Steve Avoyer (1969)

Marcello Lara (1969)

Joaquin Loyo-Mayo (1969)

Bob Lutz (1969)

Erik Van Dillen (1970)

Tom Leonard (1970)

Marcello Lara (1971)

Dick Bohrnstedt (1971)

Sashi Menon (1971)

Marcello Lara (1972)

Raul Ramirez (1972)

Dick Bohrnstedt (1972)

Raul Ramirez (1973)

John Andrews (1973)

Sashi Menon (1973)

Mike Machette (1973)

John Andrews (1974)

Sashi Menon (1974)

Mike Wayman (1974)

Bruce Manson (1975)

Butch Walts (1975)

Chris Lewis (1976)

Bruce Manson (1976)

Chris Lewis (1977)

Andy Lucches (1977)

Bruce Manson (1977)

Chris Lewis (1978)

Glenn Petrovic (1978)

Robert Van't Hof (1978)

Roger Knapp (D) (1979)

Robert Van't Hof (S,D) (1979)

Doug Adler (D) (1980)

Roger Knapp (D) (1980)

Bill Nealon (D) (1980)

Robert Van't Hof (S,D) (1980)

Matt Anger (S) (1982)

Sean Brawley (S) (1982)

Matt Anger (S) (1983)

Jorge Lozano (D) (1983)

Tim Pawsat (D) (1983)

Todd Witsken (S) (1983)

Matt Anger (S,D) (1984)

Antony Emerson (D) (1984)

Rick Leach (S,D) (1984)

Jorge Lozano (S,D) (1984)

Tim Pawsat (D) (1984)

Todd Witsken (S,D) (1984)

Rick Leach (S,D) (1985)

Jorge Lozano (S,D) (1985)

Tim Pawsat (D) (1985)

Todd Witsken (S,D) (1985)

Rick Leach (S,D) (1986)

Luke Jensen (S) (1986)

Tim Pawsat (D) (1986)

Rick Leach (S,D) (1987)

Luke Jensen (S,D) (1987)

Scott Melville (D) (1987)

Eric Amend (D) (1987)

Eric Amend (S,D) (1988)

Byron Black (D) (1988)

John Carras (S,D) (1988)

Scott Melville (S,D) (1988)

Eric Amend (D) (1989)

Byron Black (S,D) (1989)

Byron Black (S,D) (1990)

Kent Seton (D) (1990)

Byron Black (S,D) (1991)

Donny Isaak (S) (1991)

Brian MacPhie (S,D) (1991)

David Ekerot (S,D) (1992)

Andras Lanyi (D) (1992)

Jon Leach (D) (1992)

Brian MacPhie (S,D) (1992)

Wayne Black (S,D) (1993)

David Ekerot (S,D) (1993)

Andras Lanyi (D) (1993)

Jon Leach (D) (1993)

Brian MacPhie (S,D) (1993)

Kent Seton (D) (1993)

Wayne Black (S,D) (1994)

Jon Leach (S,D) (1994)

Brett Hansen (S,D) (1995)

Adam Peterson (S) (1995)

Fernando Samayoa (D) (1995)

Cecil Mamiit (S) (1996)

Adam Peterson (S) (1996)

Manny Ramirez (S) (1996)

George Bastl (S,D) (1997)

Kyle Spencer (D) (1997)

George Bastl (S) (1998)

Patrick Gottesleben (D) (1999)

Roman Kukal (D) (1999)

Ryan Moore (D) (2000)

Nick Rainey (D) (2000)

Ryan Moore (D) (2001)

Andrew Park (S) (2001)

Nick Rainey (D) (2001)

Ryan Moore (D) (2002)

Nick Rainey (S,D) (2002)

Jamil Al-Agba (S) (2005)

Robert Farah (S, D) (2008

Kaes Van't Hof (D) (2008)

Robert Farah (S,D) (2009)

Steve Johnson (S,D) (2009)

Robert Farah (S,D) (2010)

Steve Johnson (S,D) (2010)

Steve Johnson (S) (2011)

Ray Sarmiento (S) (2011)

Steve Johnson (S,D) (2012)

Ray Sarmiento (S) (2012)

Roberto Quiroz (D) (2012)

Emilio Gomez (S) (2013)

Yannick Hanfmann (S) (2013)

Ray Sarmiento (S) (2013)

Yannick Hanfmann (S,D) (2014)
Ray Sarmiento (S,D) (2014)
Yannick Hanfmann (S,D) (2015)
 Roberto Quiroz (D) (2015)
Johnny Wang (S) (2015)
Brandon Holt (S) 2017

Robert Farah (S) (2010)
Steve Johnson (S) (2010)
Steve Johnson (S) (2011)
Steve Johnson (S) (2012)
Steve Johnson & Roberto Quiroz
(D) (2010)
Yannick Hanfmann & Roberto
Quiroz (D) (2015) ITA Regional

ITA Player of the Year

Cecil Mamiit (1996)
Rick Leach (1986)
Robert Farah (2010)
Steve Johnson (2011)
Steve Johnson (2012)

Coach of the Year

Dick Leach (2002)
Peter Smith (2010)
Peter Smith (2012)

ITA/Rafael Osuna Sportsmanship Award

Joaquin Loyo-Mayo (1969)
John Andrews (1974)
Roger Knapp (1982)
Byron Black (1990)
Kaes Van't Hof (2008)
Daniel Nguyen (2012)

Arthur Ashe Leadership & Sportsmanship

Kaes Van't Hof (2007, 2008))
Ray Sarmiento (2014)

Rafael Osuna Sportsmanship (Regional)

Robert Farah (2010)
Daniel Nguyen (2012)

ITA All-Stars

Roberto Farah (2008)
Kaes Van't Hof (2008)

PAC-12 Team Titles

George Toley:
1962, 1963, 1964, 1966, 1967, 1968

Dick Leach:
1980 (tie), 1984, 1987, 1991, 1992, 1993, 1994

Peter Smith:
2004, 2008, 2010 (tie), 2011, 2012 (tournament), 2014, 2015 (regular-season tie & tournament), 2017 (tournament)

PAC-12

Singles Champions
Wayne Black (1994)
Adam Peterson (1996)
Ryan Moore (2001)
Kaes Van't Hof (2008)
Robert Farah (2010)
Steve Johnson (2011)

PAC-12

Doubles Champions
Scott Melville/Eric Amend (1988)
David Ekerot/Andras Lanyi (1993)
Wayne Black/Jon Leach (1994)
Brett Hansen/Fernando Samayoa (1995)
Parker Collins/Daniel Langre (2003)
Robert Farah/Kaes Van't Hof (2008)
Robert Farah/Steve Johnson (2010)
Steve Johnson/Ray Sarmiento (2011)

PAC-12

Coach of the Year
George Toley (1976)
Dick Leach (1987)
Dick Leach (1991)
Dick Leach (1992)
Dick Leach (1994)
Dick Leach (2002)
Peter Smith (2004)
Peter Smith (2007)
Peter Smith (2010)

Peter Smith (2011)
Peter Smith (Co) (2012)

Yannick Hanfmann/Roberto
Quiroz (2015)

PAC-12

Player of the Year
Robert Van't Hof (1980)
Rick Leach (1987)
Brian MacPhie (1993)
Wayne Black (1994)
Robert Farah (2009)
Robert Farah (2010)
Steve Johnson (2011)
Steve Johnson (2012)
Yannick Hanfmann (2014)

PAC-12

Doubles Team of the Year
Robert Farah/Kaes Van't Hof
(2008)
Robert Farah/Steve Johnson
(2009)
Robert Farah/Steve Johnson
(2010)
Steve Johnson/Roberto Quiroz
(2012)
Yannick Hanfmann/Ray
Sarmiento (2014)

PAC-12 All-Academic

Byron Black (1st team) (1991)
Donny Isaak (2nd team) (1991)
David Ekerot (1st team) (1992)
Jon Leach (1st team) (1992)
David Ekerot (1st team) (1993)
Lukas Hovorka (2nd team)
(1993)
Jon Leach (2nd team) (1993)
Lukas Hovorka (1st team) (1994)
.Jon Leach (1st team) (1994)
Lukas Hovorka (1st team) (1995)
Lukas Hovorka (1st team) (1996)
Patrick Gottesleben (2nd team)
(1998)
Andrew Park (1st team) (2000)
Andrew Park (1st team) (2001)
Andrew Park (1st team) (2002)
Ruben Torres (2nd team) (2002)
Kaes Van't Hof (1st team) (2008)
Robert Farah (2nd team) (2010)
Daniel Nguyen (2nd team)
(2010)
Jaak Poldma (2nd team) (2010)
Jaak Poldma (1st team) (2011)
Daniel Nguyen (2nd team)
(2011)

Daniel Nguyen (1st team) (2012)
Max de Vroome (2nd team)
(2015)

Academic All-American

Daniel Nguyen (3rd team)
(2012)

ITA Scholar-Athlete

Daniel Nguyen (2012)
Michael Tang (2013)
Max de Vroome (2015, 2016)

ALSO FROM
NEW CHAPTER PRESS

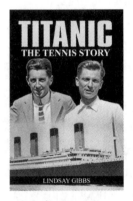

TITANIC: The Tennis Story
By Lindsay Gibbs

A stirring and remarkable story, this novel tells the tale of the intertwined life of Dick Williams and Karl Behr who survived the sinking of the *Titanic* and went on to have Hall of Fame tennis careers. Two years before they faced each other in the quarterfinals of the U.S. Nationals – the modern-day U.S. Open – the two men boarded the infamous ship as strangers. Dick, shy and gangly, was moving to America to pursue a tennis career and attend Harvard. Karl, a dashing tennis veteran, was chasing after Helen, the love of his life. The two men remarkably survived the sinking of the great vessel and met aboard the rescue ship *Carpathia*. But as they reached the shores of the United States, both men did all they could to distance themselves from the disaster. An emotional and touching work, this novel brings one of the most extraordinary sports stories to life in literary form. This real-life account – with an ending seemingly plucked out of a Hollywood screenplay – weaves the themes of love, tragedy, history, sport and perseverance.

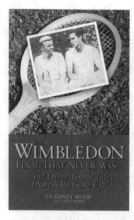

The Wimbledon Final That Never Was... And Other Tennis Tales From A Bygone Era
By Sidney Wood with David Wood

Sidney Wood tells the entertaining and fascinating tale of his Wimbledon title win 1931, capped with a strange default to his best friend, doubles partner, roommate and Davis Cup teammate Frank Shields ordered by the U.S. Tennis Association! Also included in this volume are a compilation of short stories that deliver fascinating anecdotes of old-school Hollywood and the styles of play of all 20th-century tennis legends.

The Greatest Tennis Matches of All Time
By Steve Flink

Author and tennis historian Steve Flink profiles and ranks the greatest tennis matches in the history of the sport. Roger Federer, Billie Jean King, Rafael Nadal, Bjorn Borg, John McEnroe, Martina Navratilova, Rod Laver, Don Budge and Chris Evert are all featured in this book that breaks down, analyzes, and puts into historical context the most memorable matches ever played.